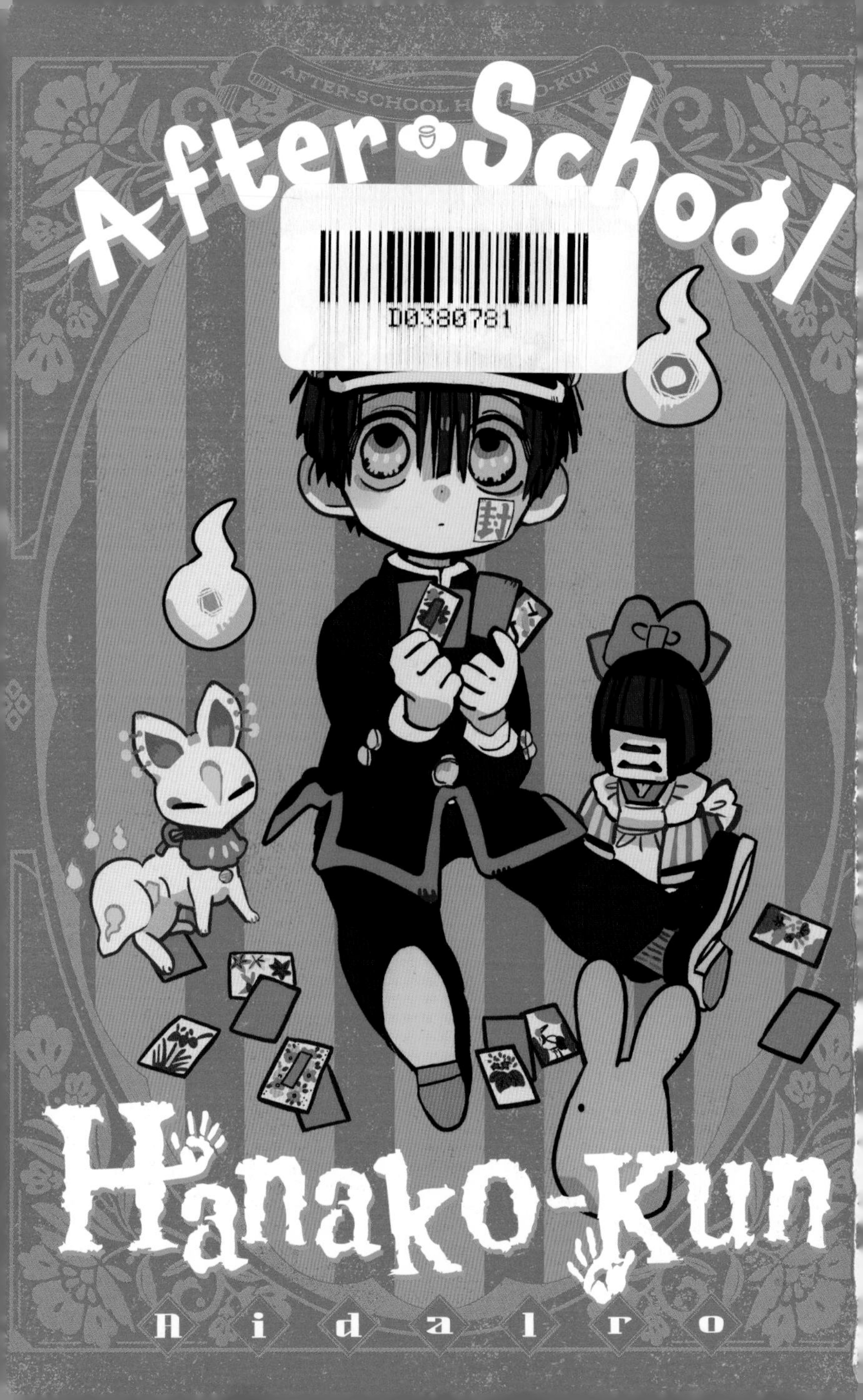
AFTER-SCHOOL HANAKO-KUN
After-School
Hanako-Kun
AidaIro

CONTENTS

AFTER-SCHOOL
HANAKO-KUN

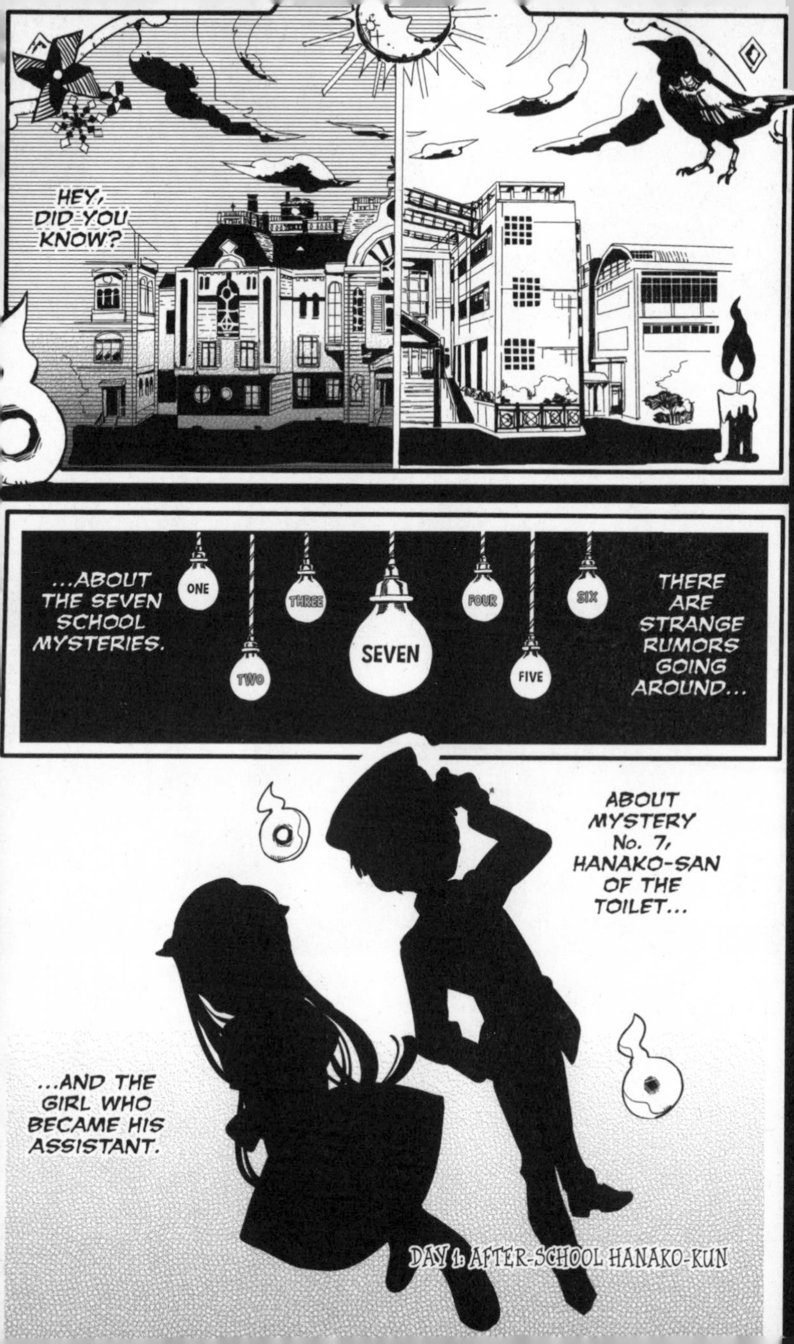
HEY, DID YOU KNOW?
THERE ARE STRANGE RUMORS GOING AROUND...
SIX
FOUR
THREE
ONE
SEVEN
FIVE
TWO
...ABOUT THE SEVEN SCHOOL MYSTERIES.
ABOUT MYSTERY No. 7, HANAKO-SAN OF THE TOILET...
...AND THE GIRL WHO BECAME HIS ASSISTANT.
DAY 1: AFTER-SCHOOL HANAKO-KUN

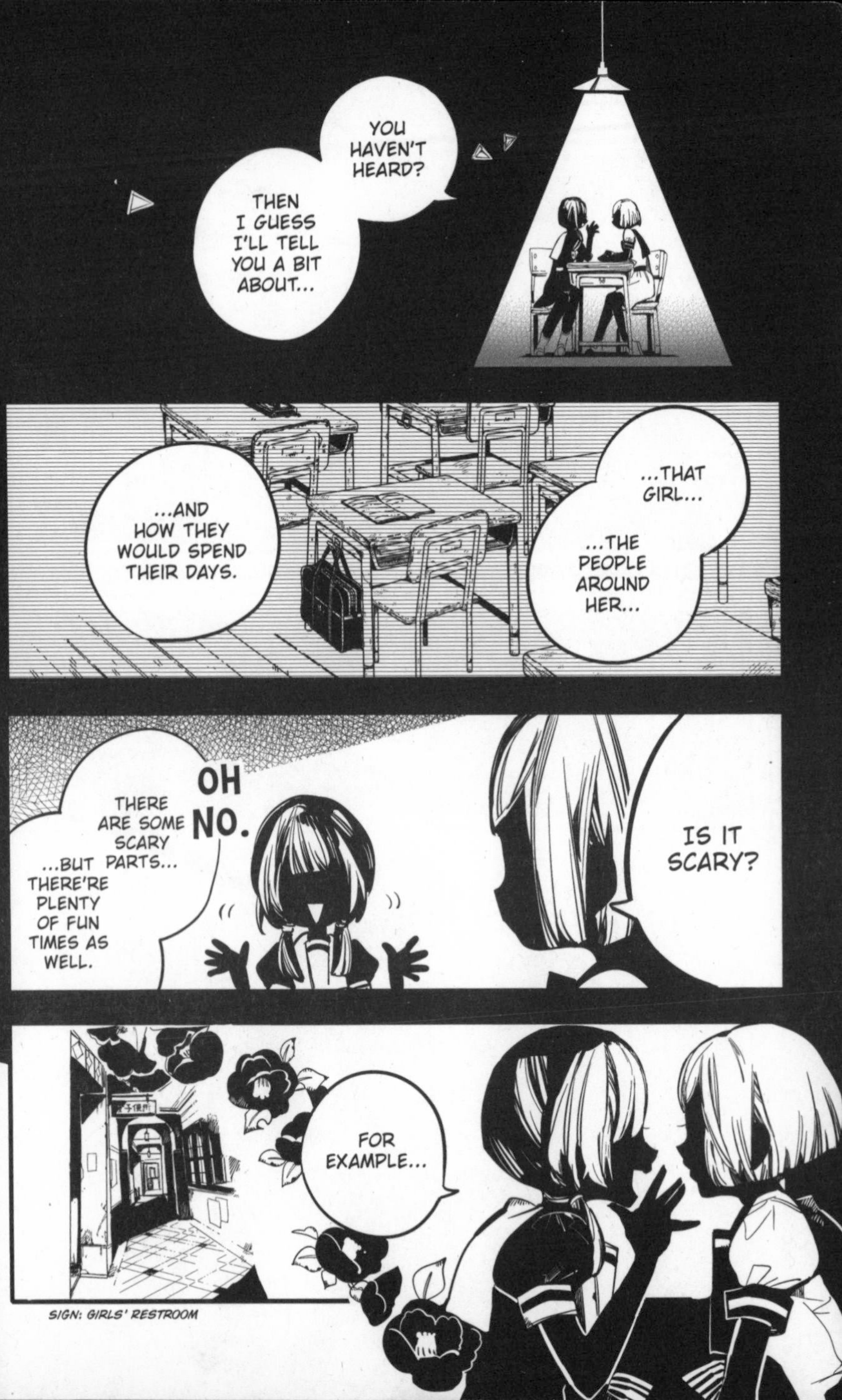
YOU HAVEN'T HEARD?
THEN I GUESS I'LL TELL YOU A BIT ABOUT...
...THAT GIRL... ...THE PEOPLE AROUND HER...
...AND HOW THEY WOULD SPEND THEIR DAYS.
IS IT SCARY?
OH NO.
THERE ARE SOME SCARY PARTS... ...BUT THERE'RE PLENTY OF FUN TIMES AS WELL.
FOR EXAMPLE...
SIGN: GIRLS' RESTROOM

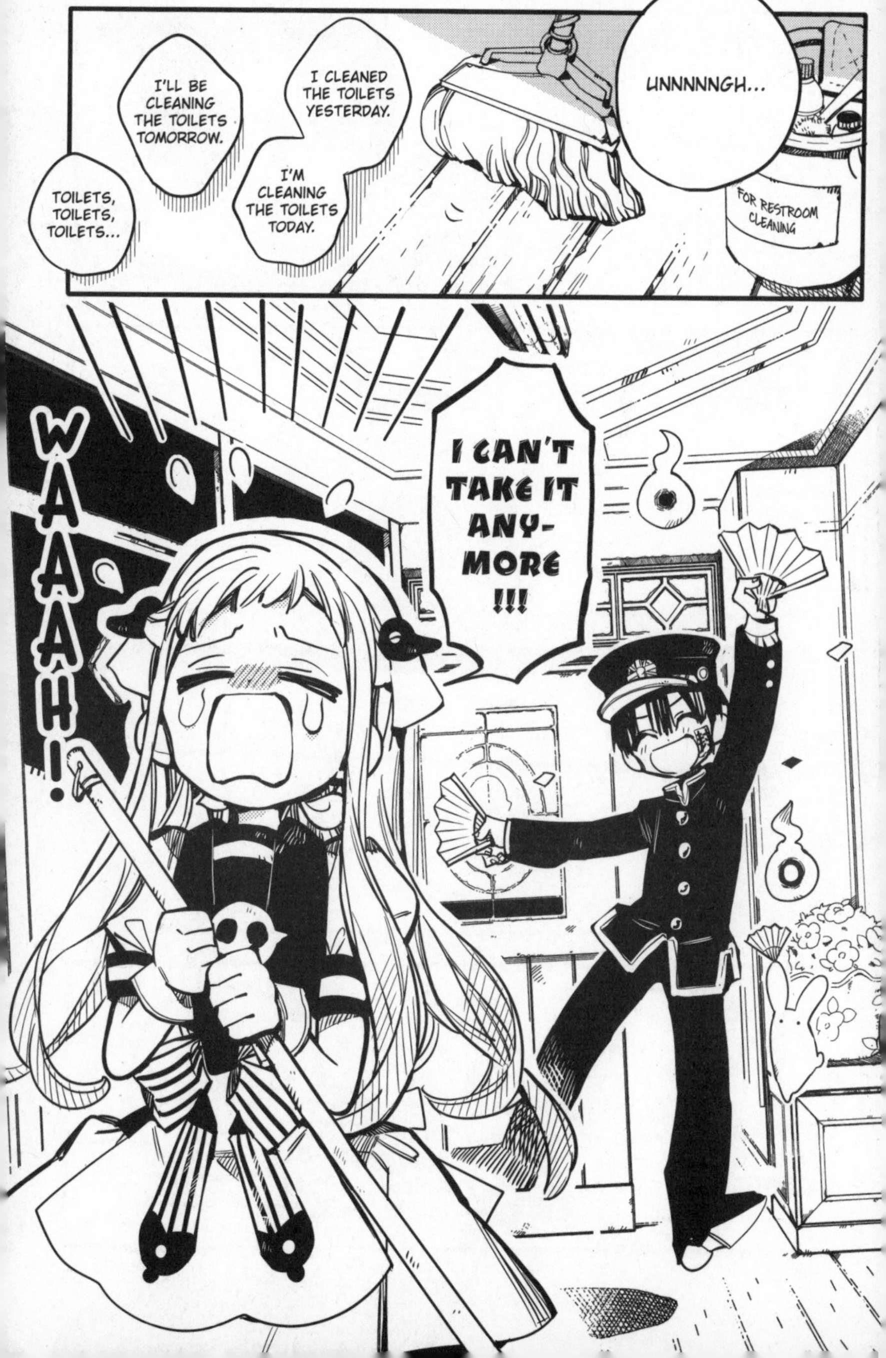
UNNNNNGH...
FOR RESTROOM CLEANING
I CLEANED THE TOILETS YESTERDAY.
I'M CLEANING THE TOILETS TODAY.
I'LL BE CLEANING THE TOILETS TOMORROW.
TOILETS, TOILETS, TOILETS...
I CAN'T TAKE IT ANY-MORE!!!
WAAAAH!

RADISH FEST

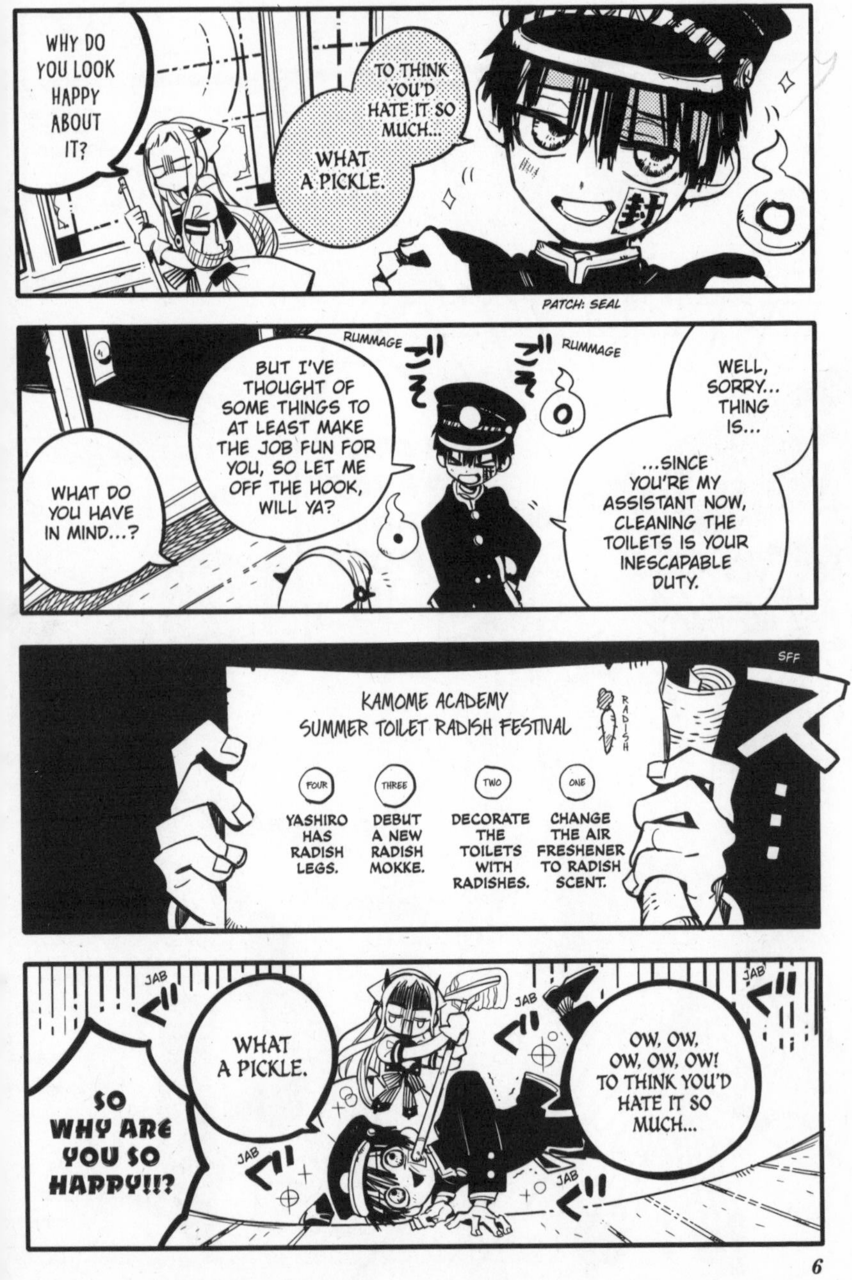
TO THINK YOU'D HATE IT SO MUCH...
WHAT A PICKLE.
WHY DO YOU LOOK HAPPY ABOUT IT?
PATCH: SEAL
WELL, SORRY... THING IS...
...SINCE YOU'RE MY ASSISTANT NOW, CLEANING THE TOILETS IS YOUR INESCAPABLE DUTY.
RUMMAGE
RUMMAGE
BUT I'VE THOUGHT OF SOME THINGS TO AT LEAST MAKE THE JOB FUN FOR YOU, SO LET ME OFF THE HOOK, WILL YA?
WHAT DO YOU HAVE IN MIND...?
SFF
KAMOME ACADEMY
SUMMER TOILET RADISH FESTIVAL
RADISH
ONE
CHANGE THE AIR FRESHENER TO RADISH SCENT.
TWO
DECORATE THE TOILETS WITH RADISHES.
THREE
DEBUT A NEW RADISH MOKKE.
FOUR
YASHIRO HAS RADISH LEGS.
JAB
OW, OW, OW, OW, OW! TO THINK YOU'D HATE IT SO MUCH...
JAB
WHAT A PICKLE.
JAB
JAB
JAB
SO WHY ARE YOU SO HAPPY!!?

SOMEONE YOU LIKE

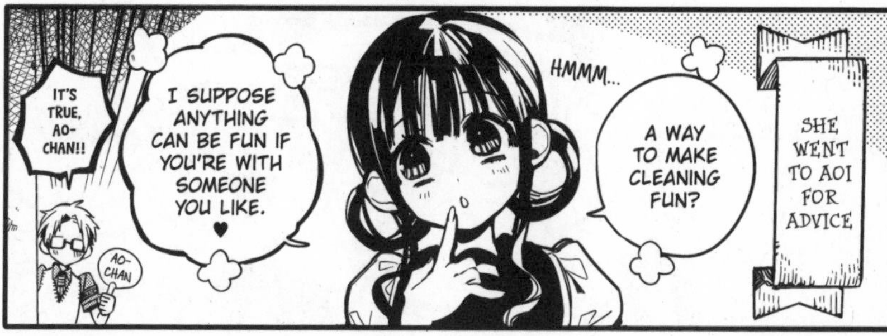
SHE WENT TO AOI FOR ADVICE
HMMM...
A WAY TO MAKE CLEANING FUN?
I SUPPOSE ANYTHING CAN BE FUN IF YOU'RE WITH SOMEONE YOU LIKE. ♥
IT'S TRUE, AO-CHAN!!
AO-CHAN

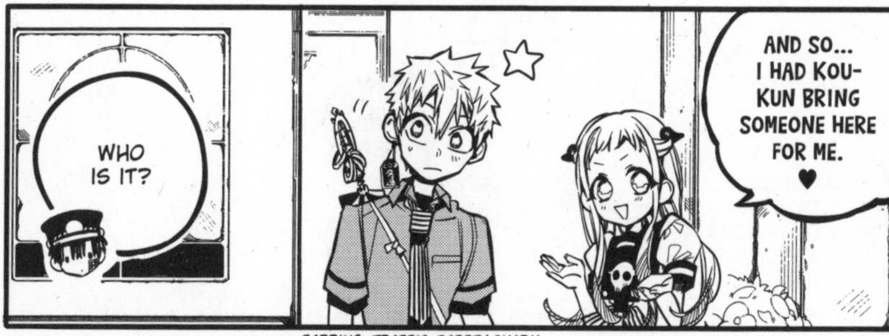
AND SO... I HAD KOU-KUN BRING SOMEONE HERE FOR ME. ♥
WHO IS IT?

EARRING: TRAFFIC-SAFETY CHARM

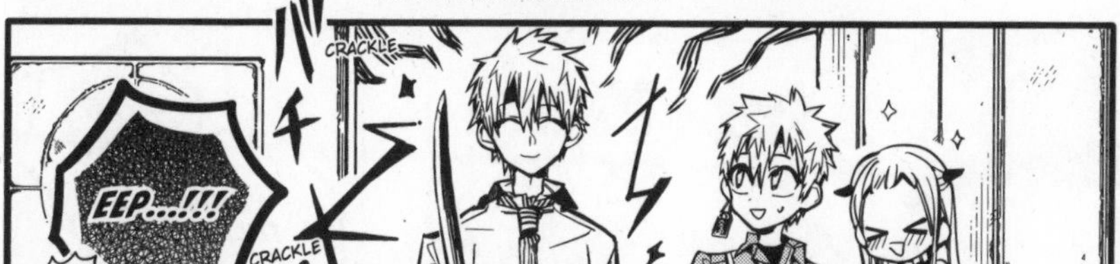
CRACKLE
CRACKLE
CRACKLE
EEP...!!!

ARMBAND: STUDENT COUNCIL

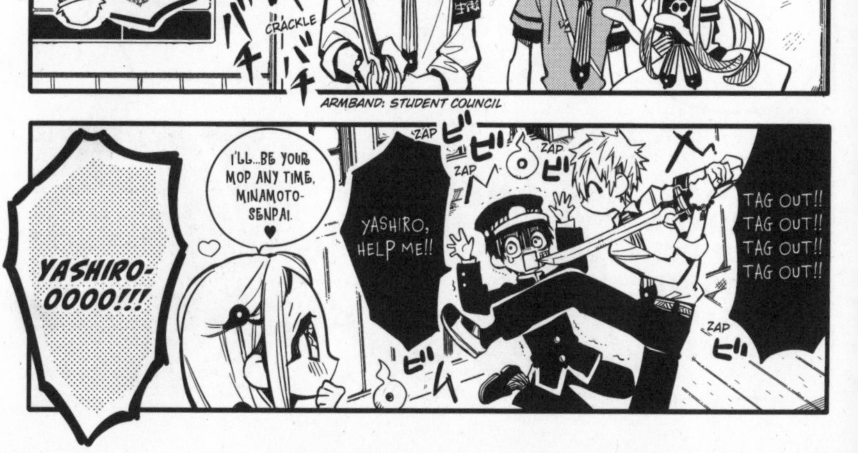
TAG OUT!! TAG OUT!! TAG OUT!! TAG OUT!!
ZAP
ZAP
ZAP
ZAP
YASHIRO, HELP ME!!
I'LL...BE YOUR MOP ANY TIME, MINAMOTO-SENPAI. ♥
YASHIRO-OOOO!!!

PLEASE LEAVE

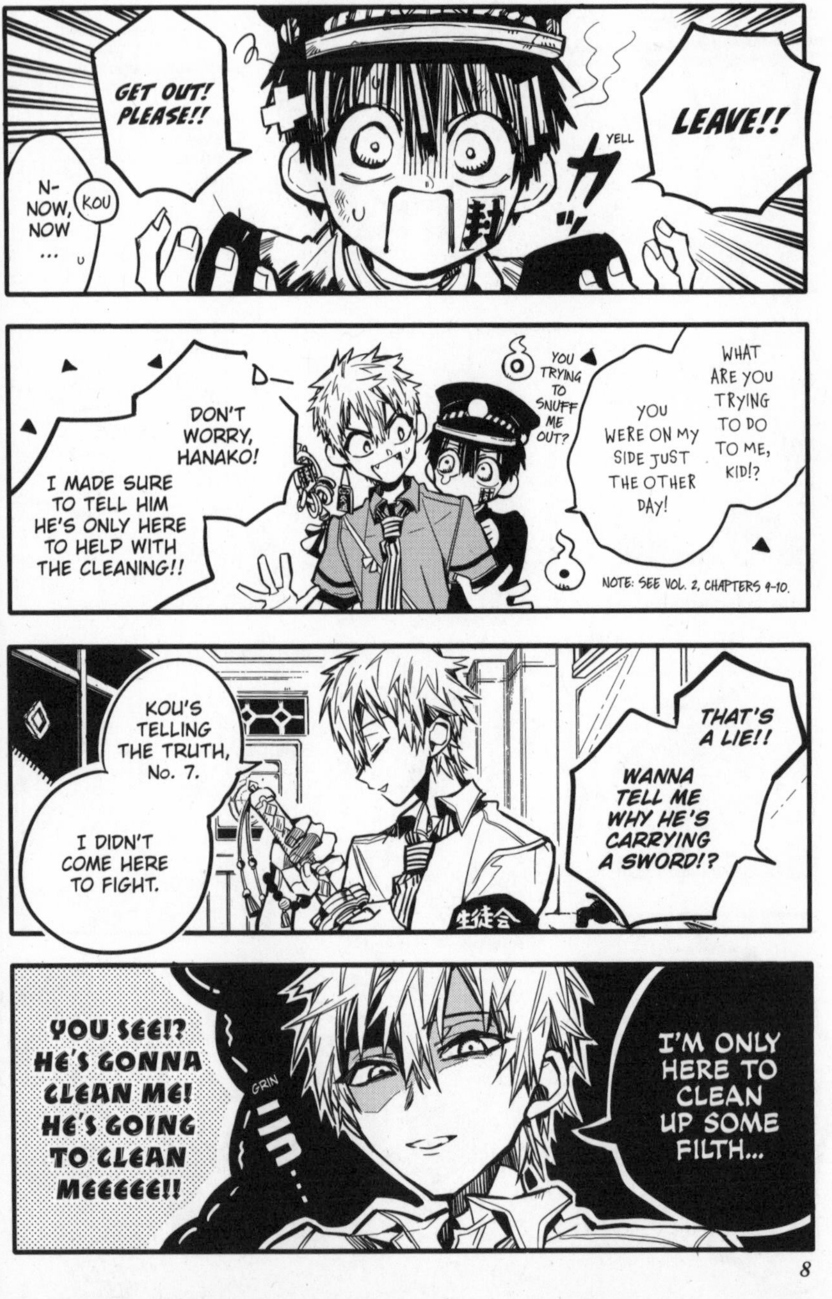
LEAVE!!
YELL
GET OUT! PLEASE!!
KOU
N-NOW, NOW ...
WHAT ARE YOU TRYING TO DO TO ME, KID!?
YOU WERE ON MY SIDE JUST THE OTHER DAY!
YOU TRYING TO SNUFF ME OUT?
D—
DON'T WORRY, HANAKO!
I MADE SURE TO TELL HIM HE'S ONLY HERE TO HELP WITH THE CLEANING!!
NOTE: SEE VOL. 2, CHAPTERS 9-10.
THAT'S A LIE!!
WANNA TELL ME WHY HE'S CARRYING A SWORD!?
KOU'S TELLING THE TRUTH, No. 7.
I DIDN'T COME HERE TO FIGHT.
I'M ONLY HERE TO CLEAN UP SOME FILTH...
GRIN
YOU SEE!? HE'S GONNA CLEAN ME! HE'S GOING TO CLEAN MEEEEEE!!

THE HEART BEATS FASTER WHEN...

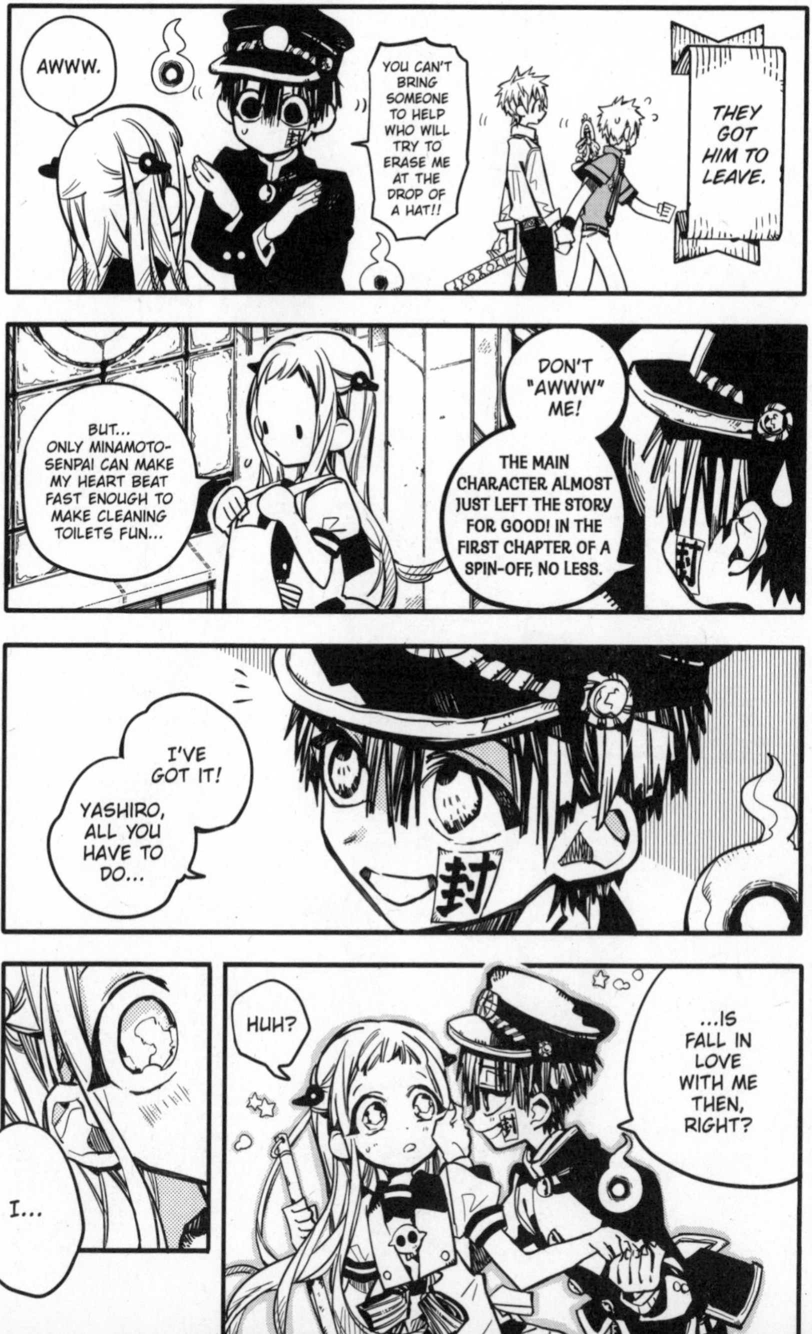
THEY GOT HIM TO LEAVE.
YOU CAN'T BRING SOMEONE TO HELP WHO WILL TRY TO ERASE ME AT THE DROP OF A HAT!!
AWWW.
DON'T "AWWW" ME!
THE MAIN CHARACTER ALMOST JUST LEFT THE STORY FOR GOOD! IN THE FIRST CHAPTER OF A SPIN-OFF, NO LESS.
BUT... ONLY MINAMOTO-SENPAI CAN MAKE MY HEART BEAT FAST ENOUGH TO MAKE CLEANING TOILETS FUN...
I'VE GOT IT!
YASHIRO, ALL YOU HAVE TO DO...
...IS FALL IN LOVE WITH ME THEN, RIGHT?
HUH?
I...

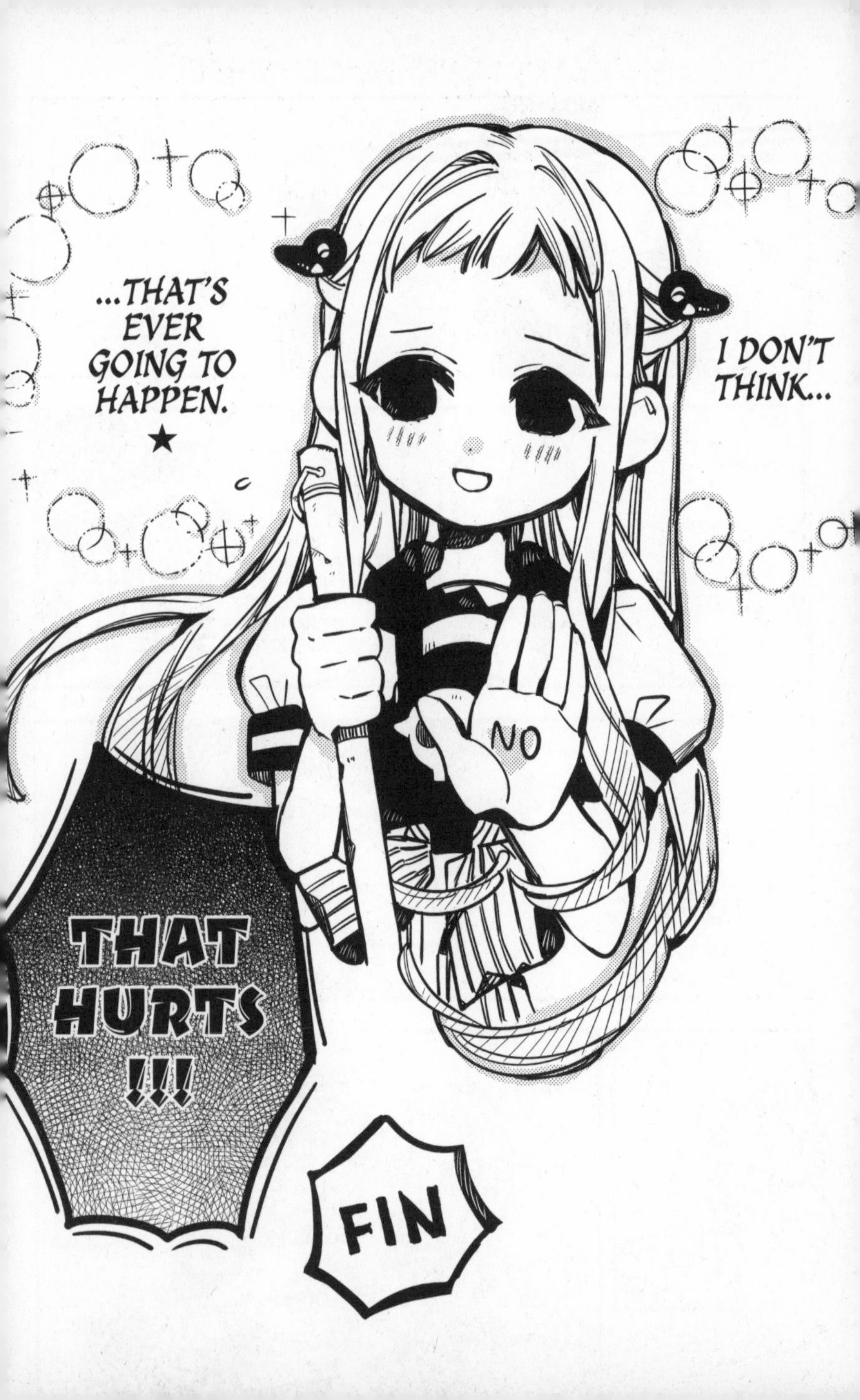
I DON'T THINK...
...THAT'S EVER GOING TO HAPPEN. ★
NO
THAT HURTS!!!
FIN

After-School
Hanako-Kun

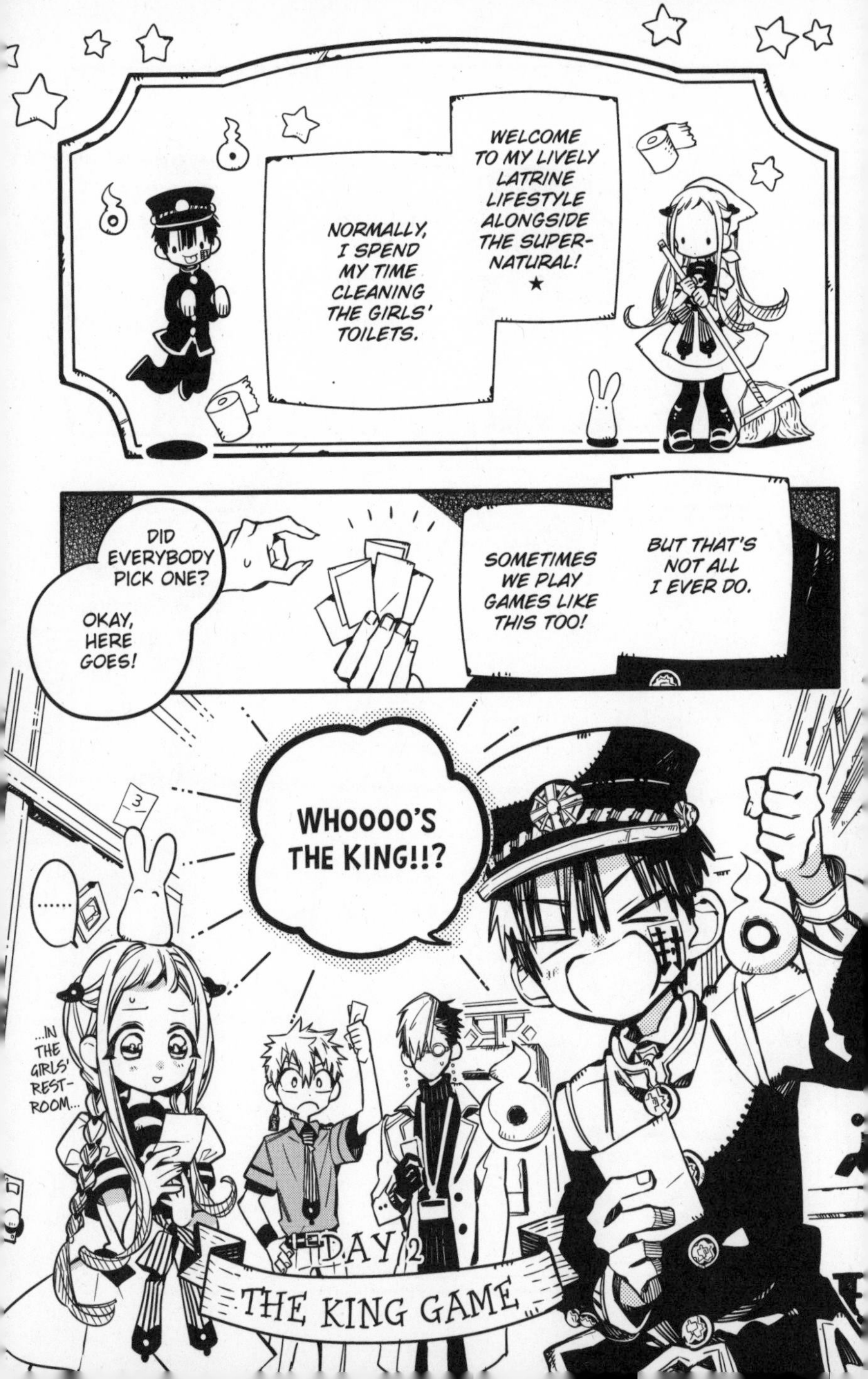
WELCOME TO MY LIVELY LATRINE LIFESTYLE ALONGSIDE THE SUPER-NATURAL! ★
NORMALLY, I SPEND MY TIME CLEANING THE GIRLS' TOILETS.
BUT THAT'S NOT ALL I EVER DO.
SOMETIMES WE PLAY GAMES LIKE THIS TOO!
DID EVERYBODY PICK ONE?
OKAY, HERE GOES!
WHOOOO'S THE KING!!?
......
...IN THE GIRLS' REST-ROOM...
DAY 2
THE KING GAME

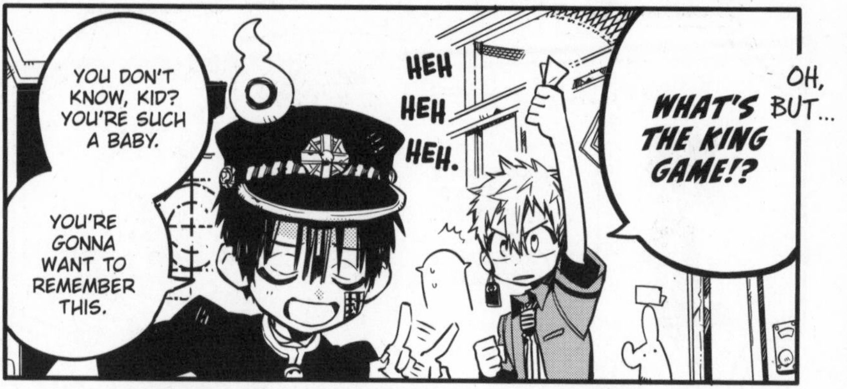
OH, BUT... WHAT'S THE KING GAME!?
HEH HEH HEH.
YOU DON'T KNOW, KID? YOU'RE SUCH A BABY.
YOU'RE GONNA WANT TO REMEMBER THIS.

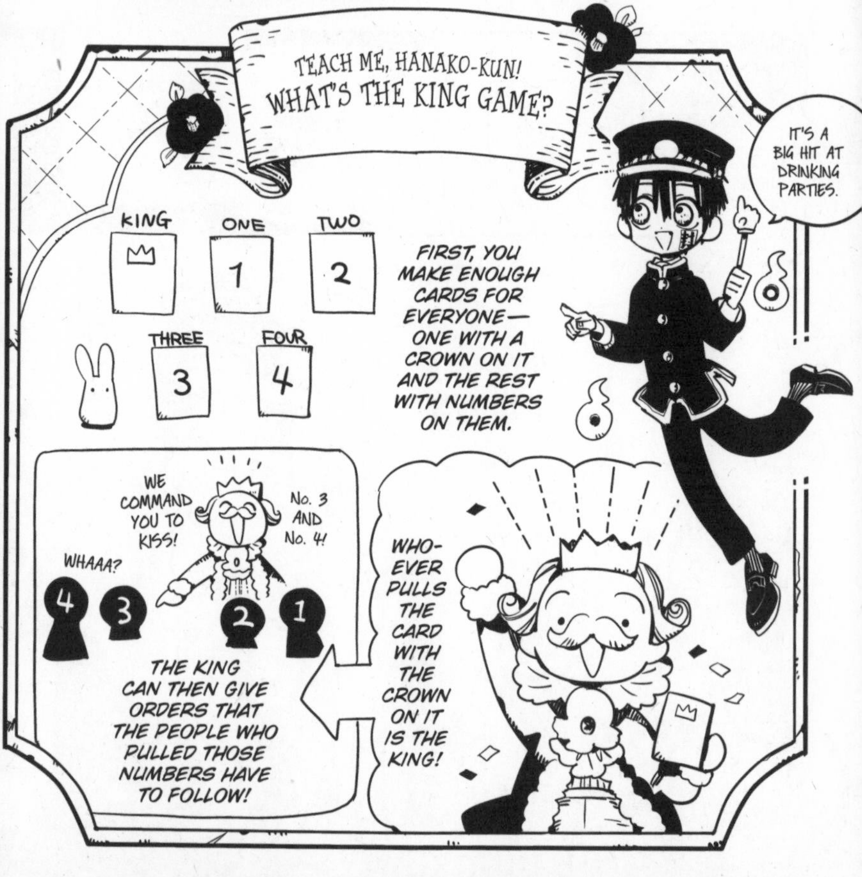
TEACH ME, HANAKO-KUN! WHAT'S THE KING GAME?
IT'S A BIG HIT AT DRINKING PARTIES.
FIRST, YOU MAKE ENOUGH CARDS FOR EVERYONE—ONE WITH A CROWN ON IT AND THE REST WITH NUMBERS ON THEM.
KING
ONE
1
TWO
2
THREE
3
FOUR
4
WHO-EVER PULLS THE CARD WITH THE CROWN ON IT IS THE KING!
No. 3 AND No. 4!
WE COMMAND YOU TO KISS!
WHAAA?
4
3
2
1
THE KING CAN THEN GIVE ORDERS THAT THE PEOPLE WHO PULLED THOSE NUMBERS HAVE TO FOLLOW!

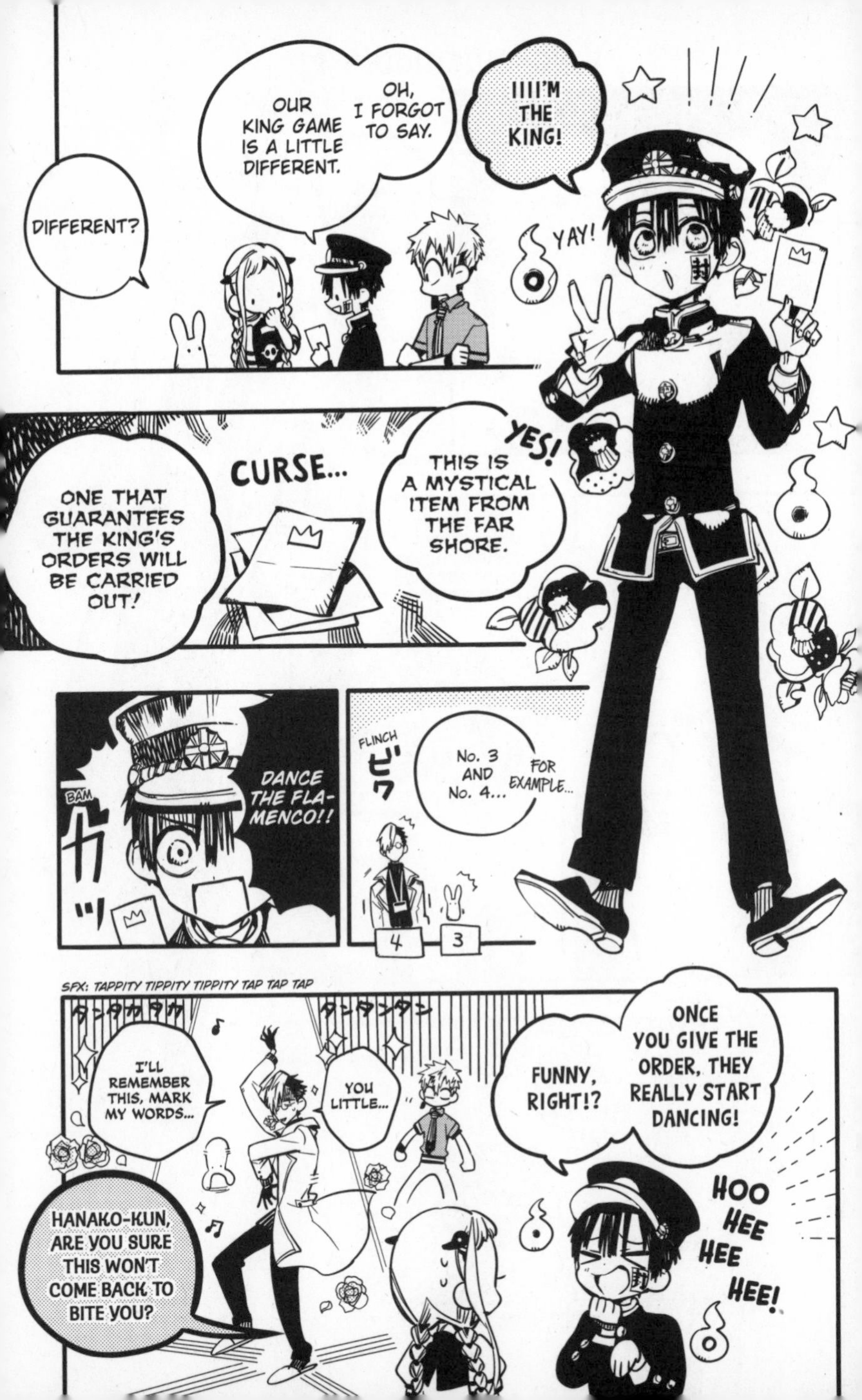
IIII'M THE KING!
YAY!
YES!
OH, I FORGOT TO SAY.
OUR KING GAME IS A LITTLE DIFFERENT.
DIFFERENT?
THIS IS A MYSTICAL ITEM FROM THE FAR SHORE.
CURSE...
ONE THAT GUARANTEES THE KING'S ORDERS WILL BE CARRIED OUT!
FLINCH
ビク
FOR EXAMPLE...
No. 3 AND No. 4...
4
3
BAM
ガッ
DANCE THE FLA-MENCO!!
SFX: TAPPITY TIPPITY TIPPITY TAP TAP TAP
ONCE YOU GIVE THE ORDER, THEY REALLY START DANCING!
FUNNY, RIGHT!?
HOO HEE HEE HEE!
YOU LITTLE...
I'LL REMEMBER THIS, MARK MY WORDS...
HANAKO-KUN, ARE YOU SURE THIS WON'T COME BACK TO BITE YOU?

KING TSUCHIGOMORI

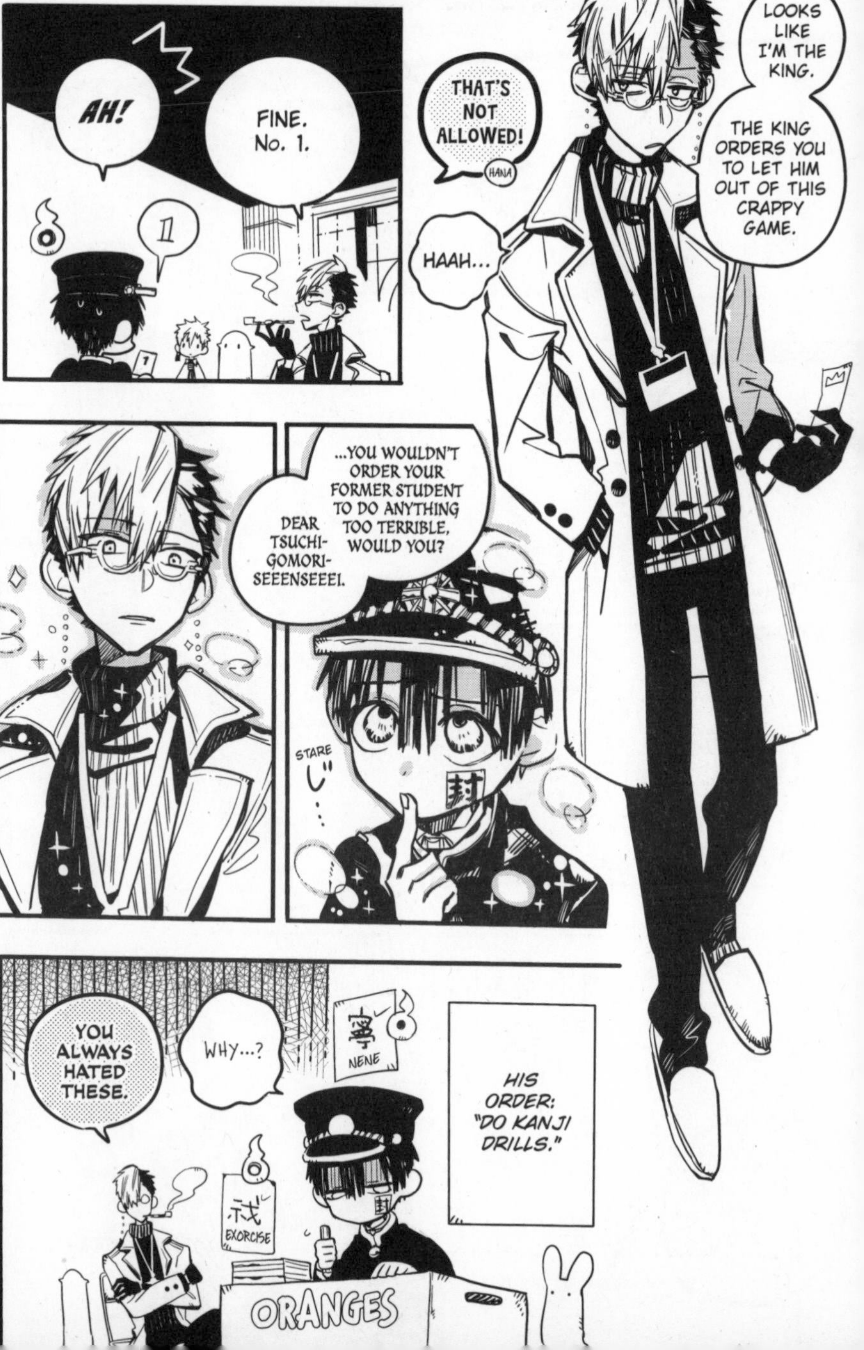
LOOKS LIKE I'M THE KING.
THE KING ORDERS YOU TO LET HIM OUT OF THIS CRAPPY GAME.
THAT'S NOT ALLOWED!
HANA
HAAH...
FINE. No. 1.
AH!
1
...YOU WOULDN'T ORDER YOUR FORMER STUDENT TO DO ANYTHING TOO TERRIBLE, WOULD YOU?
DEAR TSUCHI-GOMORI-SEEENSEEEI.
STARE
じ
HIS ORDER: "DO KANJI DRILLS."
寧
NENE
WHY...?
YOU ALWAYS HATED THESE.
祓
EXORCISE
ORANGES

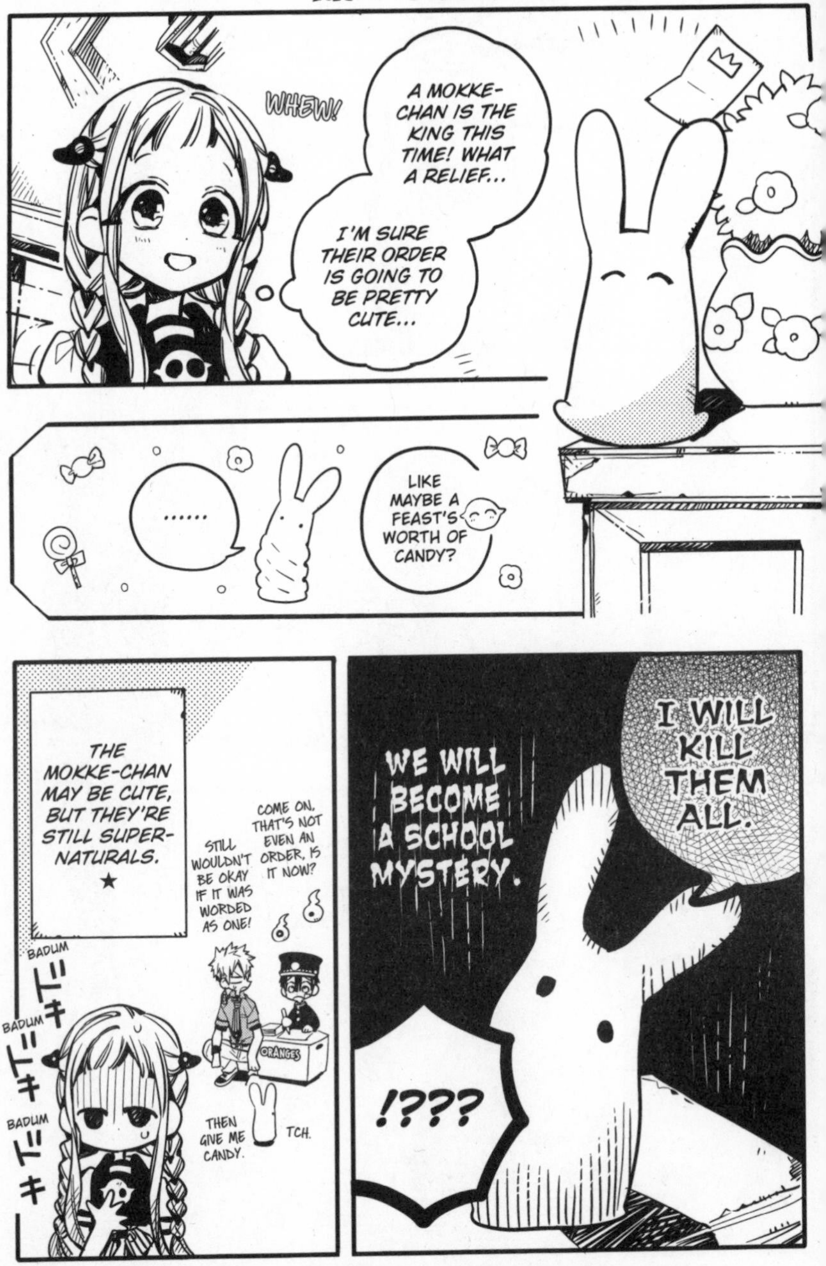
A MOKKE-CHAN IS THE KING THIS TIME! WHAT A RELIEF...
I'M SURE THEIR ORDER IS GOING TO BE PRETTY CUTE...
WHEW!
LIKE MAYBE A FEAST'S WORTH OF CANDY?
......
I WILL KILL THEM ALL.
WE WILL BECOME A SCHOOL MYSTERY.
!???
THE MOKKE-CHAN MAY BE CUTE, BUT THEY'RE STILL SUPER-NATURALS. ★
COME ON, THAT'S NOT EVEN AN ORDER, IS IT NOW?
STILL WOULDN'T BE OKAY IF IT WAS WORDED AS ONE!
ORANGES
TCH.
THEN GIVE ME CANDY.
BADUM
BADUM
BADUM

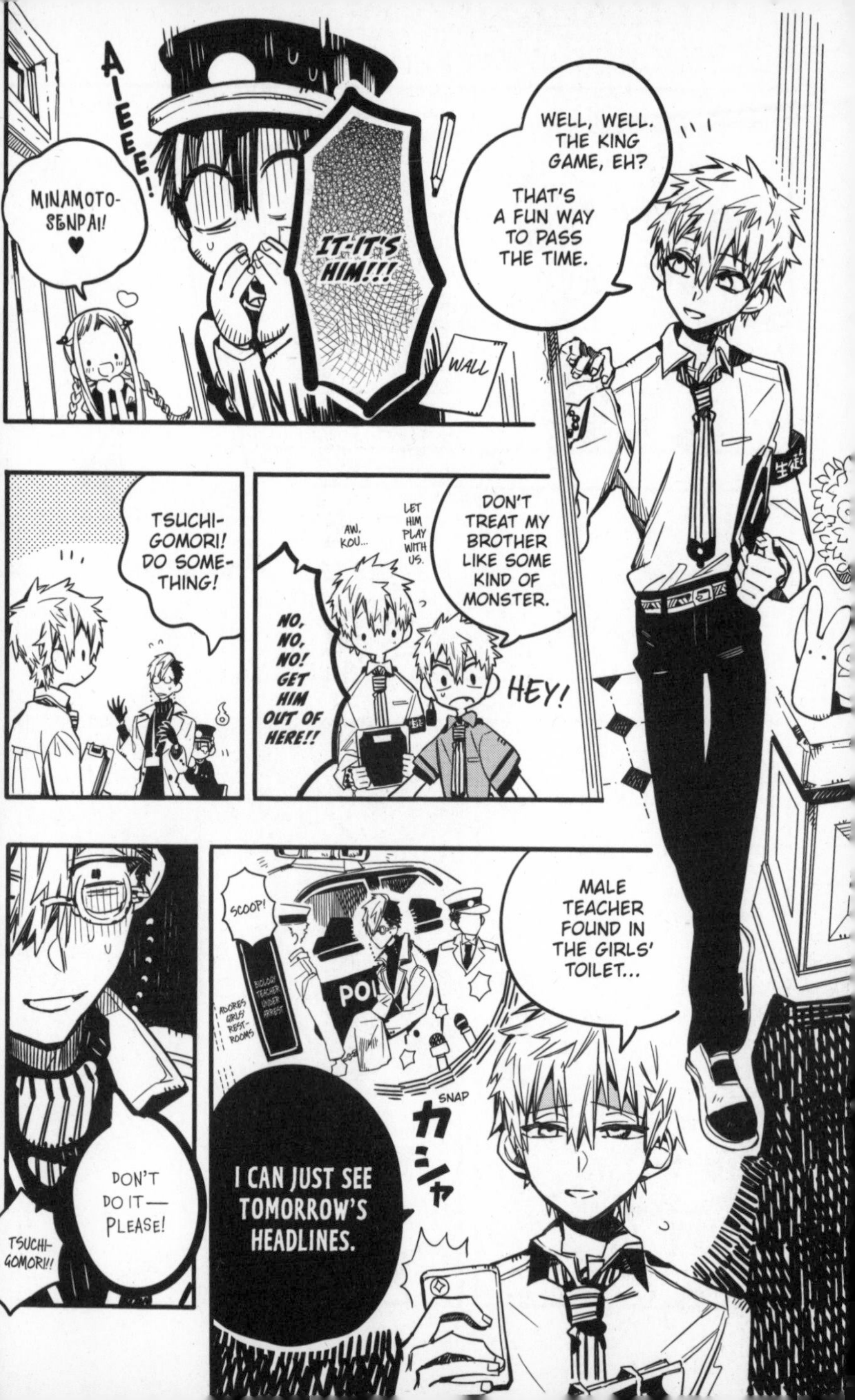
WELL, WELL. THE KING GAME, EH?
THAT'S A FUN WAY TO PASS THE TIME.
AIEEEE!
IT-IT'S HIM!!!
WALL
MINAMOTO-SENPAI! ♥
DON'T TREAT MY BROTHER LIKE SOME KIND OF MONSTER.
LET HIM PLAY WITH US.
AW, KOU...
HEY!
NO, NO, NO! GET HIM OUT OF HERE!!
TSUCHI-GOMORI! DO SOME-THING!
MALE TEACHER FOUND IN THE GIRLS' TOILET...
SCOOP!
BIOLOGY TEACHER UNDER ARREST
ADORES GIRLS' REST-ROOMS
POL
SNAP
I CAN JUST SEE TOMORROW'S HEADLINES.
DON'T DO IT— PLEASE!
TSUCHI-GOMORI!!

LOVE VIBES

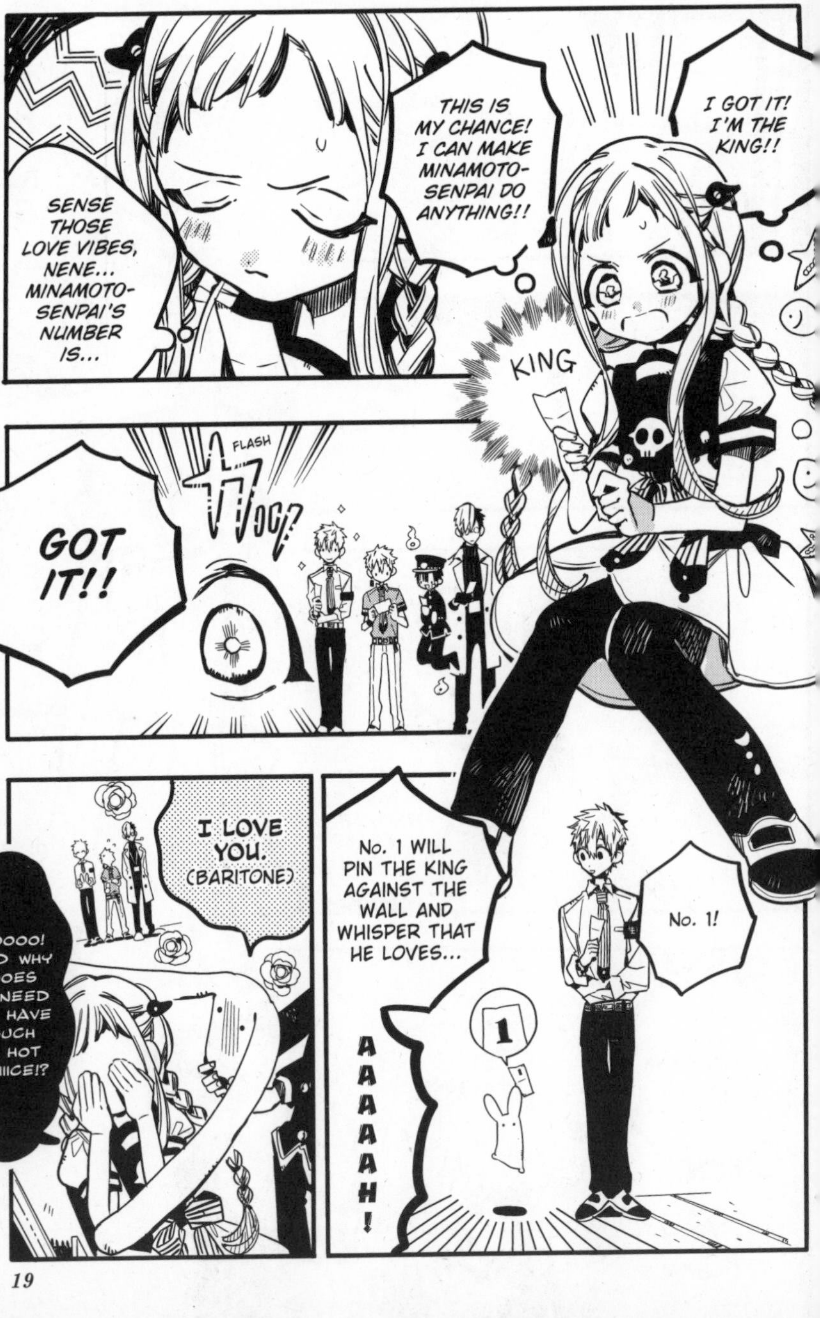
I GOT IT! I'M THE KING!!
THIS IS MY CHANCE! I CAN MAKE MINAMOTO-SENPAI DO ANYTHING!!
KING
SENSE THOSE LOVE VIBES, NENE... MINAMOTO-SENPAI'S NUMBER IS...
FLASH
GOT IT!!
No. 1!
No. 1 WILL PIN THE KING AGAINST THE WALL AND WHISPER THAT HE LOVES...
1
AAAAAAAH!
I LOVE YOU. (BARITONE)
NOOOO! AND WHY DOES IT NEED TO HAVE SUCH A HOT VOIIICE!?

CRITICAL MISS

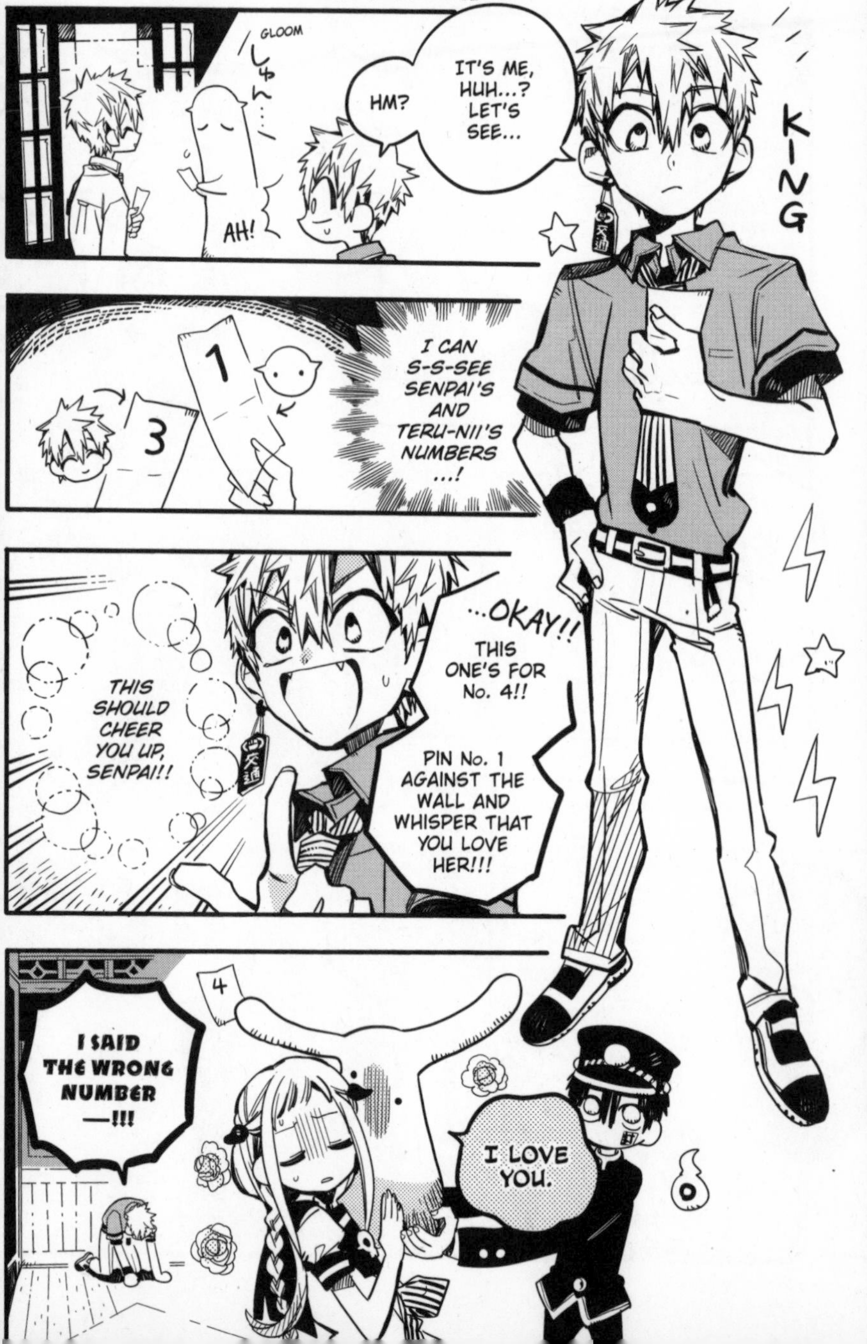
KING
HM?
IT'S ME, HUH...? LET'S SEE...
GLOOM
しゅん…
AH!
I CAN S-S-SEE SENPAI'S AND TERU-NII'S NUMBERS ...!
...OKAY!!
THIS ONE'S FOR No. 4!!
PIN No. 1 AGAINST THE WALL AND WHISPER THAT YOU LOVE HER!!!
THIS SHOULD CHEER YOU UP, SENPAI!!
I LOVE YOU.
I SAID THE WRONG NUMBER—!!!

BE NICE, PLEAZE

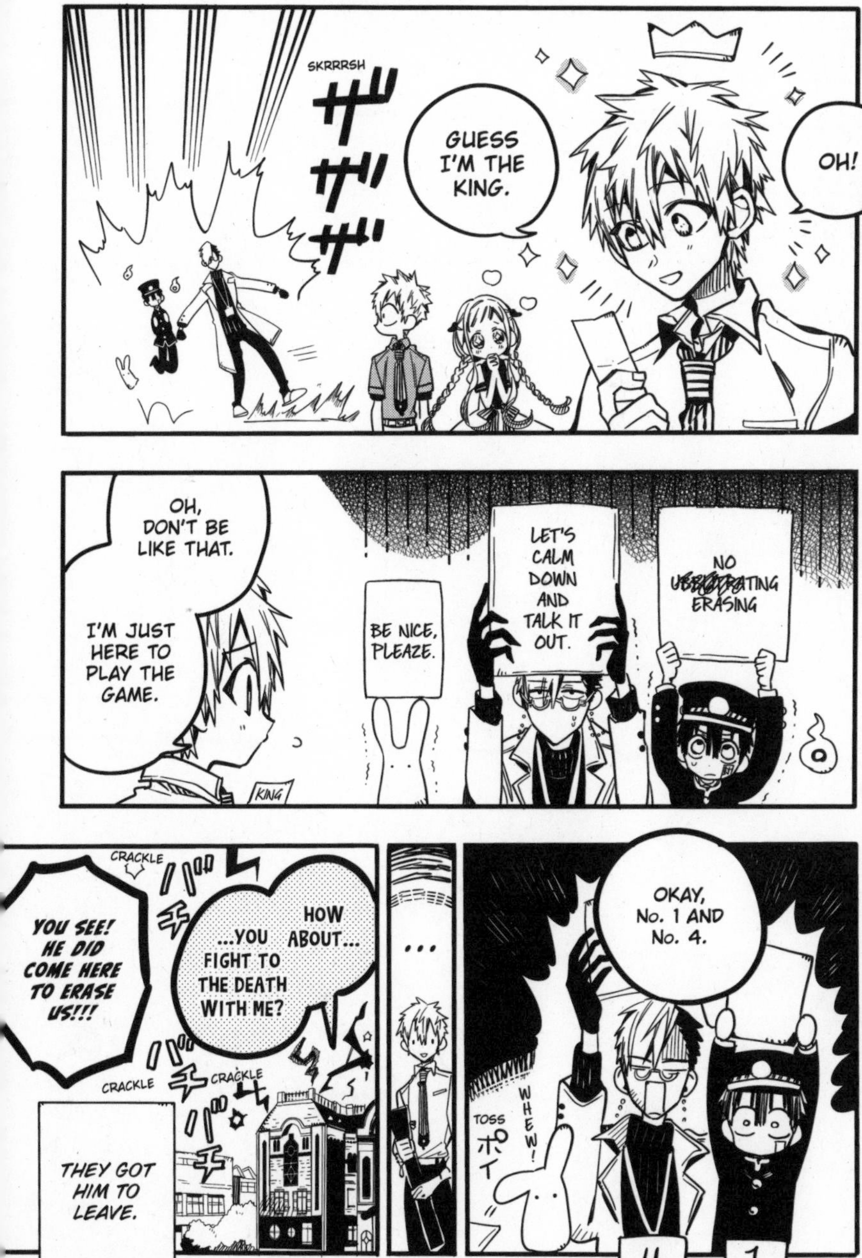
OH!
GUESS I'M THE KING.
SKRRRSH
NO ERASING
LET'S CALM DOWN AND TALK IT OUT.
BE NICE, PLEAZE.
OH, DON'T BE LIKE THAT.
I'M JUST HERE TO PLAY THE GAME.
KING
OKAY, No. 1 AND No. 4.
WHEW!
TOSS
4
1
...
HOW ABOUT...
...YOU FIGHT TO THE DEATH WITH ME?
CRACKLE
CRACKLE
CRACKLE
YOU SEE! HE DID COME HERE TO ERASE US!!!
THEY GOT HIM TO LEAVE.

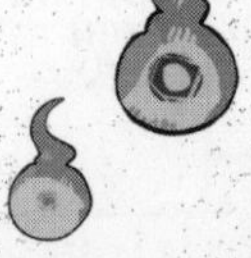

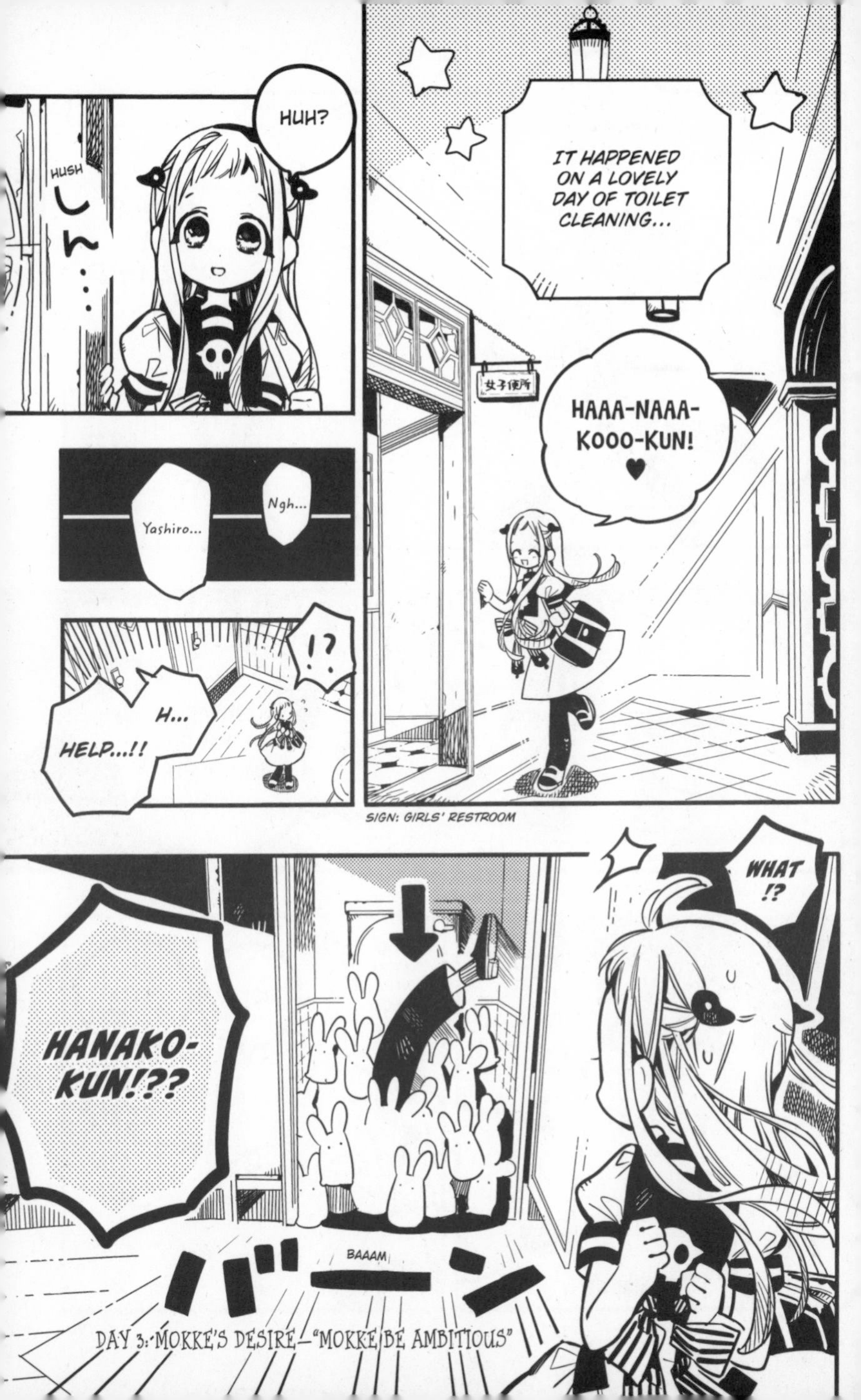
IT HAPPENED ON A LOVELY DAY OF TOILET CLEANING...
女子便所
HAAA-NAAA-KOOO-KUN! ♥
SIGN: GIRLS' RESTROOM
HUH?
HUSH
しん…
Ngh...
Yashiro...
!?
H...
HELP...!!
WHAT !?
HANAKO-KUN!??
BAAAM
DAY 3: MOKKE'S DESIRE—"MOKKE BE AMBITIOUS"

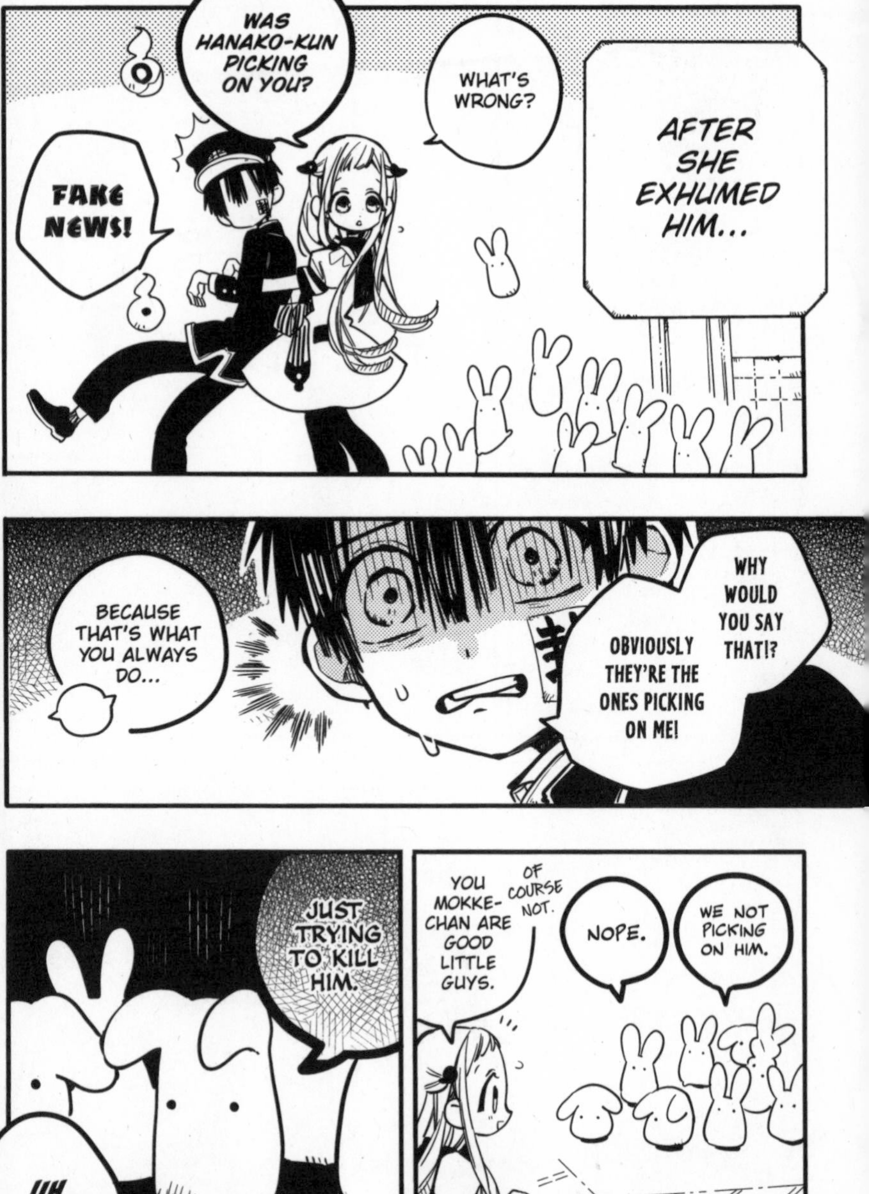
AFTER SHE EXHUMED HIM...
WHAT'S WRONG?
WAS HANAKO-KUN PICKING ON YOU?
FAKE NEWS!
WHY WOULD YOU SAY THAT!?
OBVIOUSLY THEY'RE THE ONES PICKING ON ME!
BECAUSE THAT'S WHAT YOU ALWAYS DO...
WE NOT PICKING ON HIM.
NOPE.
OF COURSE NOT.
YOU MOKKE-CHAN ARE GOOD LITTLE GUYS.
JUST TRYING TO KILL HIM.
UH...

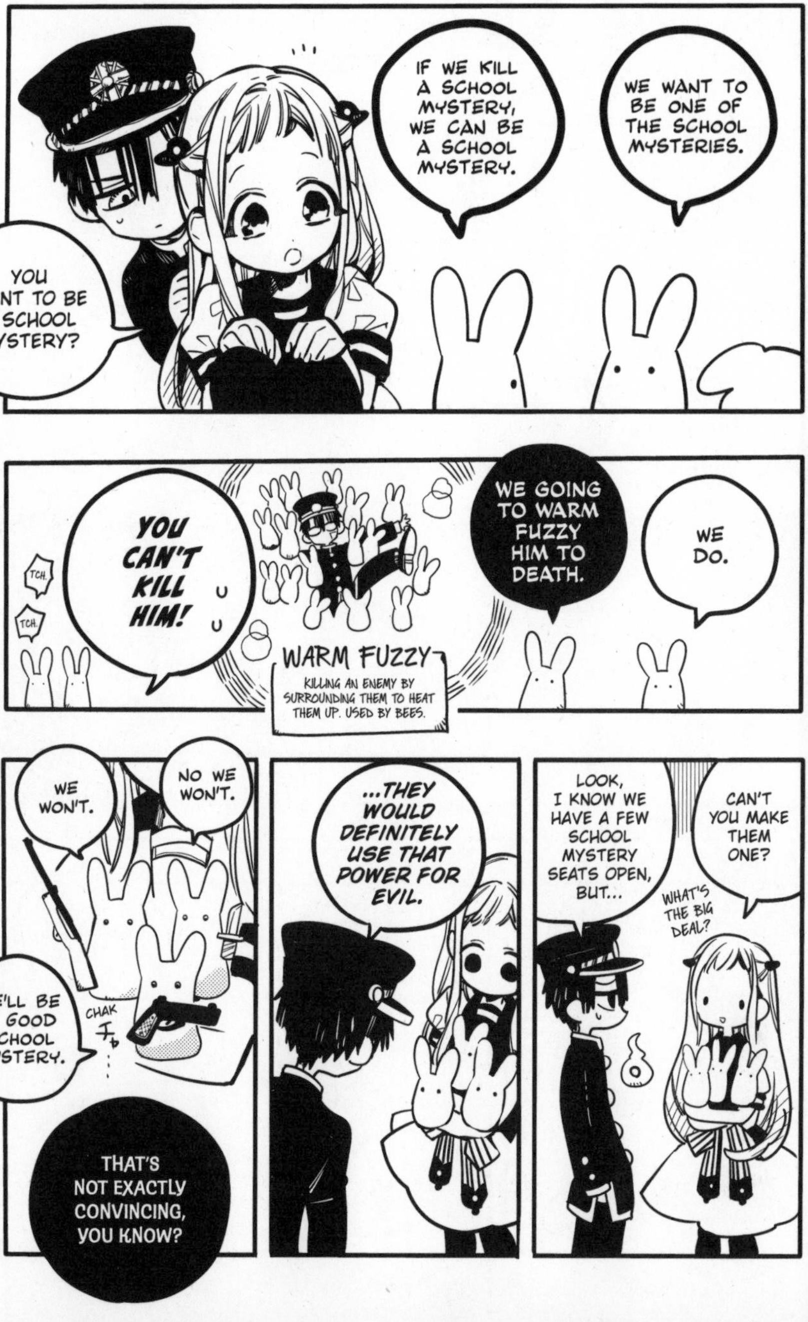
WE WANT TO BE ONE OF THE SCHOOL MYSTERIES.
IF WE KILL A SCHOOL MYSTERY, WE CAN BE A SCHOOL MYSTERY.
YOU WANT TO BE A SCHOOL MYSTERY?
WE DO.
WE GOING TO WARM FUZZY HIM TO DEATH.
WARM FUZZY
KILLING AN ENEMY BY SURROUNDING THEM TO HEAT THEM UP. USED BY BEES.
YOU CAN'T KILL HIM!
TCH.
TCH.
CAN'T YOU MAKE THEM ONE?
LOOK, I KNOW WE HAVE A FEW SCHOOL MYSTERY SEATS OPEN, BUT...
WHAT'S THE BIG DEAL?
...THEY WOULD DEFINITELY USE THAT POWER FOR EVIL.
NO WE WON'T.
WE WON'T.
WE'LL BE A GOOD SCHOOL MYSTERY.
CHAK
THAT'S NOT EXACTLY CONVINCING, YOU KNOW?

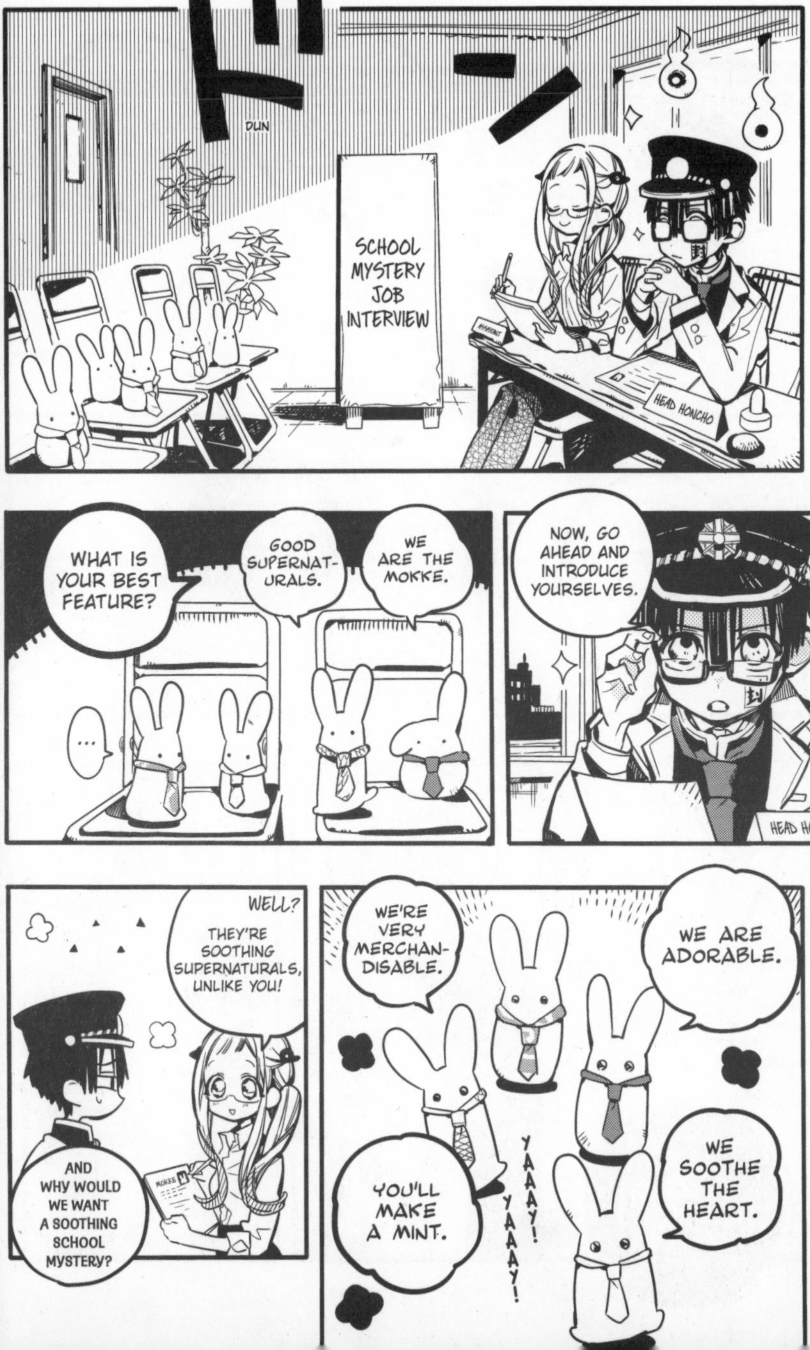
ドーン
DUN
SCHOOL MYSTERY JOB INTERVIEW
HEAD HONCHO
NOW, GO AHEAD AND INTRODUCE YOURSELVES.
HEAD HONCHO
WE ARE THE MOKKE.
GOOD SUPERNATURALS.
WHAT IS YOUR BEST FEATURE?
...
WE ARE ADORABLE.
WE'RE VERY MERCHANDISABLE.
WE SOOTHE THE HEART.
YAAAY!
YAAAY!
YOU'LL MAKE A MINT.
WELL?
THEY'RE SOOTHING SUPERNATURALS, UNLIKE YOU!
MOKKE
AND WHY WOULD WE WANT A SOOTHING SCHOOL MYSTERY?

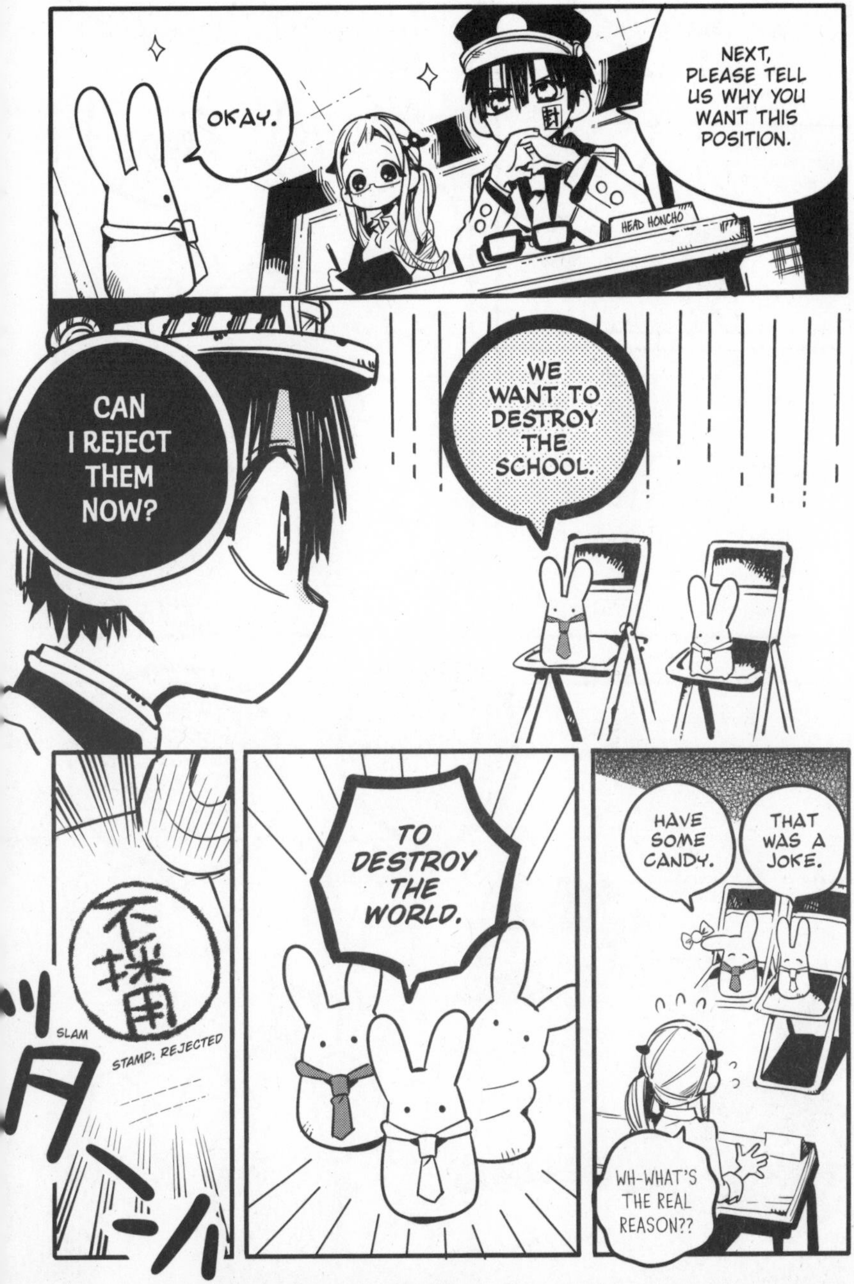
NEXT, PLEASE TELL US WHY YOU WANT THIS POSITION.
OKAY.
HEAD HONCHO
WE WANT TO DESTROY THE SCHOOL.
CAN I REJECT THEM NOW?
THAT WAS A JOKE.
HAVE SOME CANDY.
WH-WHAT'S THE REAL REASON??
TO DESTROY THE WORLD.
不採用
STAMP: REJECTED
SLAM
ダン!

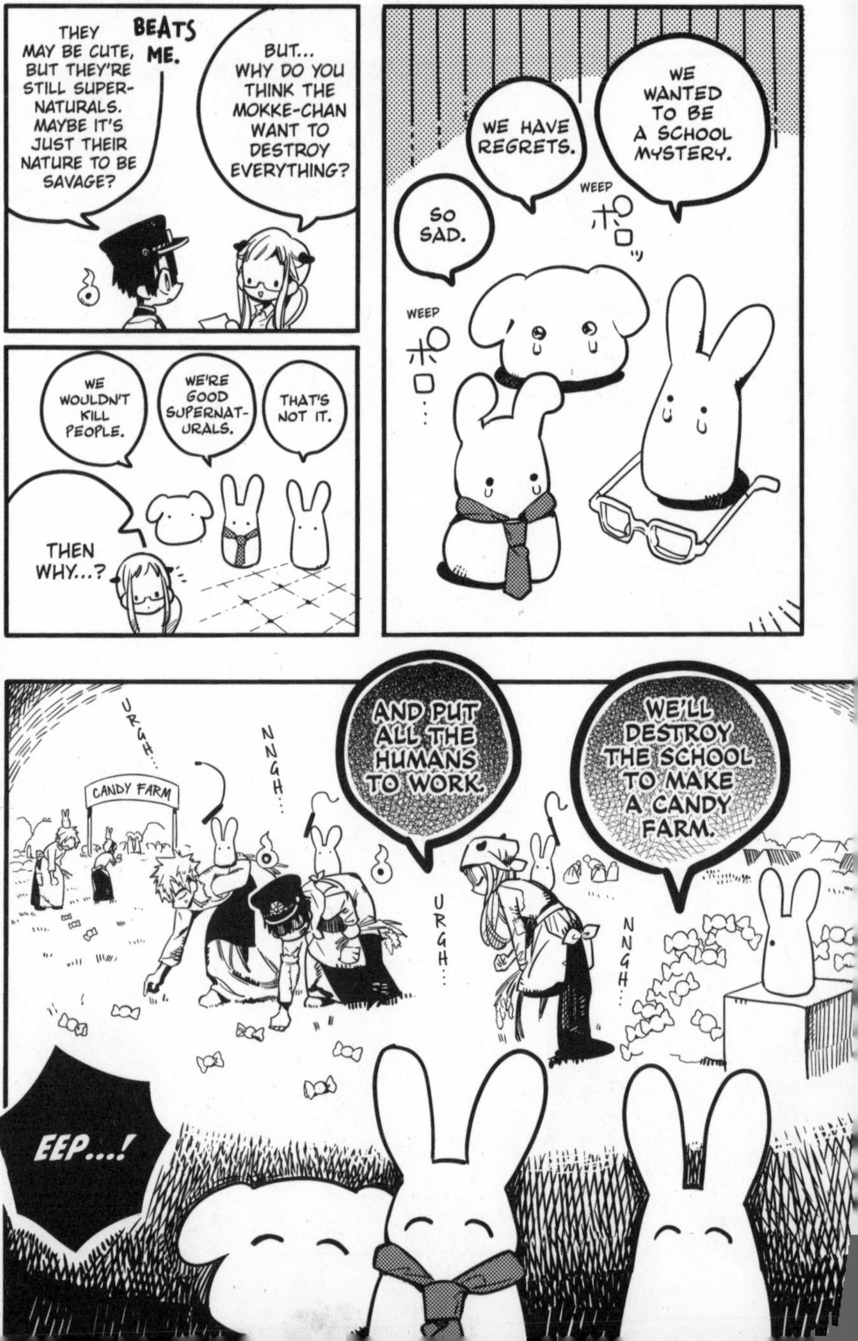
BUT... WHY DO YOU THINK THE MOKKE-CHAN WANT TO DESTROY EVERYTHING?
BEATS ME.
THEY MAY BE CUTE, BUT THEY'RE STILL SUPER-NATURALS. MAYBE IT'S JUST THEIR NATURE TO BE SAVAGE?
THAT'S NOT IT.
WE'RE GOOD SUPERNAT-URALS.
WE WOULDN'T KILL PEOPLE.
THEN WHY...?
WE WANTED TO BE A SCHOOL MYSTERY.
WE HAVE REGRETS.
WEEP
ポロッ
SO SAD.
WEEP
ポロ…
WE'LL DESTROY THE SCHOOL TO MAKE A CANDY FARM.
AND PUT ALL THE HUMANS TO WORK.
NNGH...
URGH...
NNGH...
URGH...
CANDY FARM
EEP...!

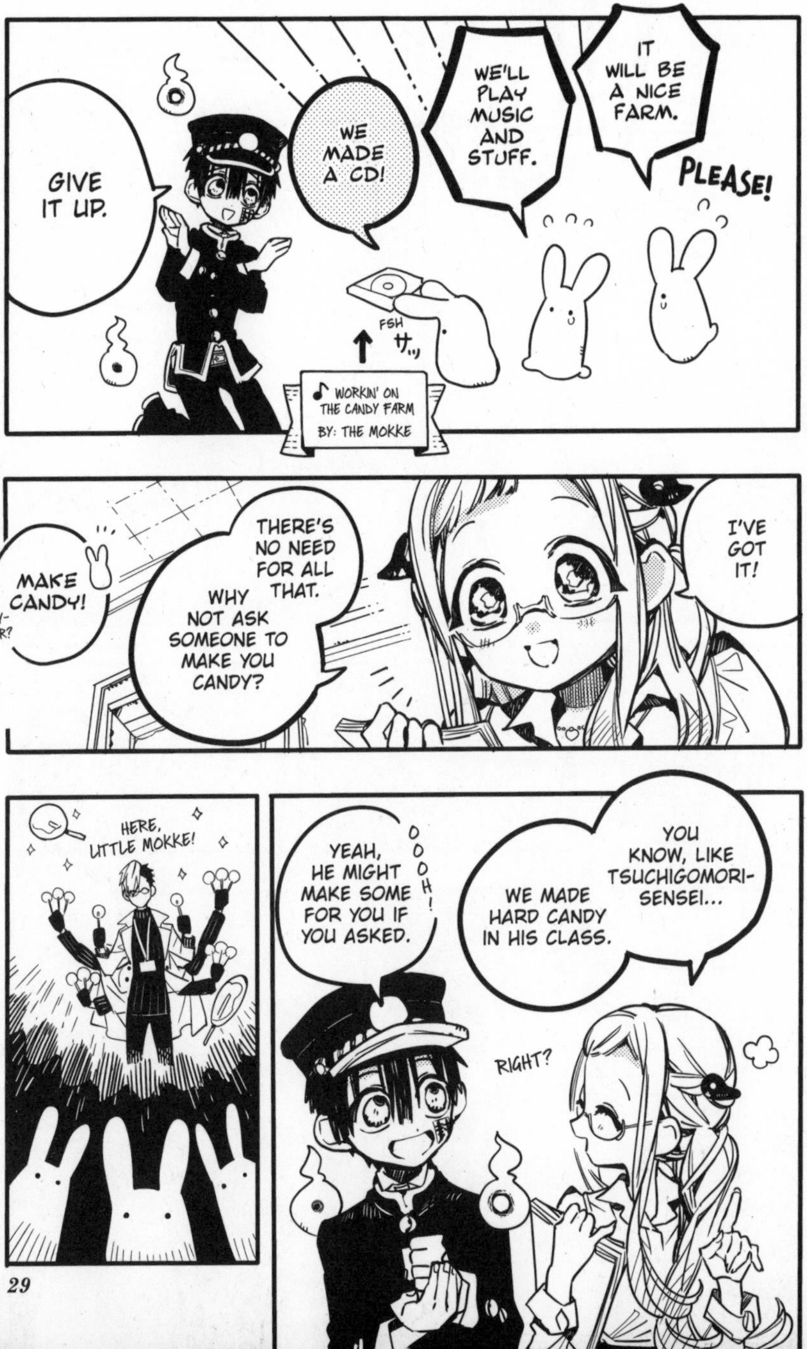
IT WILL BE A NICE FARM.
PLEASE!
WE'LL PLAY MUSIC AND STUFF.
WE MADE A CD!
FSH
サッ
WORKIN' ON THE CANDY FARM BY: THE MOKKE
GIVE IT UP.
I'VE GOT IT!
THERE'S NO NEED FOR ALL THAT.
WHY NOT ASK SOMEONE TO MAKE YOU CANDY?
MAKE CANDY!
A CANDY-MAKER?
YOU KNOW, LIKE TSUCHIGOMORI-SENSEI...
WE MADE HARD CANDY IN HIS CLASS.
RIGHT?
OOOH!
YEAH, HE MIGHT MAKE SOME FOR YOU IF YOU ASKED.
HERE, LITTLE MOKKE!

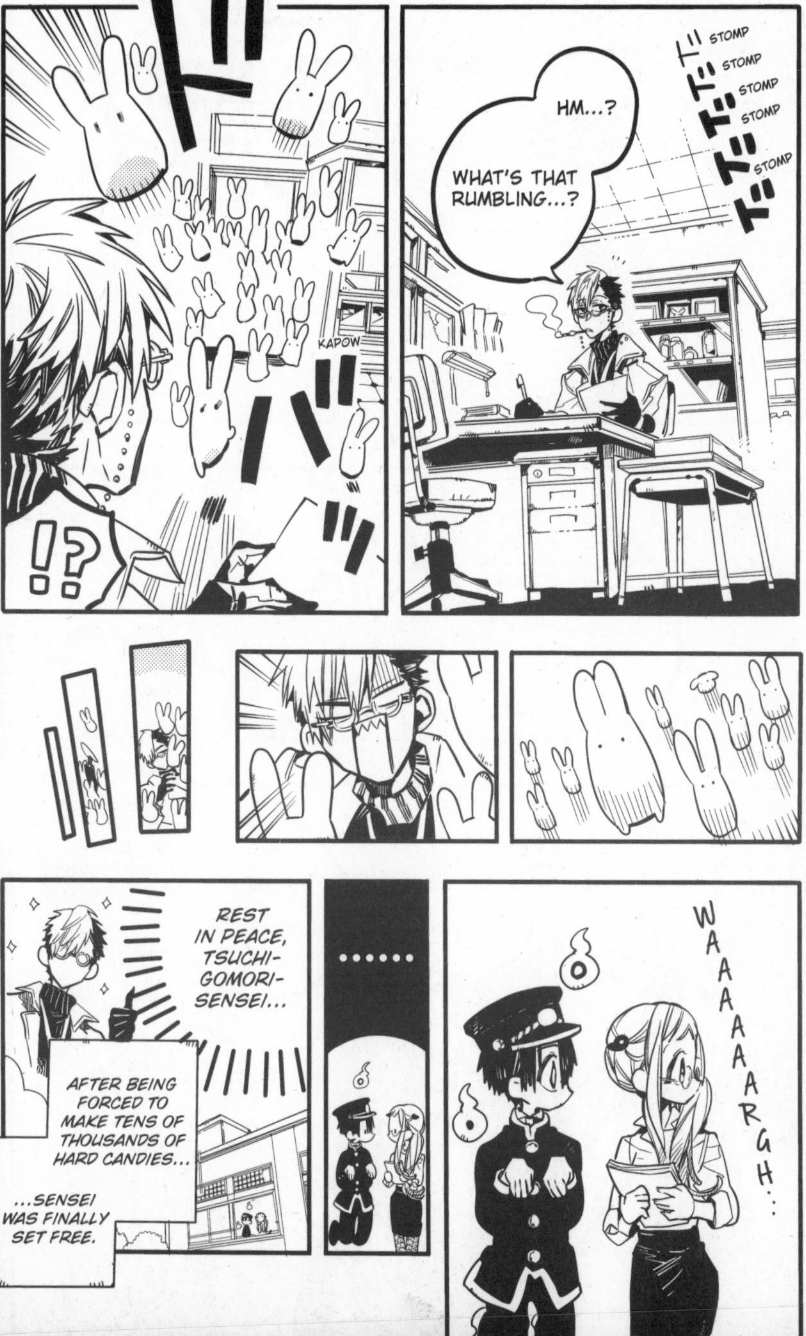
STOMP
STOMP
STOMP
STOMP
STOMP
HM...?
WHAT'S THAT RUMBLING...?
KAPOW
!?
REST IN PEACE, TSUCHIGOMORI-SENSEI...
AFTER BEING FORCED TO MAKE TENS OF THOUSANDS OF HARD CANDIES...
...SENSEI WAS FINALLY SET FREE.
WAAAAAAAARGH...
......

After-School
Hanako-Kun

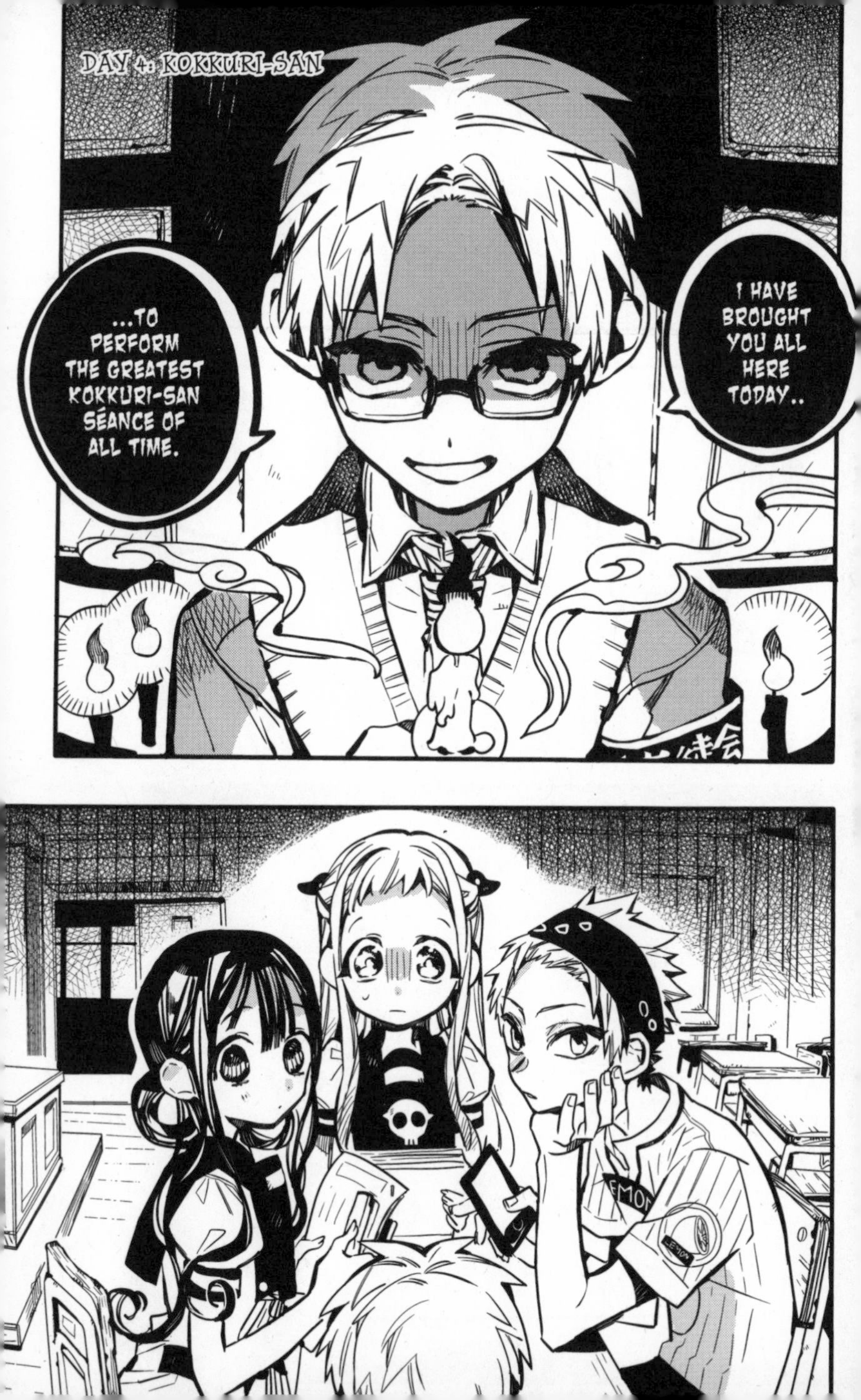
DAY 4: KOKKURI-SAN
I HAVE BROUGHT YOU ALL HERE TODAY..
...TO PERFORM THE GREATEST KOKKURI-SAN SÉANCE OF ALL TIME.

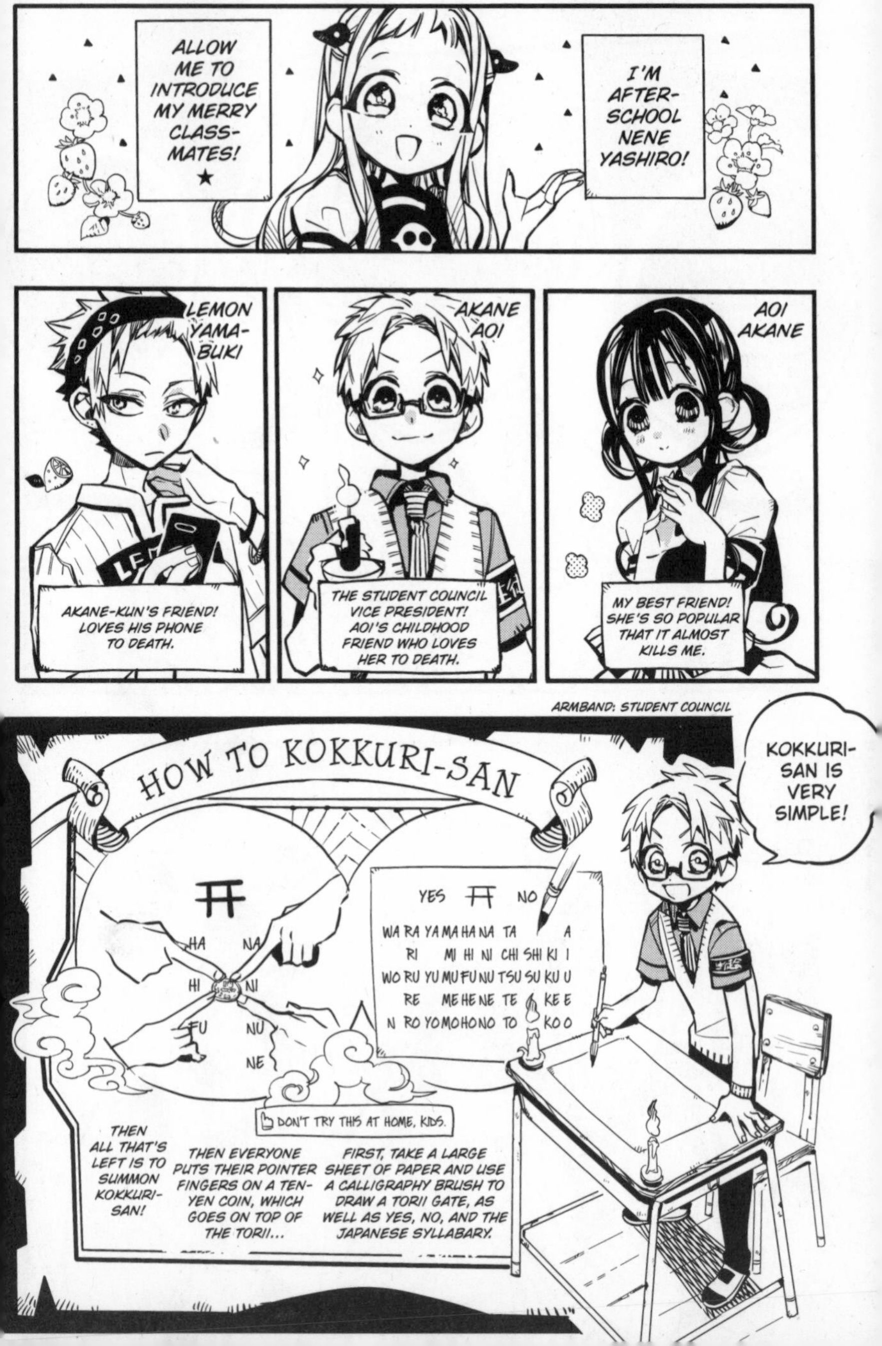
I'M AFTER-SCHOOL NENE YASHIRO!
ALLOW ME TO INTRODUCE MY MERRY CLASSMATES! ★
AOI AKANE
MY BEST FRIEND! SHE'S SO POPULAR THAT IT ALMOST KILLS ME.
AKANE AOI
THE STUDENT COUNCIL VICE PRESIDENT! AOI'S CHILDHOOD FRIEND WHO LOVES HER TO DEATH.
LEMON YAMABUKI
AKANE-KUN'S FRIEND! LOVES HIS PHONE TO DEATH.
ARMBAND: STUDENT COUNCIL
KOKKURI-SAN IS VERY SIMPLE!
HOW TO KOKKURI-SAN
YES 开 NO
WA RA YA MA HA NA TA A
RI MI HI NI CHI SHI KI I
WO RU YU MU FU NU TSU SU KU U
RE ME HE NE TE KE E
N RO YO MO HO NO TO KO O
开
HA NA
HI NI
FU NU
NE
DON'T TRY THIS AT HOME, KIDS.
FIRST, TAKE A LARGE SHEET OF PAPER AND USE A CALLIGRAPHY BRUSH TO DRAW A TORII GATE, AS WELL AS YES, NO, AND THE JAPANESE SYLLABARY.
THEN EVERYONE PUTS THEIR POINTER FINGERS ON A TEN-YEN COIN, WHICH GOES ON TOP OF THE TORII...
THEN ALL THAT'S LEFT IS TO SUMMON KOKKURI-SAN!

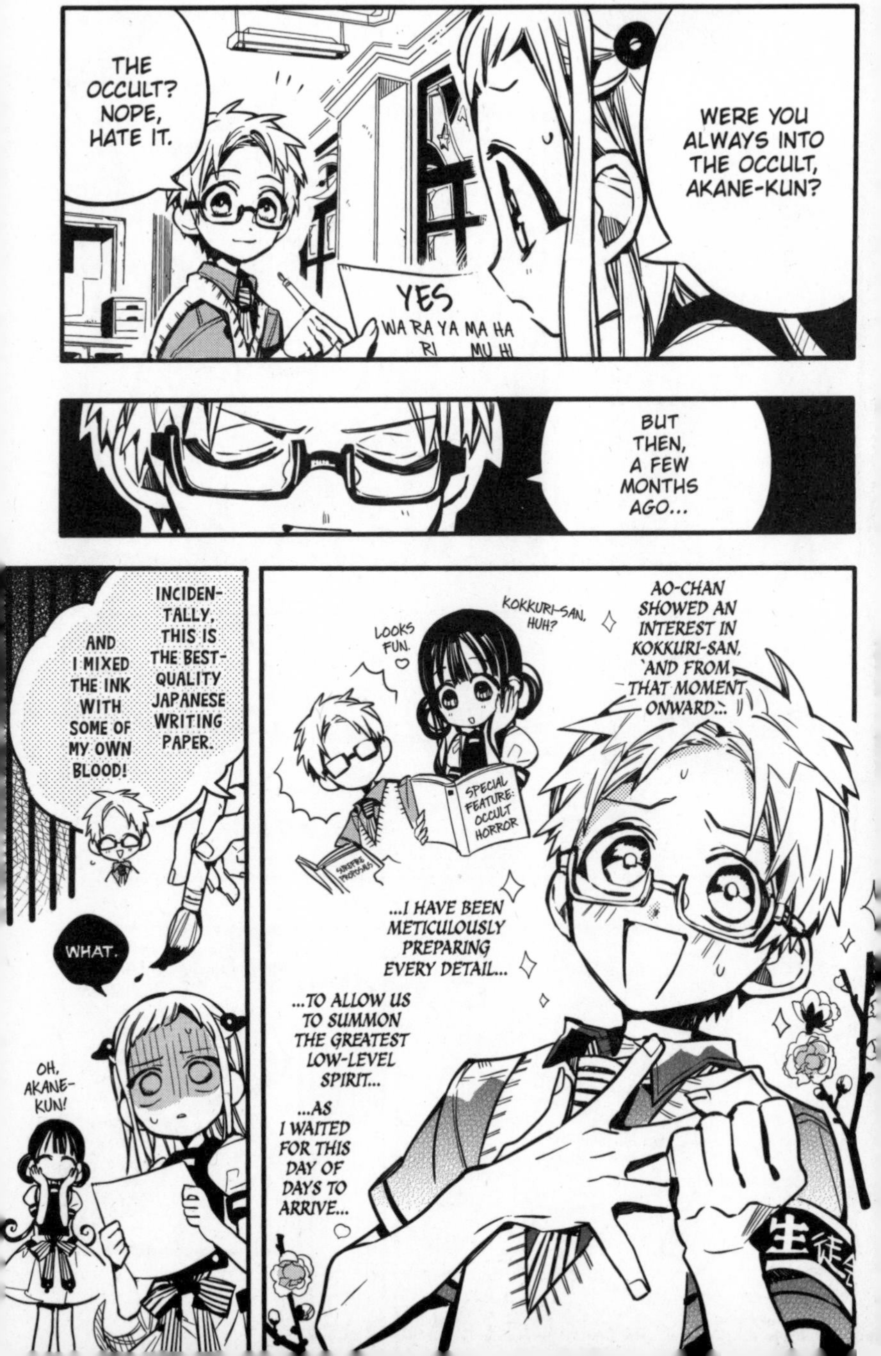
WERE YOU ALWAYS INTO THE OCCULT, AKANE-KUN?
THE OCCULT? NOPE, HATE IT.
YES
WA RA YA MA HA
RI MU HI
BUT THEN, A FEW MONTHS AGO...
AO-CHAN SHOWED AN INTEREST IN KOKKURI-SAN, AND FROM THAT MOMENT ONWARD...
KOKKURI-SAN, HUH?
LOOKS FUN.
SPECIAL FEATURE: OCCULT HORROR
...I HAVE BEEN METICULOUSLY PREPARING EVERY DETAIL...
...TO ALLOW US TO SUMMON THE GREATEST LOW-LEVEL SPIRIT...
...AS I WAITED FOR THIS DAY OF DAYS TO ARRIVE...
INCIDENTALLY, THIS IS THE BEST-QUALITY JAPANESE WRITING PAPER.
AND I MIXED THE INK WITH SOME OF MY OWN BLOOD!
WHAT.
OH, AKANE-KUN!

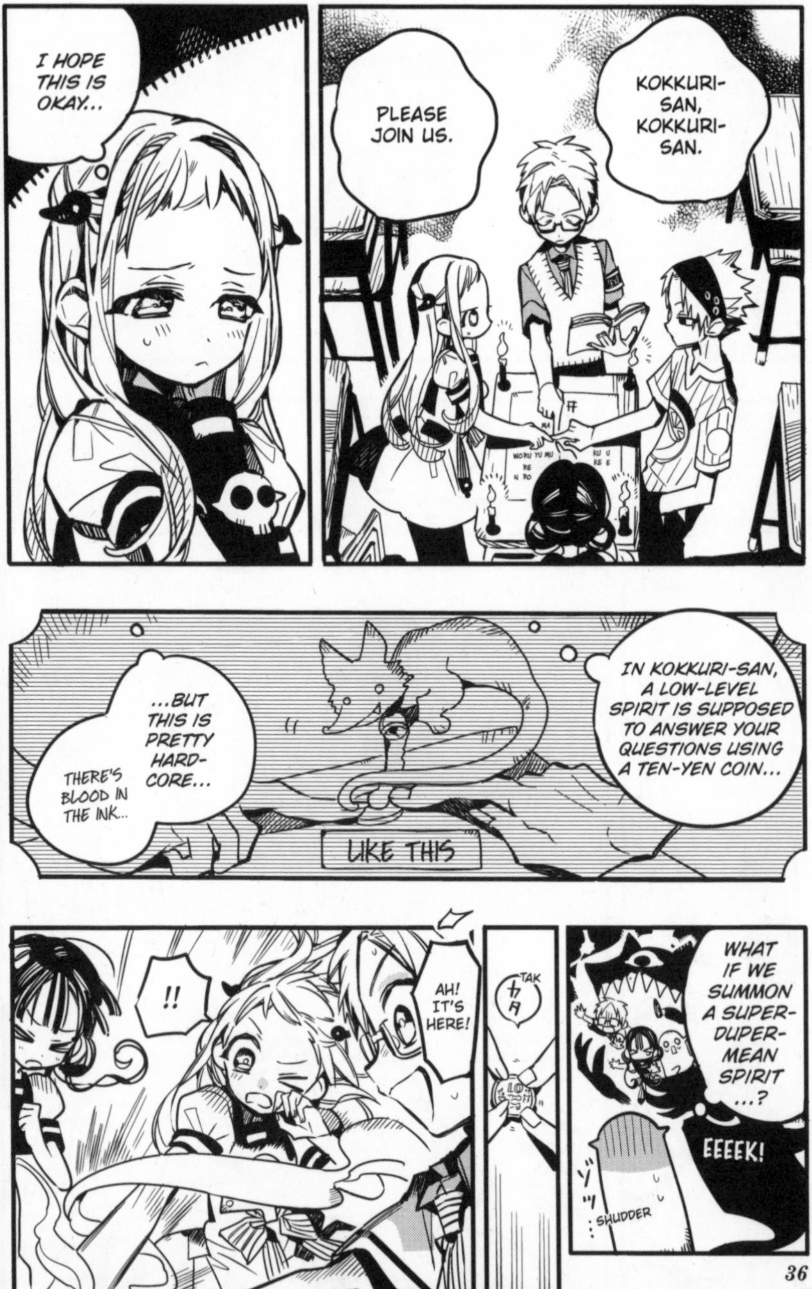

KOKKURI-SAN, KOKKURI-SAN.
PLEASE JOIN US.
I HOPE THIS IS OKAY...
IN KOKKURI-SAN, A LOW-LEVEL SPIRIT IS SUPPOSED TO ANSWER YOUR QUESTIONS USING A TEN-YEN COIN...
...BUT THIS IS PRETTY HARDCORE...
THERE'S BLOOD IN THE INK...
LIKE THIS
WHAT IF WE SUMMON A SUPER-DUPER-MEAN SPIRIT ...?
EEEEK!
SHUDDER
TAK
AH! IT'S HERE!
!!

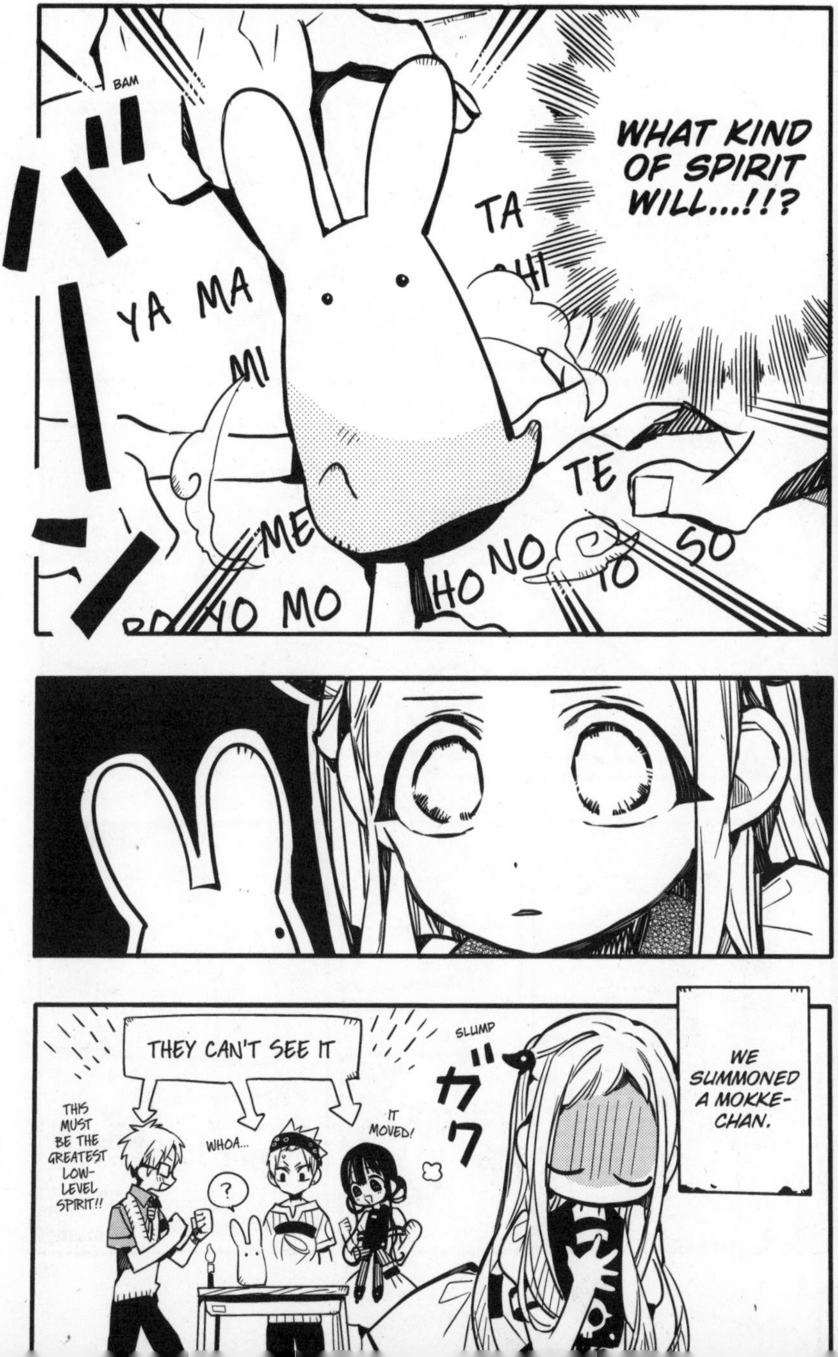
WHAT KIND OF SPIRIT WILL...!!?
BAM
YA MA
MI
TA
HI
TE
ME
NO
HO
MO
SO
WE SUMMONED A MOKKE-CHAN.
SLUMP
THEY CAN'T SEE IT
IT MOVED!
WHOA...
THIS MUST BE THE GREATEST LOW-LEVEL SPIRIT!!
?

MOKKE-CHAN IS THE GREATEST LOW-LEVEL SPIRIT...!?

WHAT KIND OF ANSWERS WILL IT GIVE US...!?

GULP

ALL RIGHT. OUR FIRST QUESTION IS...

WHAT WILL THE WEATHER BE TOMORROW?

*AME: JAPANESE FOR "RAIN" AND "CANDY"

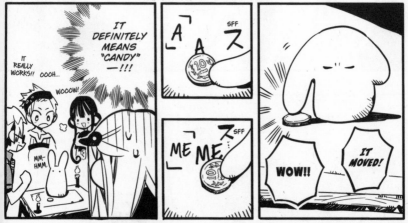

IT DEFINITELY MEANS "CANDY"—!!!

IT REALLY WORKS!! OOOH...

WOOOW!!

MM-HMM.

「A」 ス SFF

「ME ME」ス SFF

WOW!!

IT MOVED!

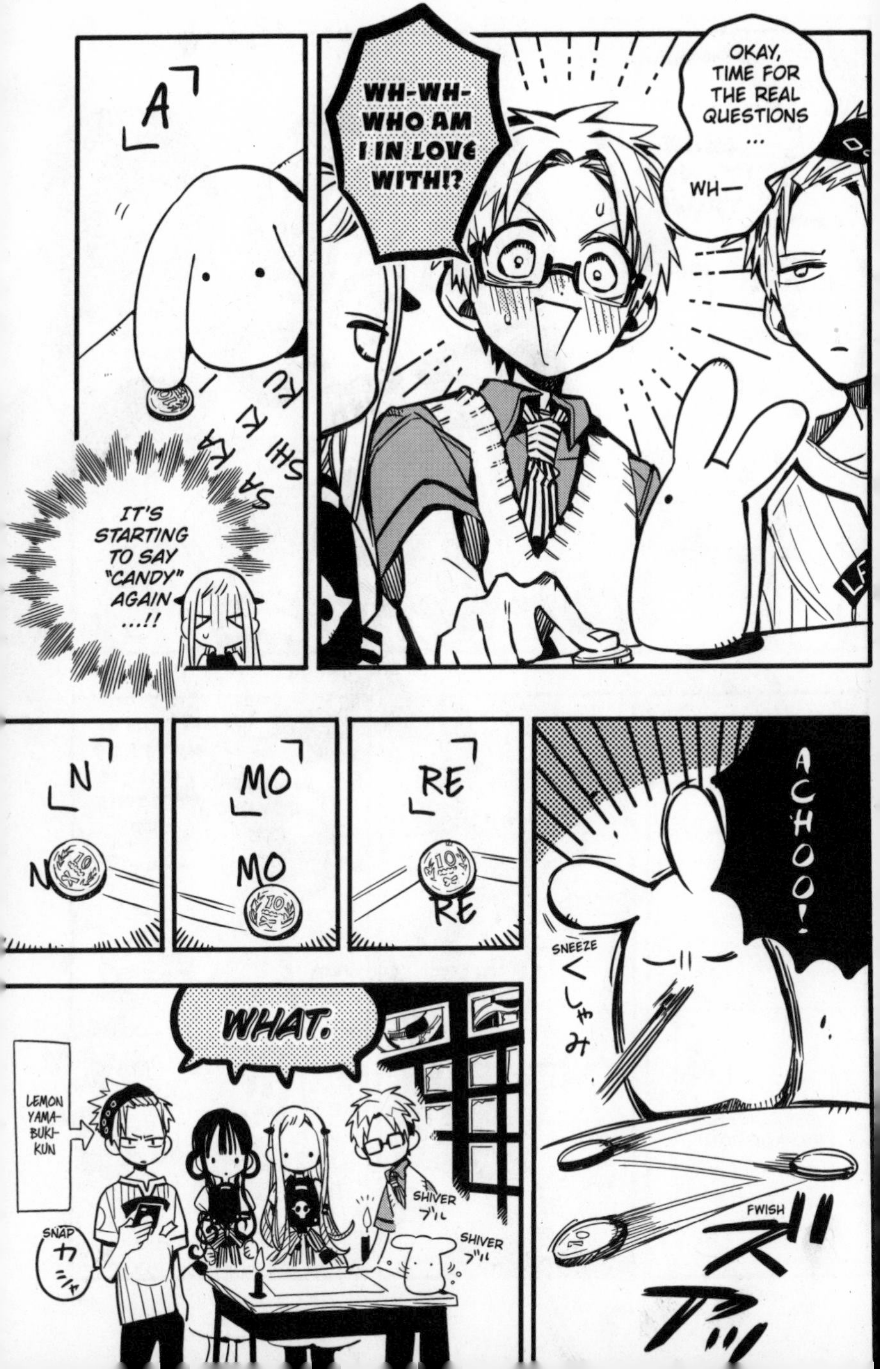
OKAY, TIME FOR THE REAL QUESTIONS ...
WH—
WH-WH-WHO AM I IN LOVE WITH!?
A
IT'S STARTING TO SAY "CANDY" AGAIN ...!!
ACHOO!
SNEEZE
くしゃみ
FWISH
ズバッ
RE
RE
MO
MO
N
N
WHAT.
LEMON YAMABUKI-KUN
SHIVER
ブル
SHIVER
ブル
SNAP
カシャ

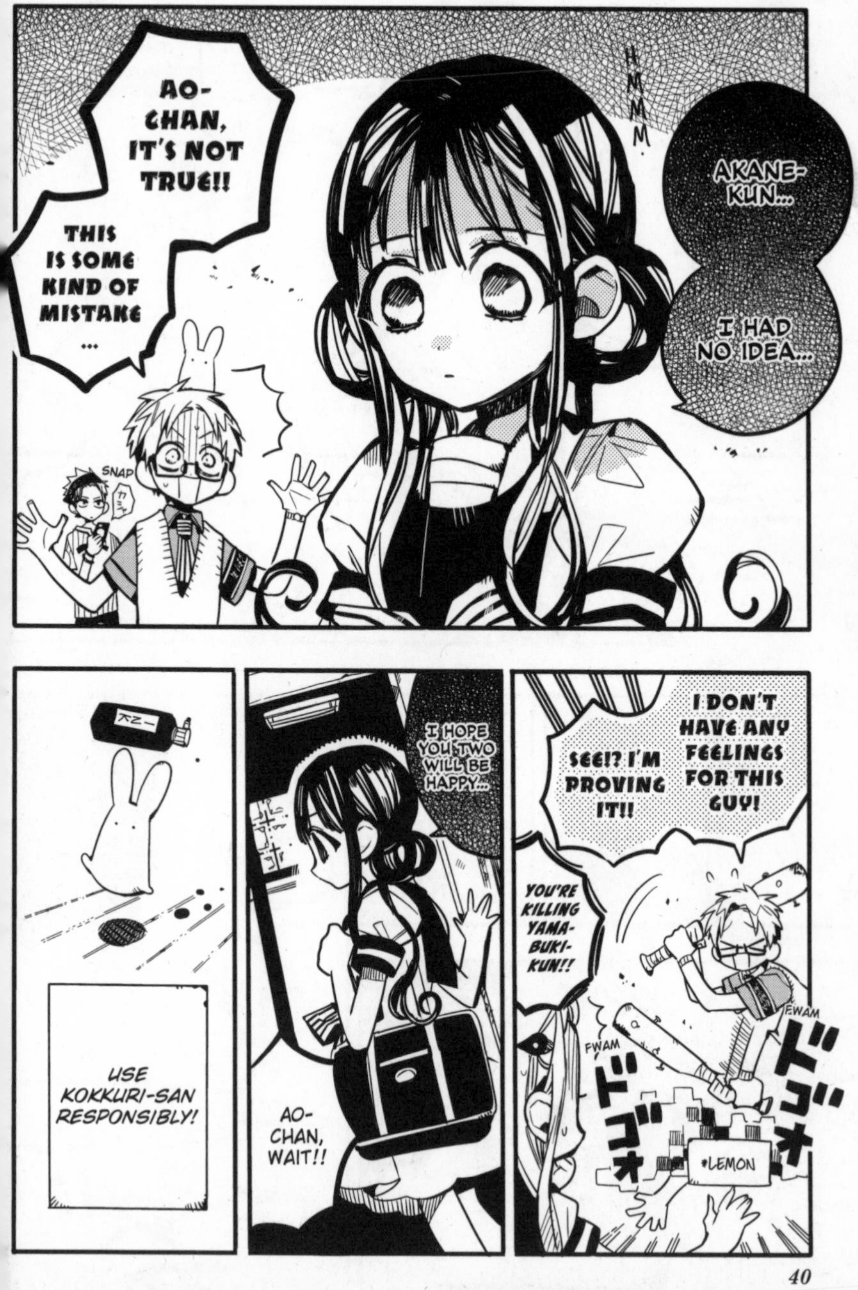
HMMMM
AKANE-KUN...
I HAD NO IDEA...
AO-CHAN, IT'S NOT TRUE!!
THIS IS SOME KIND OF MISTAKE ...
SNAP
I DON'T HAVE ANY FEELINGS FOR THIS GUY!
SEE!? I'M PROVING IT!!
YOU'RE KILLING YAMA-BUKI-KUN!!
FWAM
ドゴォ
FWAM
ドゴォ
#LEMON
I HOPE YOU TWO WILL BE HAPPY...
AO-CHAN, WAIT!!
USE KOKKURI-SAN RESPONSIBLY!

After•School
Hanako-Kun

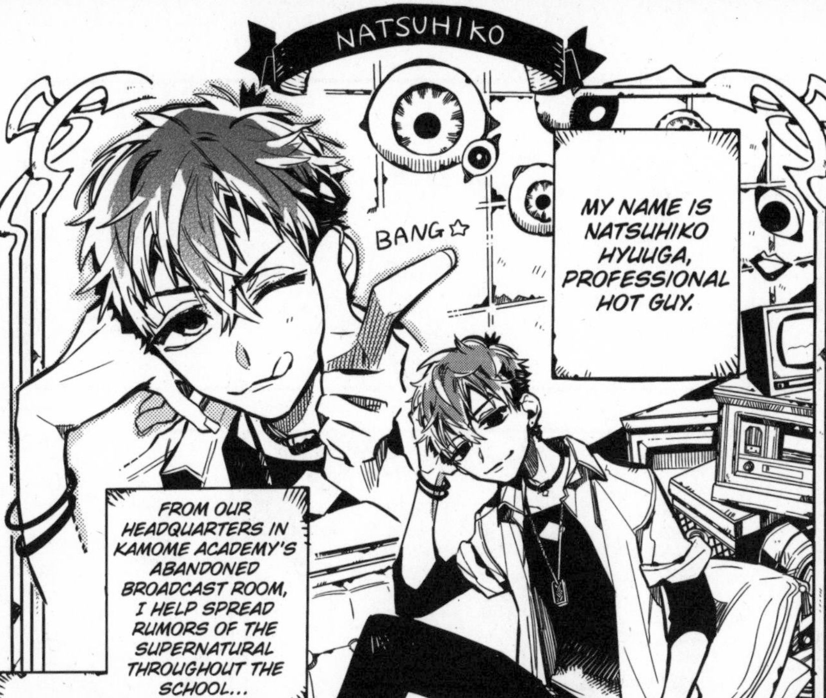
NATSUHIKO
MY NAME IS NATSUHIKO HYUUGA, PROFESSIONAL HOT GUY.
BANG☆
FROM OUR HEADQUARTERS IN KAMOME ACADEMY'S ABANDONED BROADCAST ROOM, I HELP SPREAD RUMORS OF THE SUPERNATURAL THROUGHOUT THE SCHOOL...
...BLURRING THE LINES BETWEEN THE NEAR AND FAR SHORES.
DAY 5: AFTER-SCHOOL BROADCAST ROOM

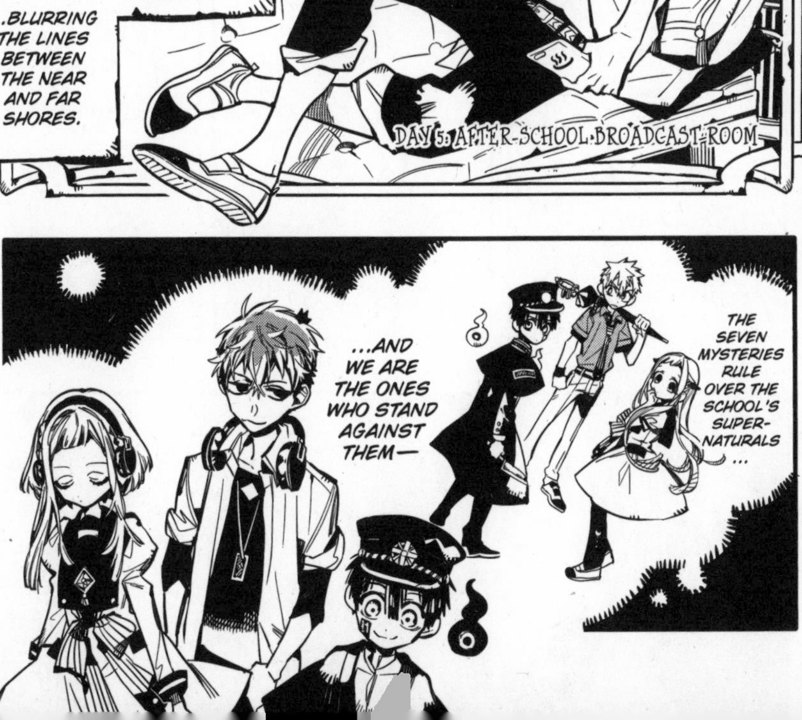
THE SEVEN MYSTERIES RULE OVER THE SCHOOL'S SUPER-NATURALS...
...AND WE ARE THE ONES WHO STAND AGAINST THEM—

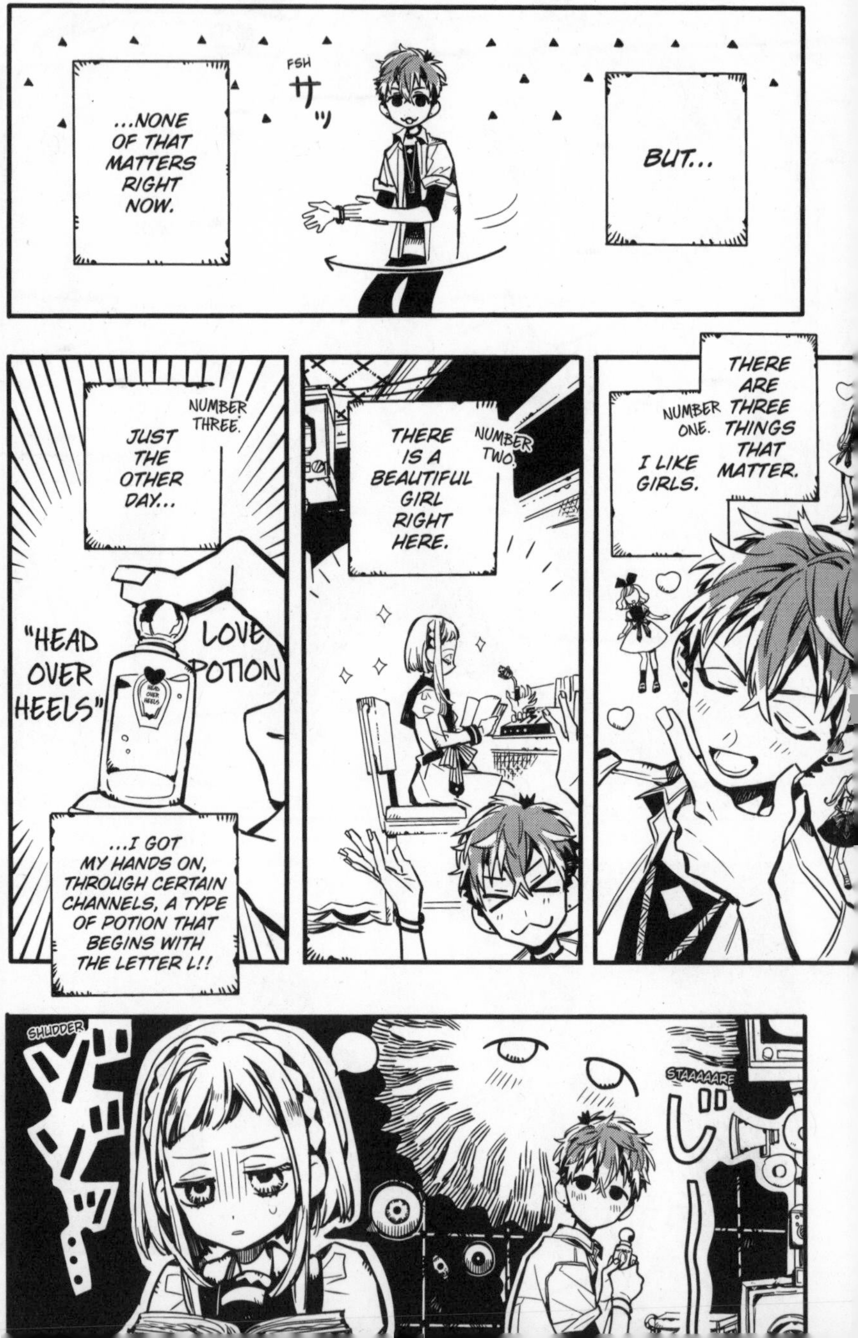
BUT...
FSH
サッ
...NONE OF THAT MATTERS RIGHT NOW.
THERE ARE THREE THINGS THAT MATTER.
NUMBER ONE.
I LIKE GIRLS.
NUMBER TWO.
THERE IS A BEAUTIFUL GIRL RIGHT HERE.
NUMBER THREE.
JUST THE OTHER DAY...
LOVE POTION
"HEAD OVER HEELS"
HEAD OVER HEELS
...I GOT MY HANDS ON, THROUGH CERTAIN CHANNELS, A TYPE OF POTION THAT BEGINS WITH THE LETTER L!!
STAAAAARE
SHUDDER

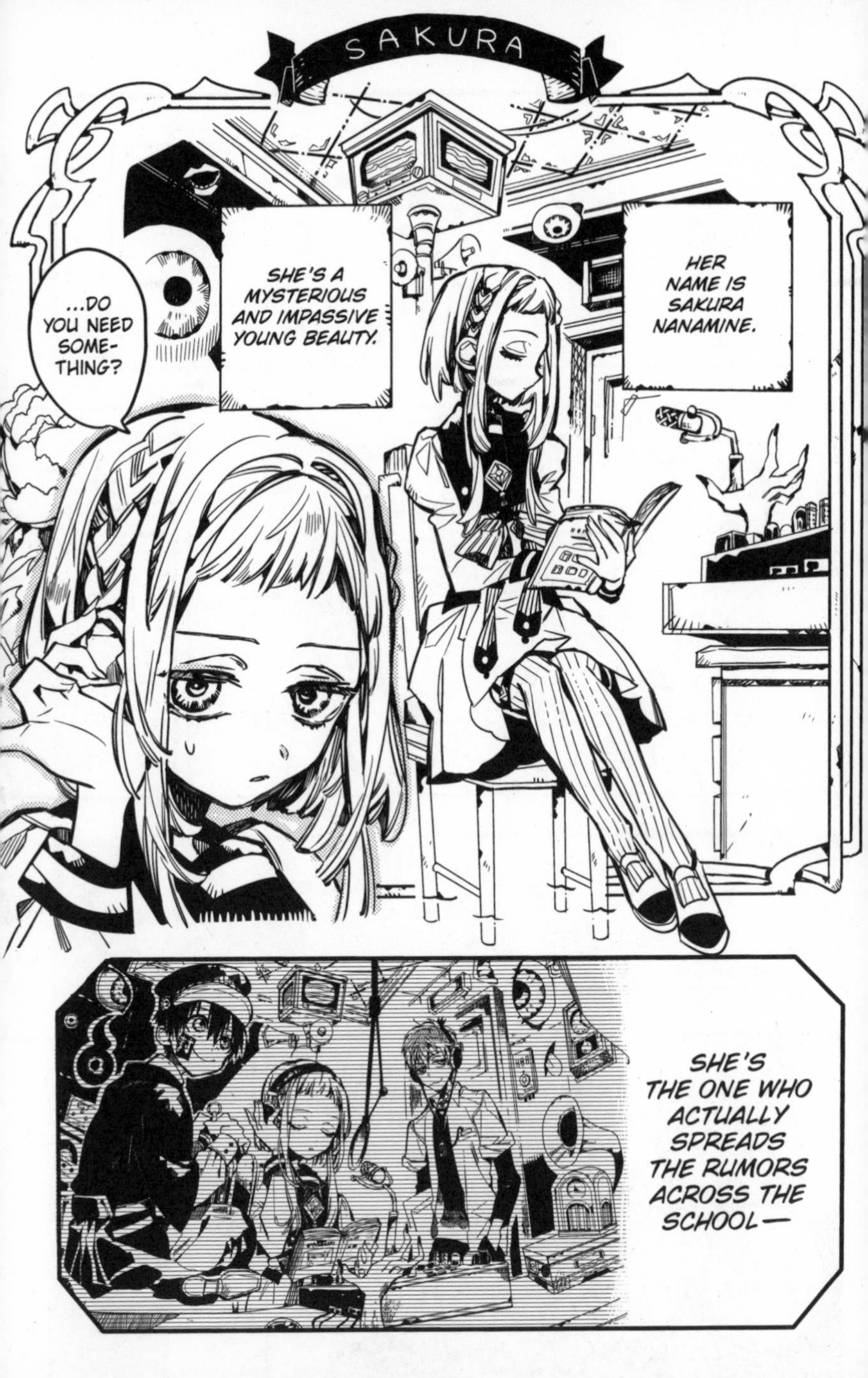
SAKURA
HER NAME IS SAKURA NANAMINE.
SHE'S A MYSTERIOUS AND IMPASSIVE YOUNG BEAUTY.
...DO YOU NEED SOME-THING?
SHE'S THE ONE WHO ACTUALLY SPREADS THE RUMORS ACROSS THE SCHOOL—

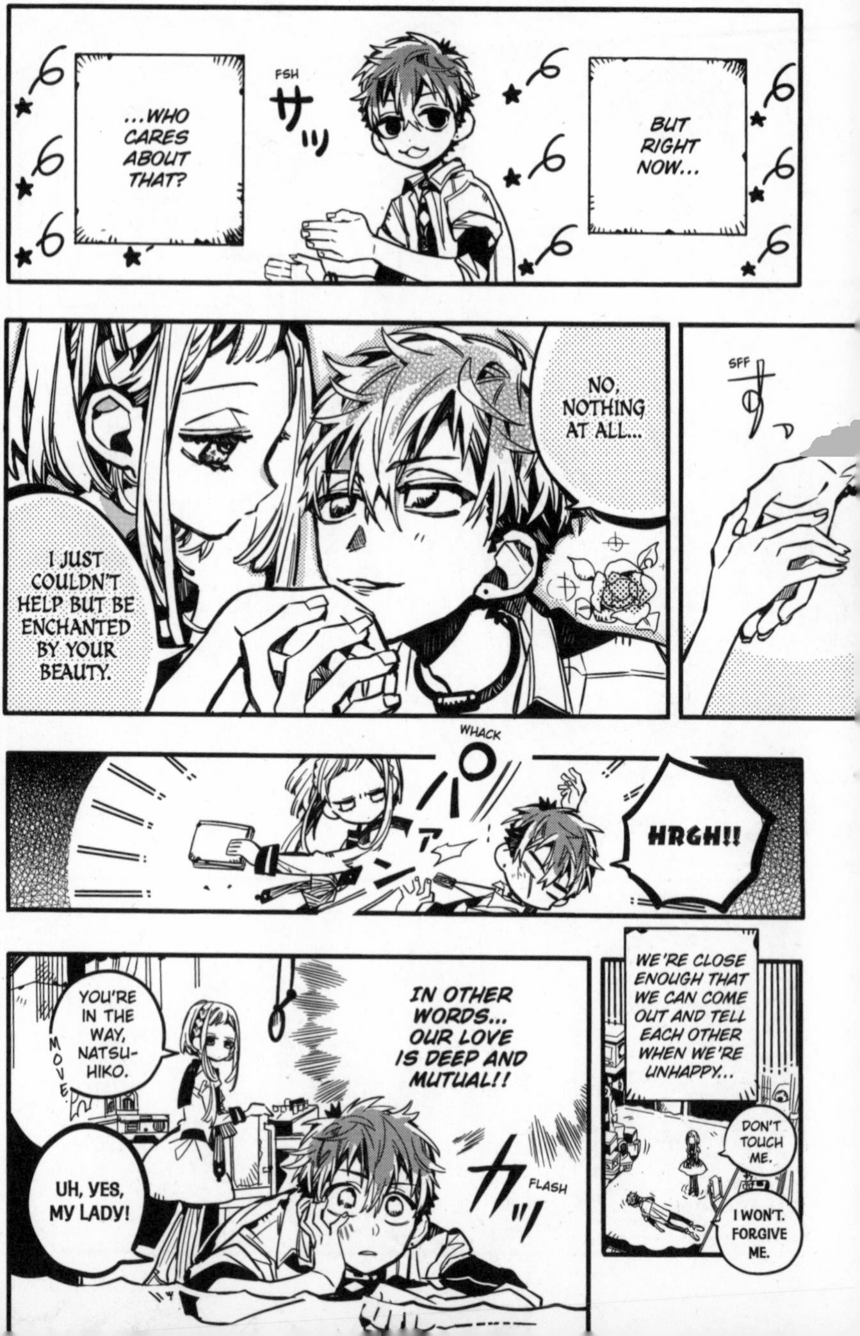
BUT RIGHT NOW...
FSH
サッ
...WHO CARES ABOUT THAT?
SFF
すっ
NO, NOTHING AT ALL...
I JUST COULDN'T HELP BUT BE ENCHANTED BY YOUR BEAUTY.
WHACK
パァン
HRGH!!
WE'RE CLOSE ENOUGH THAT WE CAN COME OUT AND TELL EACH OTHER WHEN WE'RE UNHAPPY...
DON'T TOUCH ME.
I WON'T. FORGIVE ME.
IN OTHER WORDS... OUR LOVE IS DEEP AND MUTUAL!!
FLASH
カッ
YOU'RE IN THE WAY, NATSU-HIKO.
MOVE
UH, YES, MY LADY!

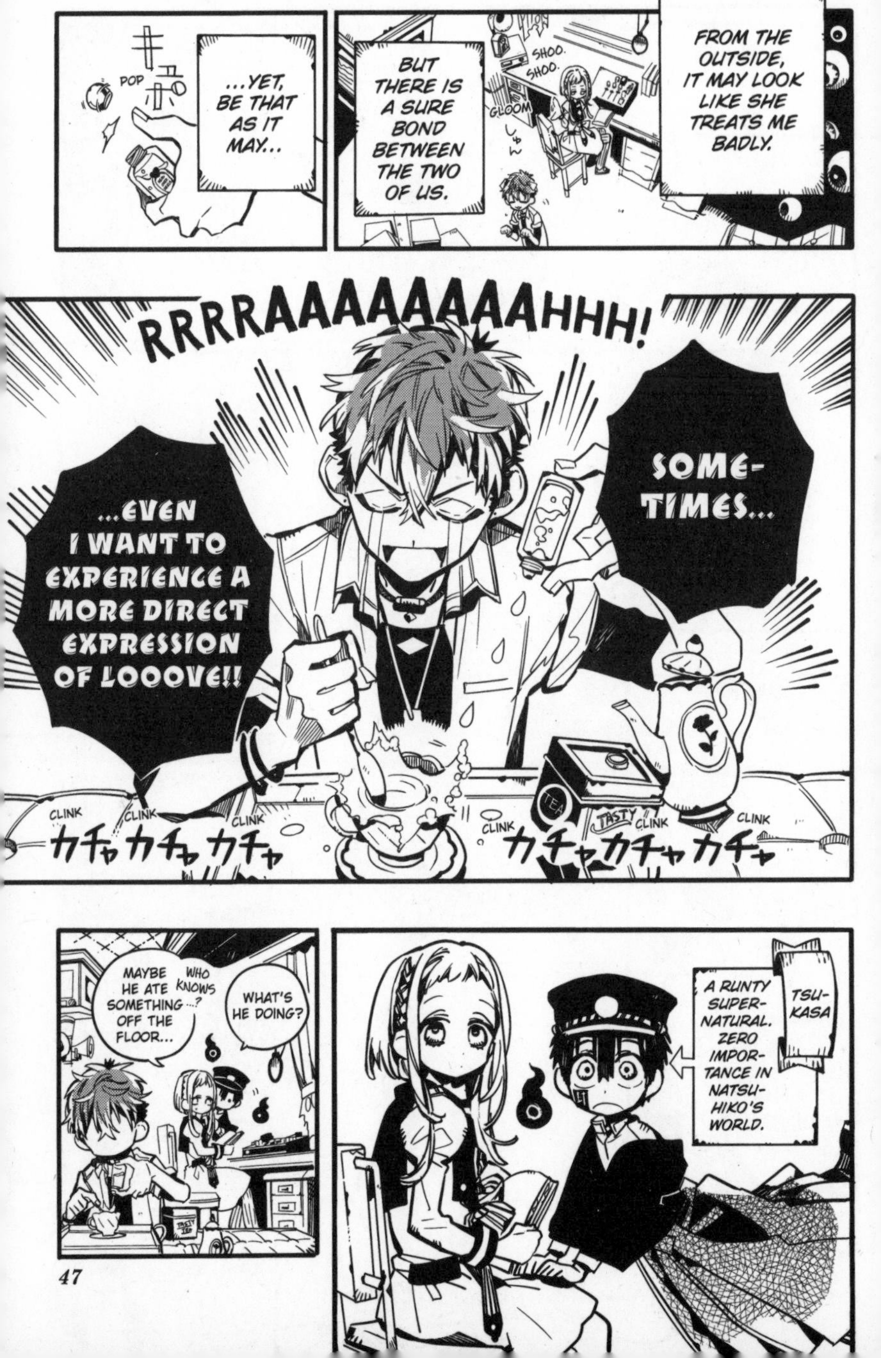
FROM THE OUTSIDE, IT MAY LOOK LIKE SHE TREATS ME BADLY.
BUT THERE IS A SURE BOND BETWEEN THE TWO OF US.
SHOO. SHOO.
GLOOM
...YET, BE THAT AS IT MAY...
POP
RRRRAAAAAAAAAHHH!
SOME-TIMES...
...EVEN I WANT TO EXPERIENCE A MORE DIRECT EXPRESSION OF LOOOVE!!
CLINK CLINK CLINK
CLINK CLINK CLINK
TASTY
TSU-KASA
A RUNTY SUPER-NATURAL. ZERO IMPOR-TANCE IN NATSU-HIKO'S WORLD.
WHAT'S HE DOING?
WHO KNOWS...?
MAYBE HE ATE SOMETHING OFF THE FLOOR...

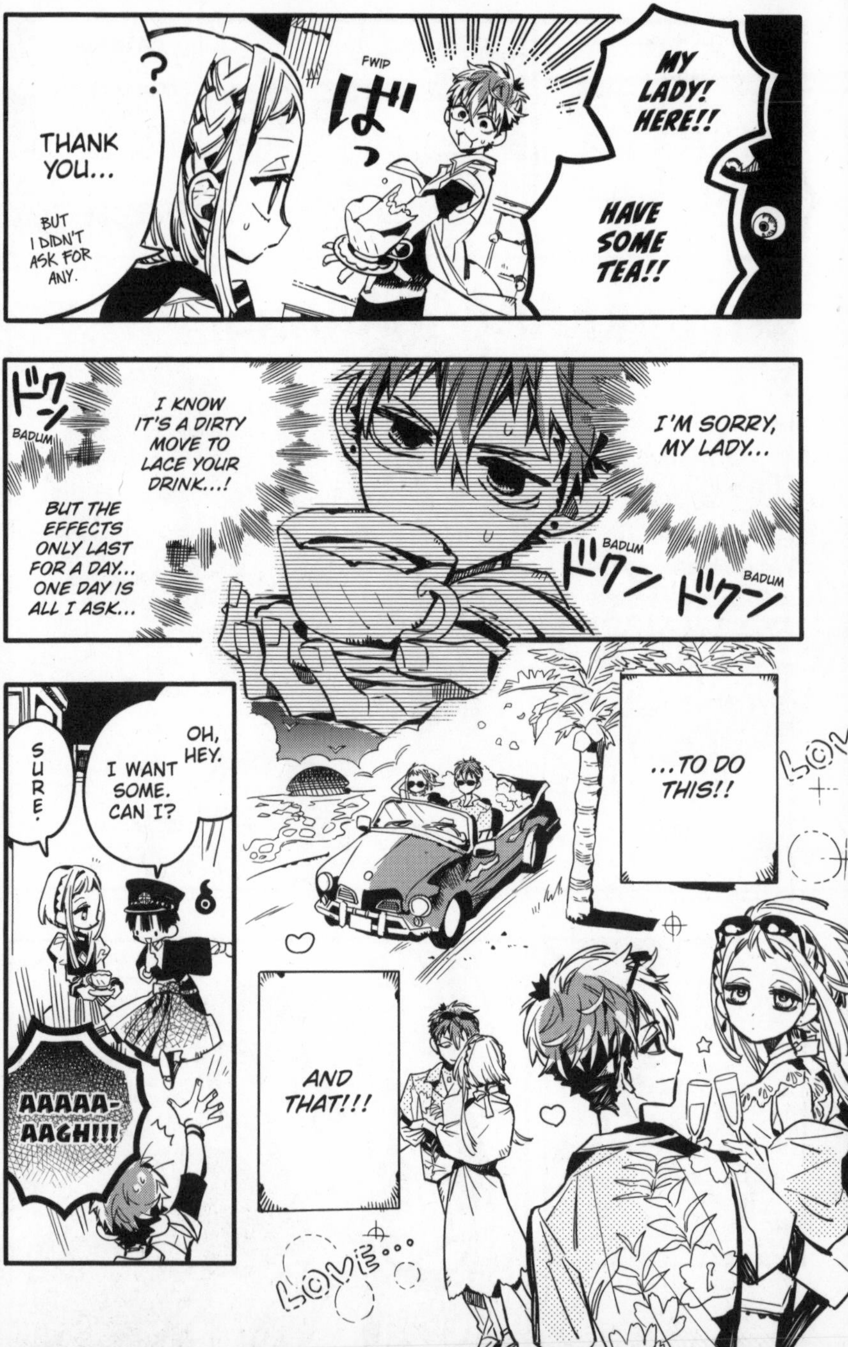
MY LADY! HERE!!
HAVE SOME TEA!!
FWIP
ばっ
THANK YOU...
BUT I DIDN'T ASK FOR ANY.
I'M SORRY, MY LADY...
BADUM
ドクン
BADUM
ドクン
I KNOW IT'S A DIRTY MOVE TO LACE YOUR DRINK...!
BUT THE EFFECTS ONLY LAST FOR A DAY... ONE DAY IS ALL I ASK...
ドクン
BADUM
...TO DO THIS!!
AND THAT!!!
LOVE...
OH, HEY.
I WANT SOME. CAN I?
SURE.
AAAAA-AAGH!!!

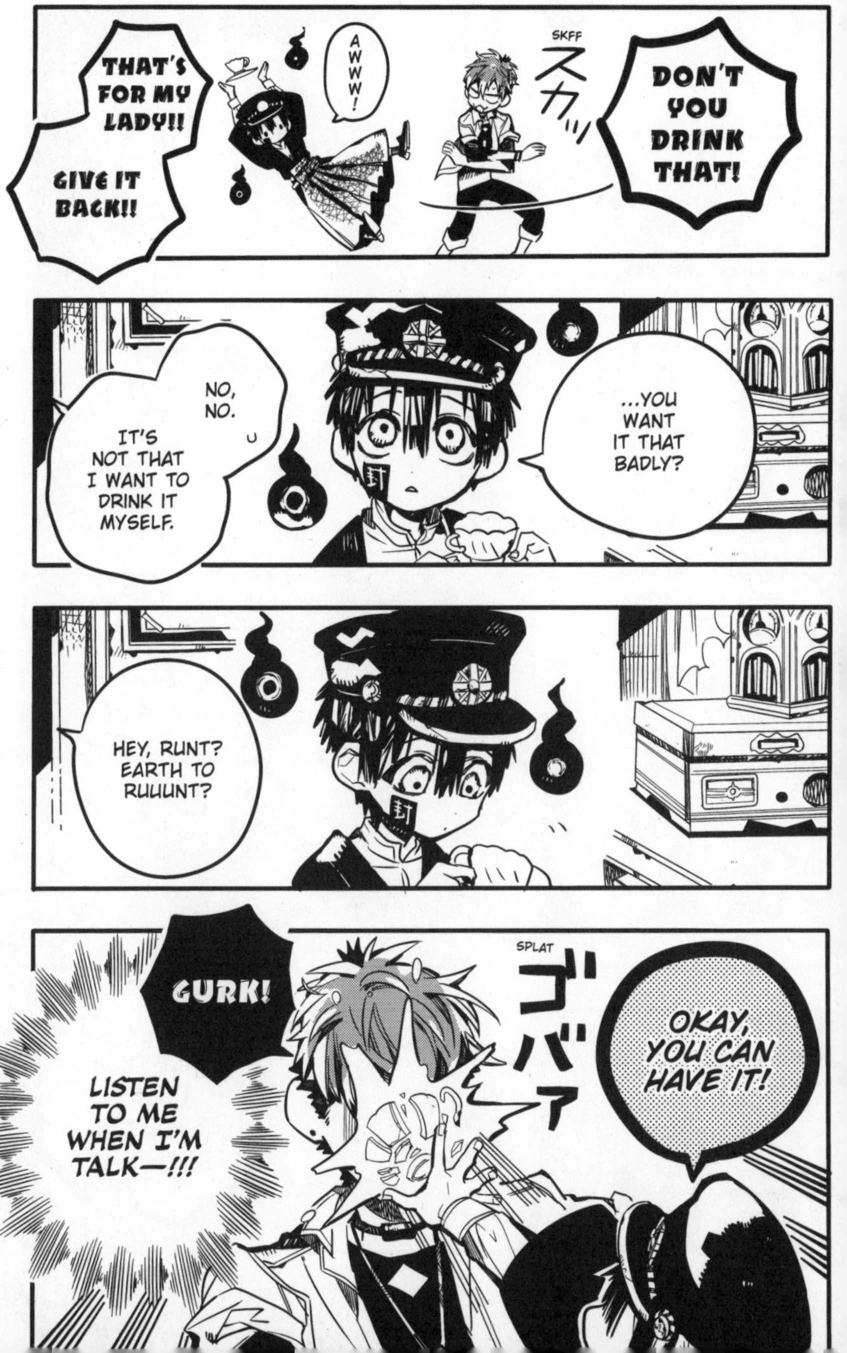
SKFF
スカッ
DON'T YOU DRINK THAT!
AWWW!
THAT'S FOR MY LADY!!
GIVE IT BACK!!
...YOU WANT IT THAT BADLY?
NO, NO.
IT'S NOT THAT I WANT TO DRINK IT MYSELF.
HEY, RUNT? EARTH TO RUUUNT?
SPLAT
ゴバア
OKAY, YOU CAN HAVE IT!
GURK!
LISTEN TO ME WHEN I'M TALK—!!!

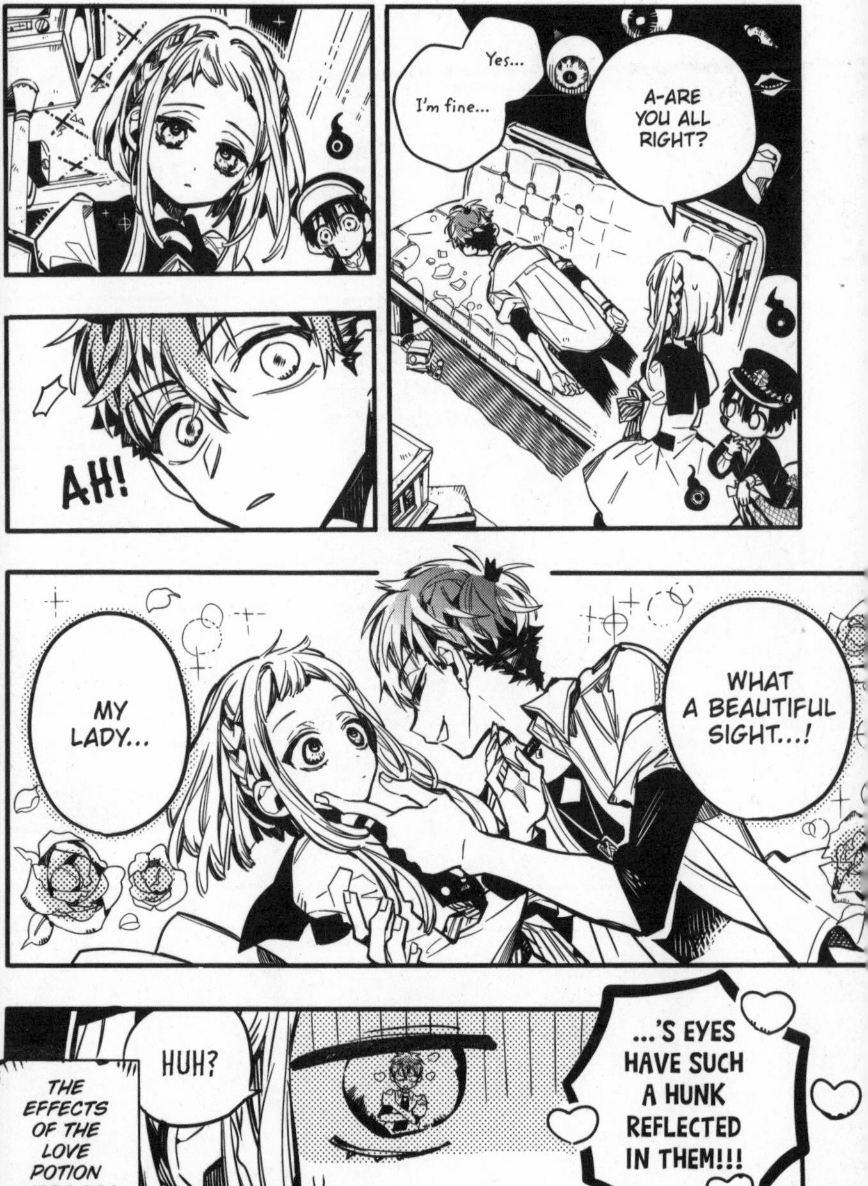
A-ARE YOU ALL RIGHT?
Yes... I'm fine...
AH!
WHAT A BEAUTIFUL SIGHT...!
MY LADY...
...'S EYES HAVE SUCH A HUNK REFLECTED IN THEM!!!
HUH?
THE EFFECTS OF THE LOVE POTION WORE OFF A DAY LATER.

After•School
Hanako-Kun

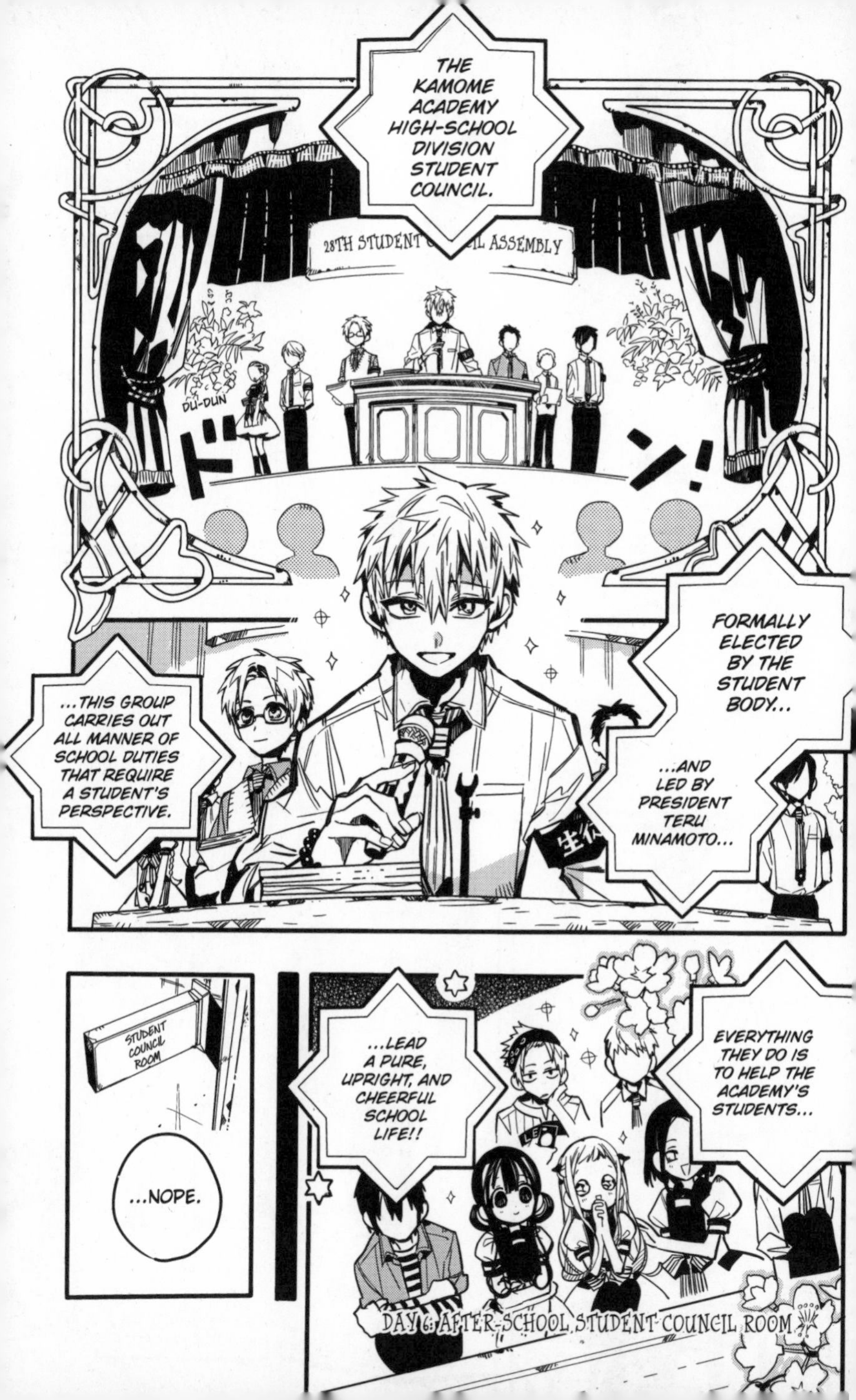
THE KAMOME ACADEMY HIGH-SCHOOL DIVISION STUDENT COUNCIL.
28TH STUDENT
IL ASSEMBLY
DU-DUN
FORMALLY ELECTED BY THE STUDENT BODY...
...AND LED BY PRESIDENT TERU MINAMOTO...
...THIS GROUP CARRIES OUT ALL MANNER OF SCHOOL DUTIES THAT REQUIRE A STUDENT'S PERSPECTIVE.
EVERYTHING THEY DO IS TO HELP THE ACADEMY'S STUDENTS...
...LEAD A PURE, UPRIGHT, AND CHEERFUL SCHOOL LIFE!!
DAY 6: AFTER-SCHOOL STUDENT COUNCIL ROOM
STUDENT COUNCIL ROOM
...NOPE.

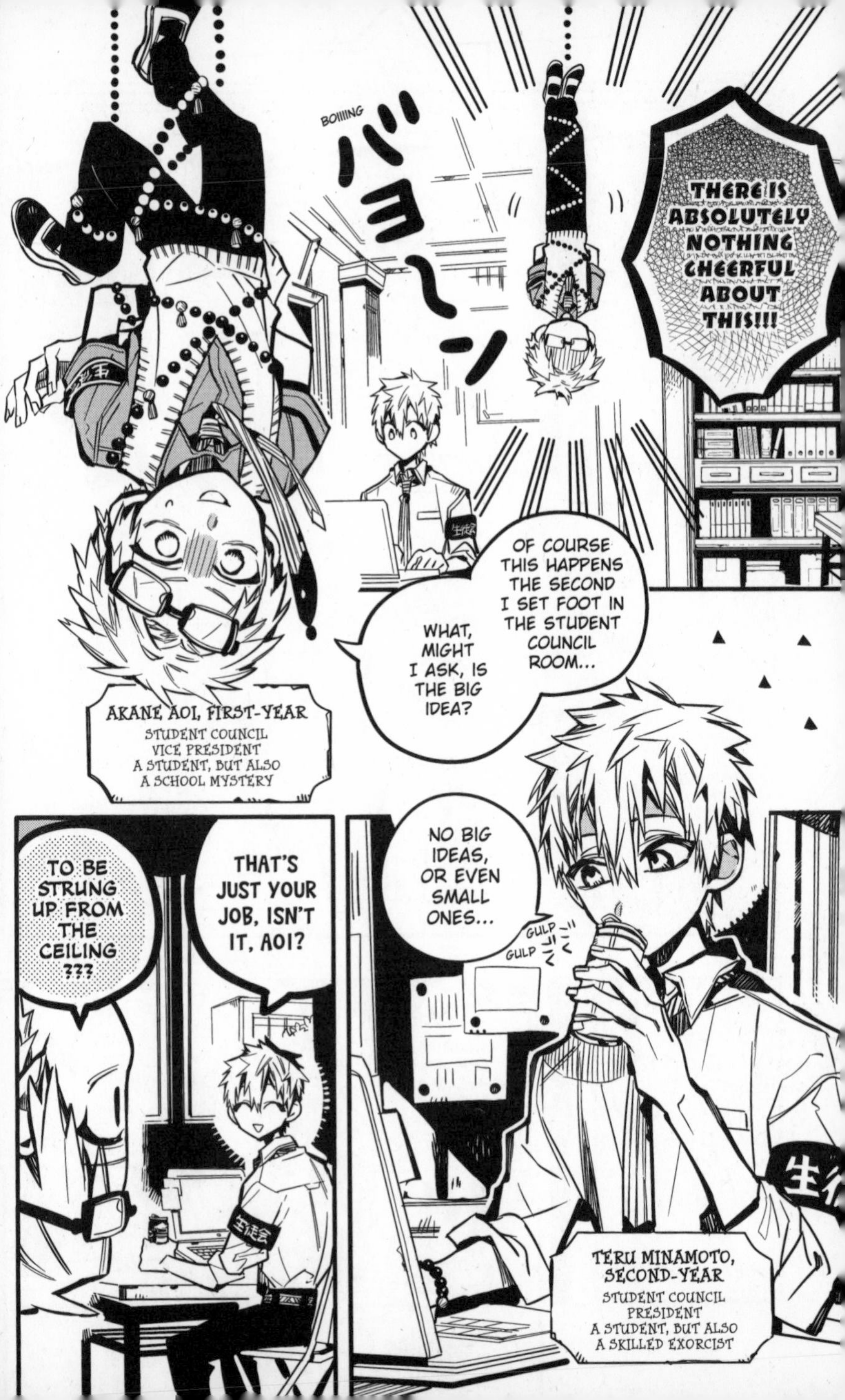
BOIIIING
バヨ〜ン
THERE IS ABSOLUTELY NOTHING CHEERFUL ABOUT THIS!!!
OF COURSE THIS HAPPENS THE SECOND I SET FOOT IN THE STUDENT COUNCIL ROOM...
WHAT, MIGHT I ASK, IS THE BIG IDEA?
AKANE AOI, FIRST-YEAR
STUDENT COUNCIL VICE PRESIDENT
A STUDENT, BUT ALSO A SCHOOL MYSTERY
NO BIG IDEAS, OR EVEN SMALL ONES...
GULP
GULP
TERU MINAMOTO, SECOND-YEAR
STUDENT COUNCIL PRESIDENT
A STUDENT, BUT ALSO A SKILLED EXORCIST
THAT'S JUST YOUR JOB, ISN'T IT, AOI?
TO BE STRUNG UP FROM THE CEILING???

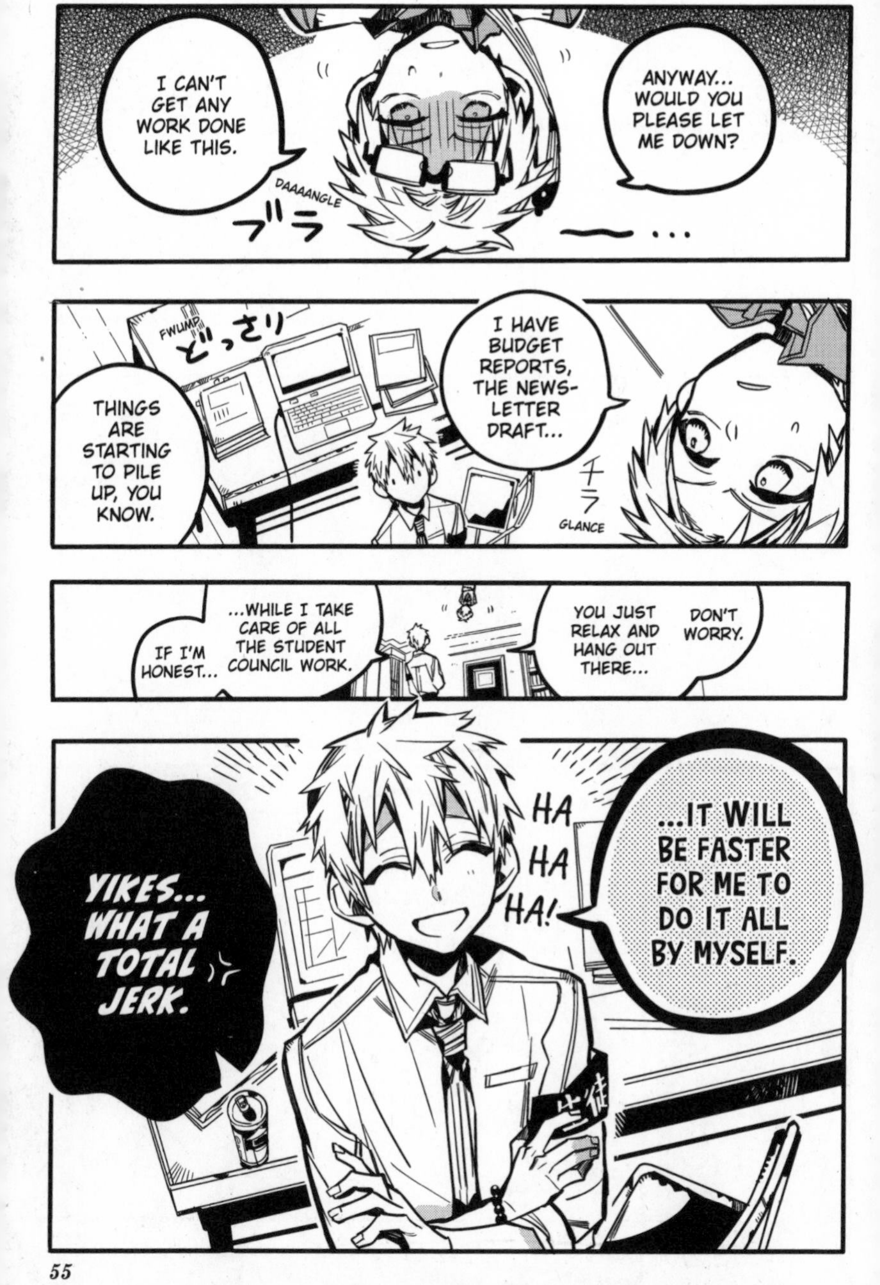
ANYWAY... WOULD YOU PLEASE LET ME DOWN?
—...
ブラ
DAAAANGLE
I CAN'T GET ANY WORK DONE LIKE THIS.
I HAVE BUDGET REPORTS, THE NEWS-LETTER DRAFT...
チラ
GLANCE
FWUMP
どっさり
THINGS ARE STARTING TO PILE UP, YOU KNOW.
DON'T WORRY.
YOU JUST RELAX AND HANG OUT THERE...
...WHILE I TAKE CARE OF ALL THE STUDENT COUNCIL WORK.
IF I'M HONEST...
...IT WILL BE FASTER FOR ME TO DO IT ALL BY MYSELF.
HA HA HA!
YIKES... WHAT A TOTAL JERK.

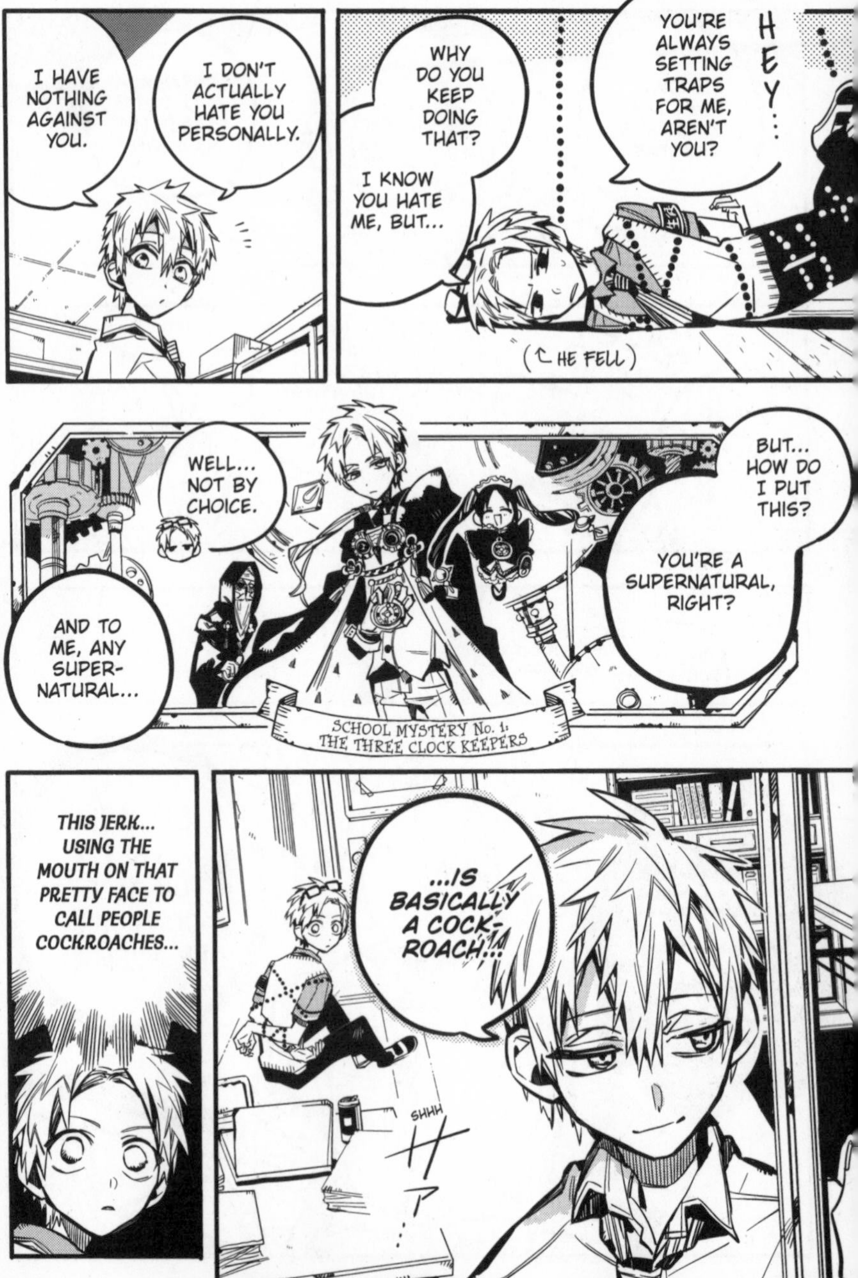
HEY...
YOU'RE ALWAYS SETTING TRAPS FOR ME, AREN'T YOU?
WHY DO YOU KEEP DOING THAT?
I KNOW YOU HATE ME, BUT...
(↑ HE FELL)
I DON'T ACTUALLY HATE YOU PERSONALLY.
I HAVE NOTHING AGAINST YOU.
BUT... HOW DO I PUT THIS?
YOU'RE A SUPERNATURAL, RIGHT?
WELL... NOT BY CHOICE.
AND TO ME, ANY SUPER-NATURAL...
SCHOOL MYSTERY No. 1: THE THREE CLOCK KEEPERS
...IS BASICALLY A COCK-ROACH!!
SHHH
THIS JERK... USING THE MOUTH ON THAT PRETTY FACE TO CALL PEOPLE COCKROACHES...

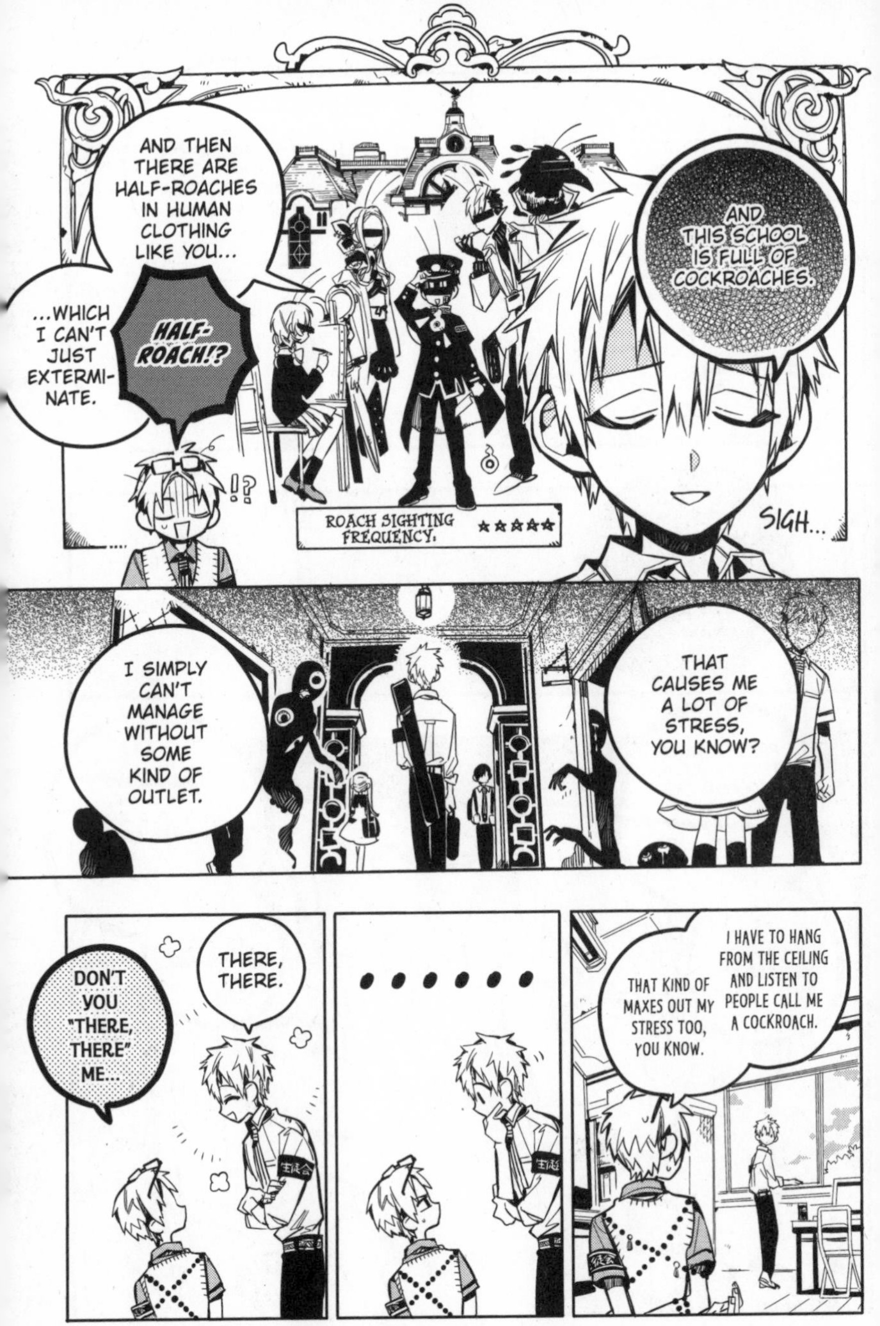
AND THIS SCHOOL IS FULL OF COCKROACHES.
SIGH...
AND THEN THERE ARE HALF-ROACHES IN HUMAN CLOTHING LIKE YOU...
HALF-ROACH!?
...WHICH I CAN'T JUST EXTERMI-NATE.
ROACH SIGHTING FREQUENCY: ★★★★★
!?
THAT CAUSES ME A LOT OF STRESS, YOU KNOW?
I SIMPLY CAN'T MANAGE WITHOUT SOME KIND OF OUTLET.
I HAVE TO HANG FROM THE CEILING AND LISTEN TO PEOPLE CALL ME A COCKROACH.
THAT KIND OF MAXES OUT MY STRESS TOO, YOU KNOW.
......
THERE, THERE.
DON'T YOU "THERE, THERE" ME...

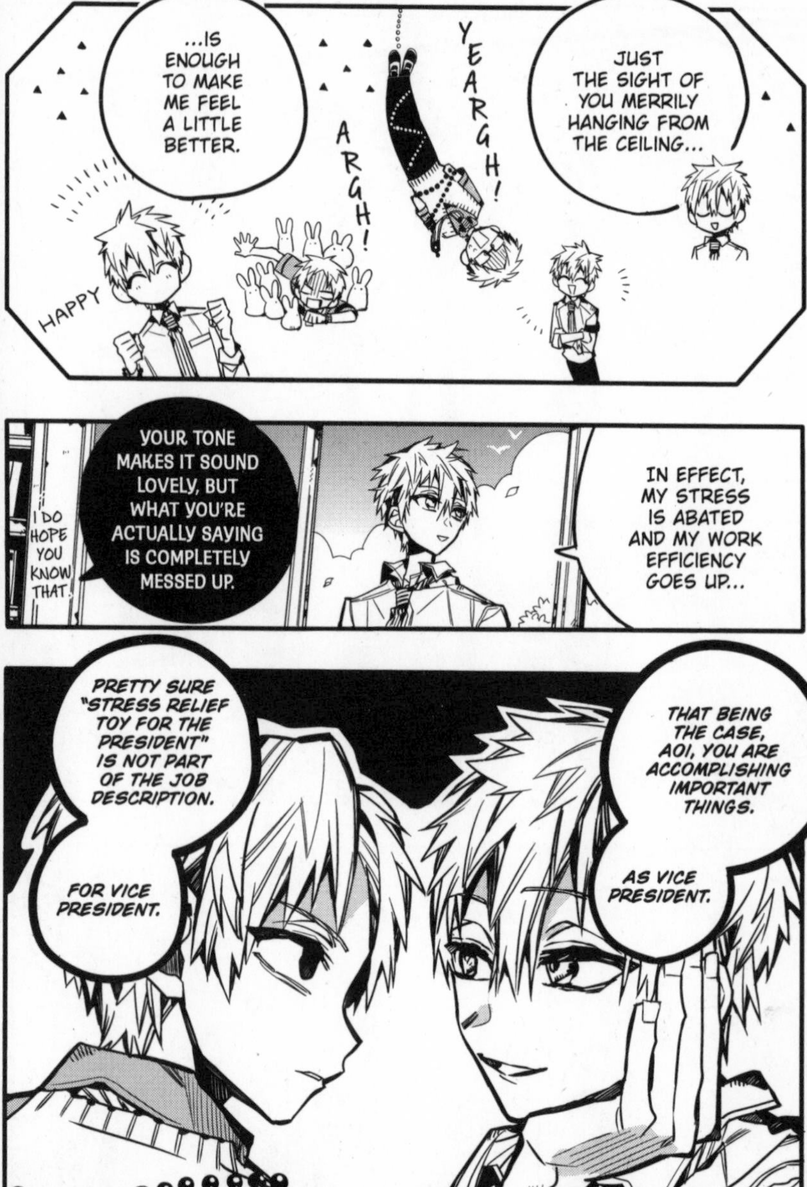
JUST THE SIGHT OF YOU MERRILY HANGING FROM THE CEILING...
YEARGH!
ARGH!
...IS ENOUGH TO MAKE ME FEEL A LITTLE BETTER.
HAPPY
IN EFFECT, MY STRESS IS ABATED AND MY WORK EFFICIENCY GOES UP...
YOUR TONE MAKES IT SOUND LOVELY, BUT WHAT YOU'RE ACTUALLY SAYING IS COMPLETELY MESSED UP.
I DO HOPE YOU KNOW THAT.
THAT BEING THE CASE, AOI, YOU ARE ACCOMPLISHING IMPORTANT THINGS.
AS VICE PRESIDENT.
PRETTY SURE "STRESS RELIEF TOY FOR THE PRESIDENT" IS NOT PART OF THE JOB DESCRIPTION.
FOR VICE PRESIDENT.

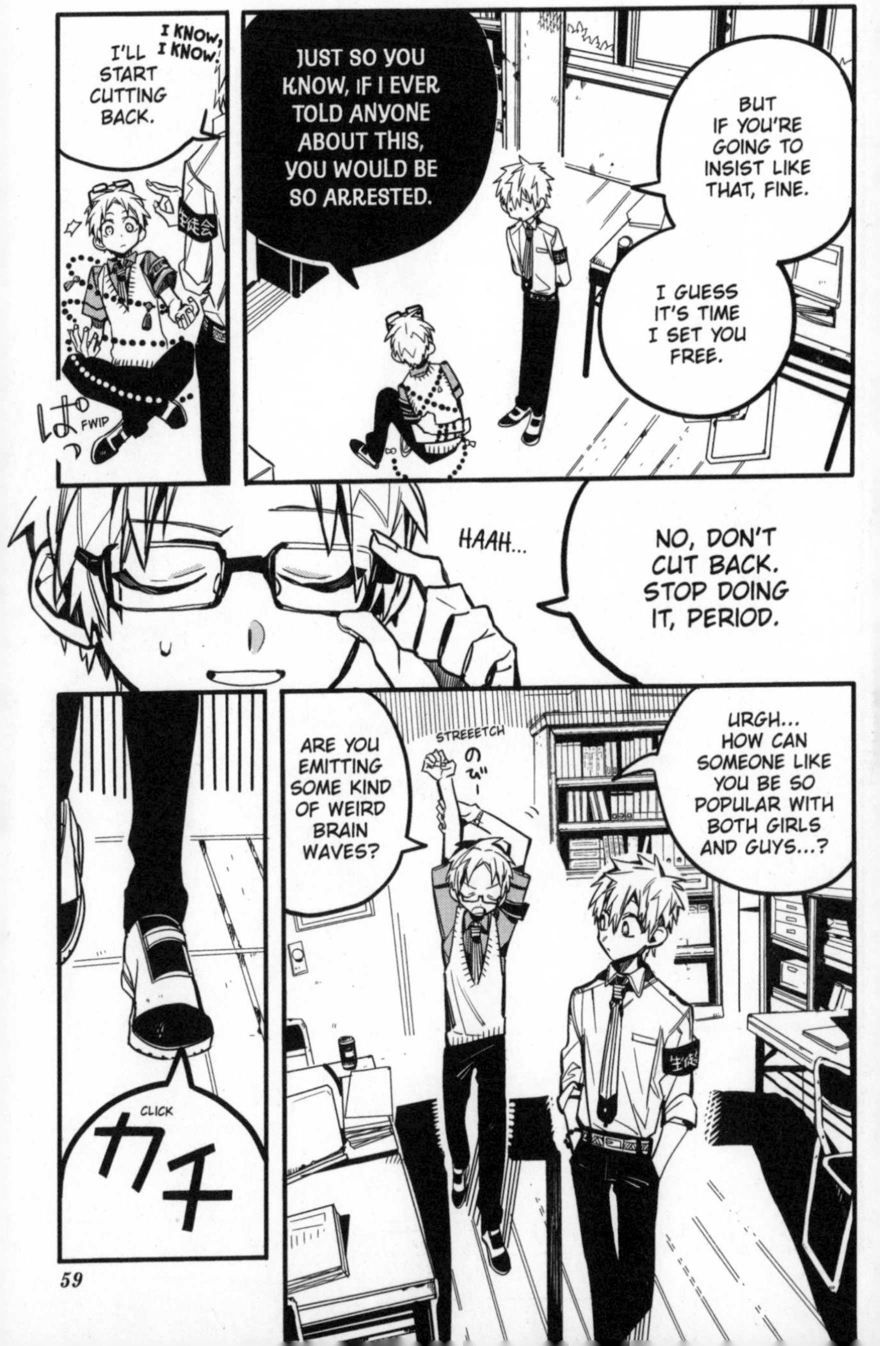
BUT IF YOU'RE GOING TO INSIST LIKE THAT, FINE.
I GUESS IT'S TIME I SET YOU FREE.
JUST SO YOU KNOW, IF I EVER TOLD ANYONE ABOUT THIS, YOU WOULD BE SO ARRESTED.
I KNOW, I KNOW!
I'LL START CUTTING BACK.
ぱっ
FWIP
NO, DON'T CUT BACK. STOP DOING IT, PERIOD.
HAAH...
URGH... HOW CAN SOMEONE LIKE YOU BE SO POPULAR WITH BOTH GIRLS AND GUYS...?
のびー
STREEETCH
ARE YOU EMITTING SOME KIND OF WEIRD BRAIN WAVES?
カチ
CLICK

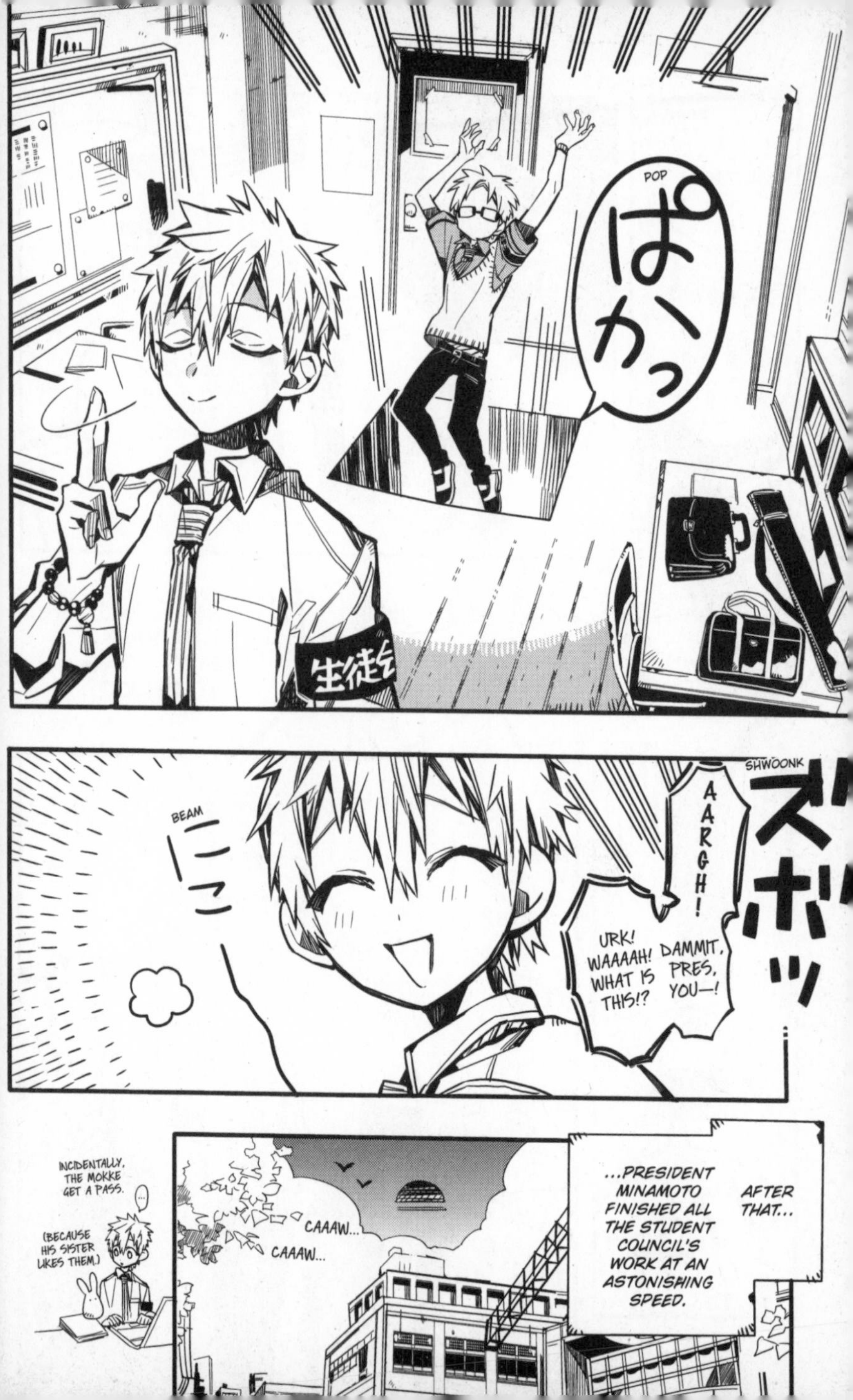
POP
ぱかっ
SHWOONK
ズボッ
AARGH!
URK! WAAAAH! WHAT IS THIS!?
DAMMIT, PRES, YOU—!
BEAM
にこっ
AFTER THAT...
...PRESIDENT MINAMOTO FINISHED ALL THE STUDENT COUNCIL'S WORK AT AN ASTONISHING SPEED.
CAAAW...
CAAAW...
INCIDENTALLY, THE MOKKE GET A PASS.
...
(BECAUSE HIS SISTER LIKES THEM.)

After•School
Hanako-Kun

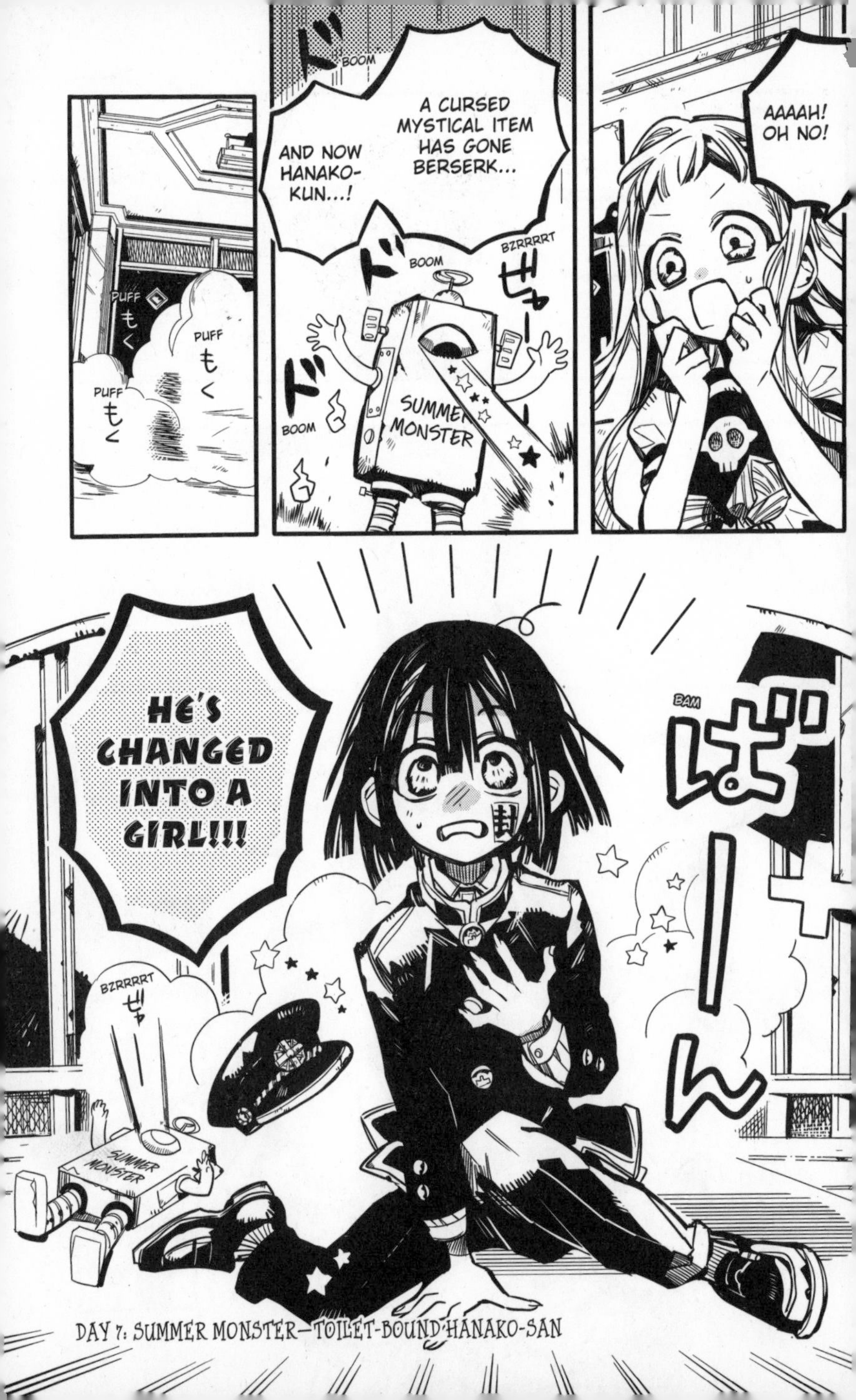
AAAAH! OH NO!
ド BOOM
A CURSED MYSTICAL ITEM HAS GONE BERSERK...
AND NOW HANAKO-KUN...!
ド BOOM
ぜャー BZRRRRT
ド BOOM
SUMMER MONSTER
もく PUFF
もく PUFF
もく PUFF
HE'S CHANGED INTO A GIRL!!!
ばーん BAM
ぜャ BZRRRRT
SUMMER MONSTER

DAY 7: SUMMER MONSTER—TOILET-BOUND HANAKO-SAN

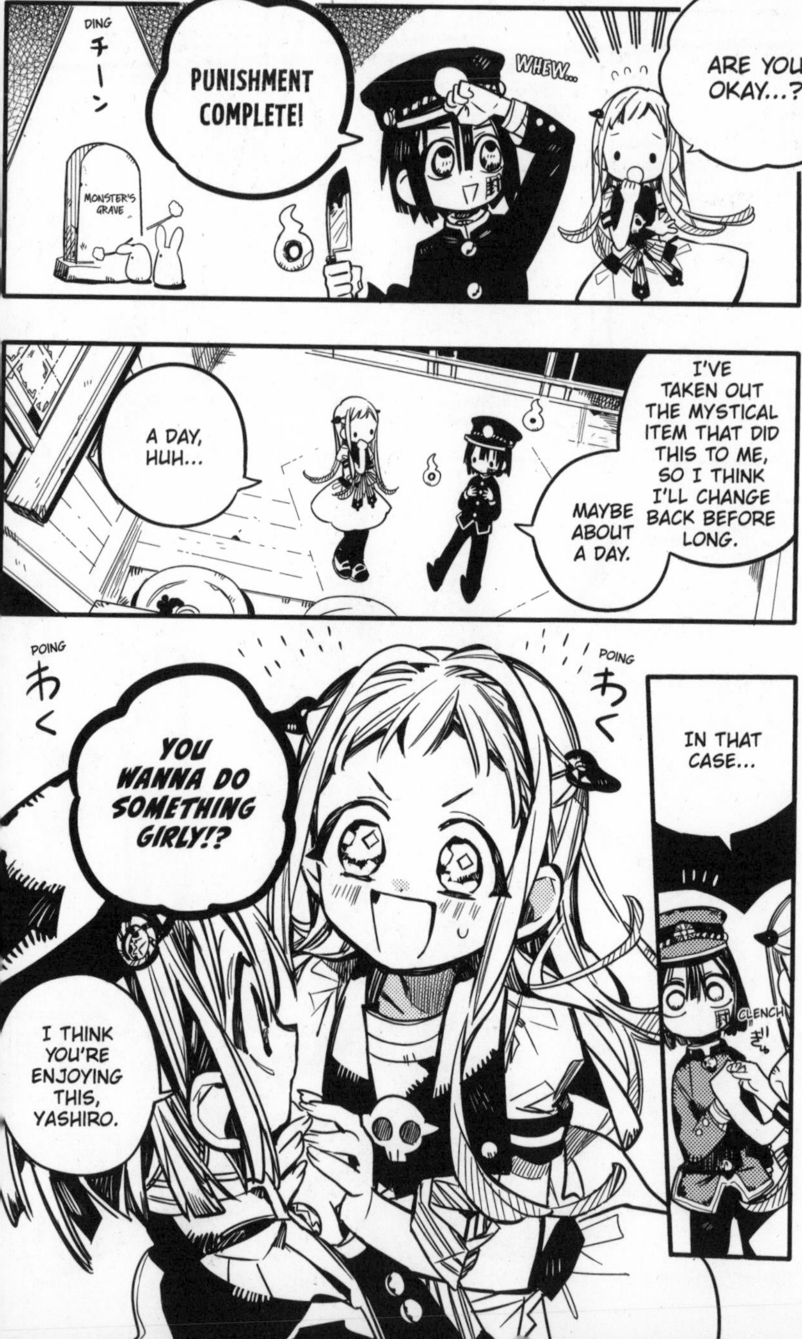
ARE YOU OKAY...?
WHEW...
PUNISHMENT COMPLETE!
DING
チーン
MONSTER'S GRAVE
I'VE TAKEN OUT THE MYSTICAL ITEM THAT DID THIS TO ME, SO I THINK I'LL CHANGE BACK BEFORE LONG.
MAYBE ABOUT A DAY.
A DAY, HUH...
IN THAT CASE...
CLENCH
ぎゅ
POING
わく
YOU WANNA DO SOMETHING GIRLY!?
POING
わく
I THINK YOU'RE ENJOYING THIS, YASHIRO.

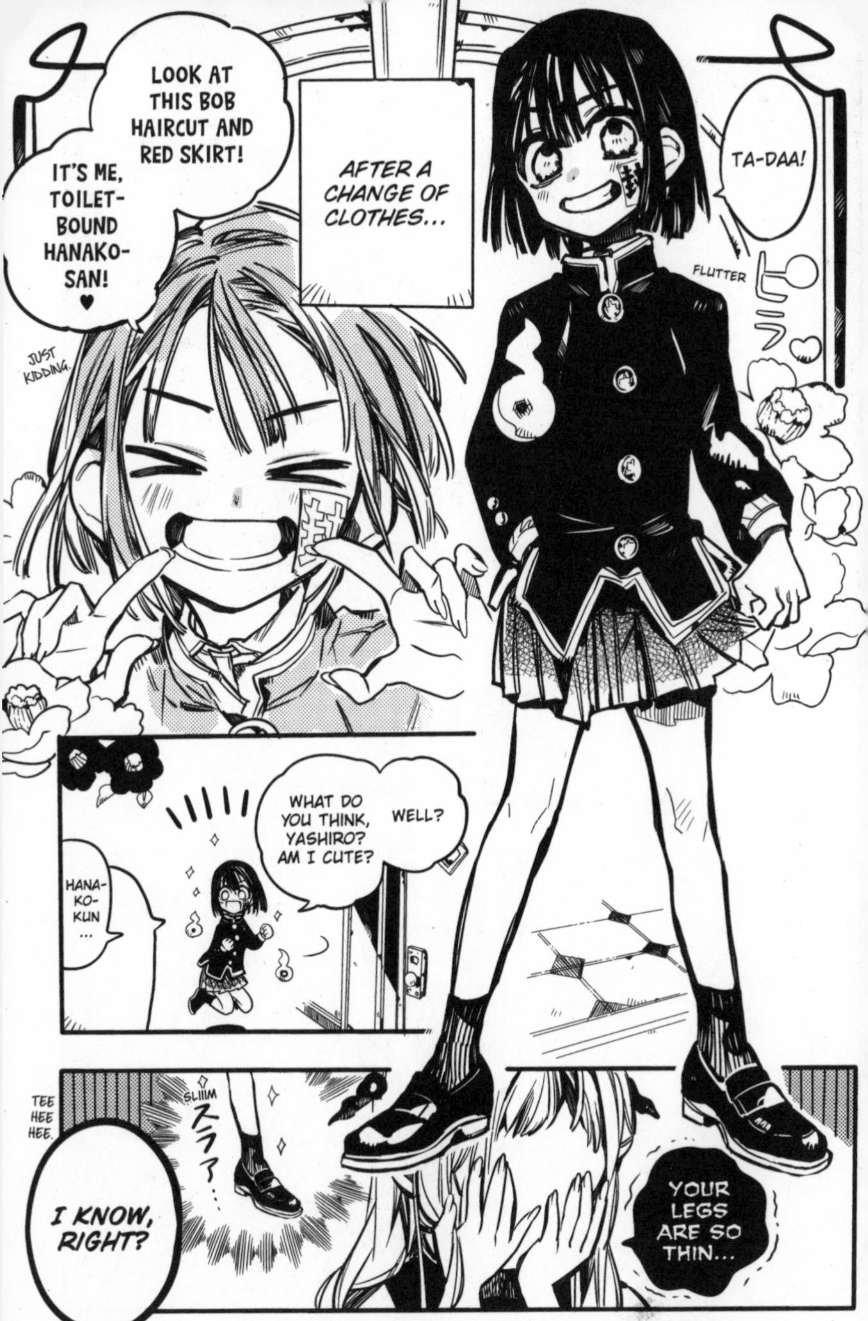
TA-DAA!
FLUTTER
AFTER A CHANGE OF CLOTHES...
LOOK AT THIS BOB HAIRCUT AND RED SKIRT!
IT'S ME, TOILET-BOUND HANAKO-SAN! ♥
JUST KIDDING.
WELL?
WHAT DO YOU THINK, YASHIRO? AM I CUTE?
HANA-KO-KUN ...
YOUR LEGS ARE SO THIN...
SLIIIM
TEE HEE HEE.
I KNOW, RIGHT?

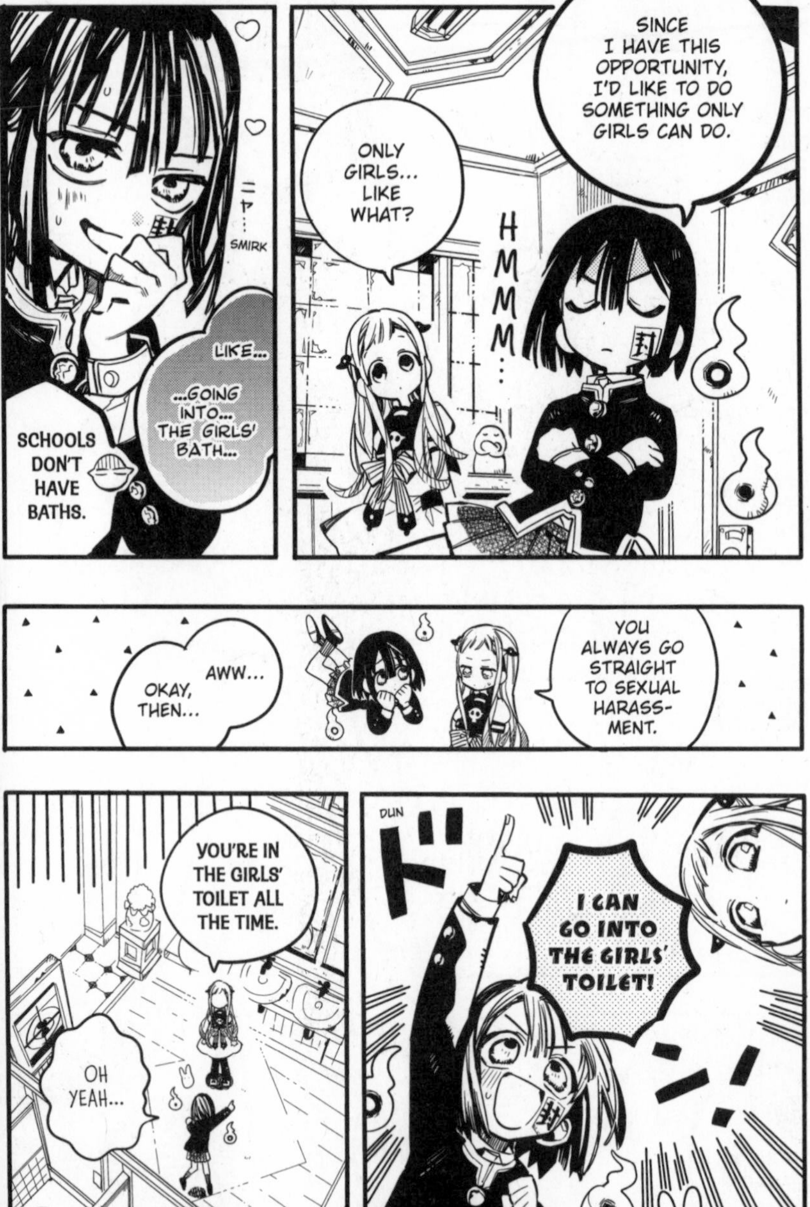
SINCE I HAVE THIS OPPORTUNITY, I'D LIKE TO DO SOMETHING ONLY GIRLS CAN DO.
ONLY GIRLS... LIKE WHAT?
HMMM...
ニヤ…
SMIRK
LIKE...
...GOING INTO... THE GIRLS' BATH...
SCHOOLS DON'T HAVE BATHS.
YOU ALWAYS GO STRAIGHT TO SEXUAL HARASS-MENT.
AWW... OKAY, THEN...
DUN
ド
I CAN GO INTO THE GIRLS' TOILET!
YOU'RE IN THE GIRLS' TOILET ALL THE TIME.
OH YEAH...

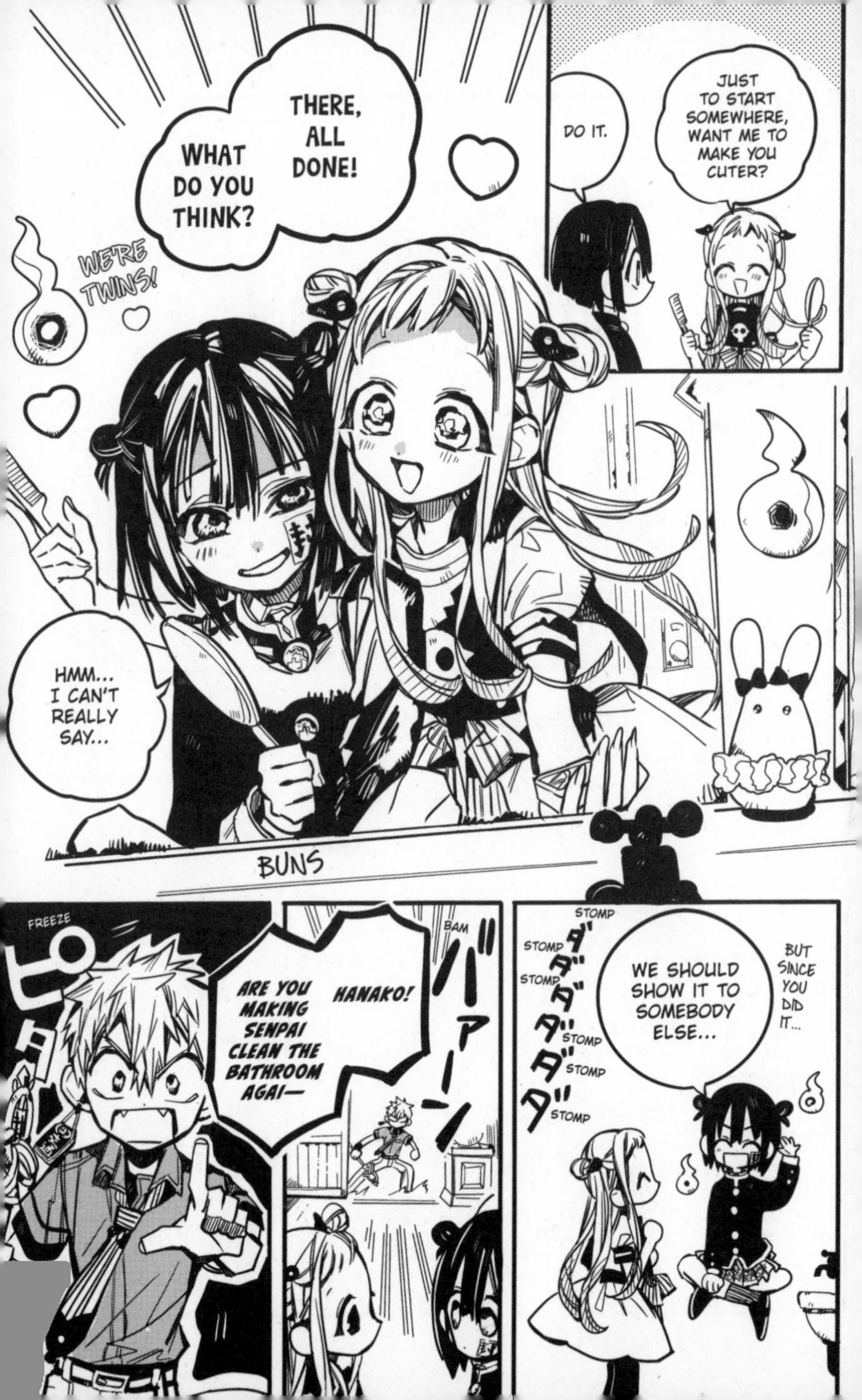
JUST TO START SOMEWHERE, WANT ME TO MAKE YOU CUTER?
DO IT.
THERE, ALL DONE!
WHAT DO YOU THINK?
WE'RE TWINS!
HMM... I CAN'T REALLY SAY...
BUNS
BUT SINCE YOU DID IT...
WE SHOULD SHOW IT TO SOMEBODY ELSE...
STOMP
STOMP
STOMP
STOMP
STOMP
STOMP
BAM
HANAKO!
ARE YOU MAKING SENPAI CLEAN THE BATHROOM AGAI—
FREEZE

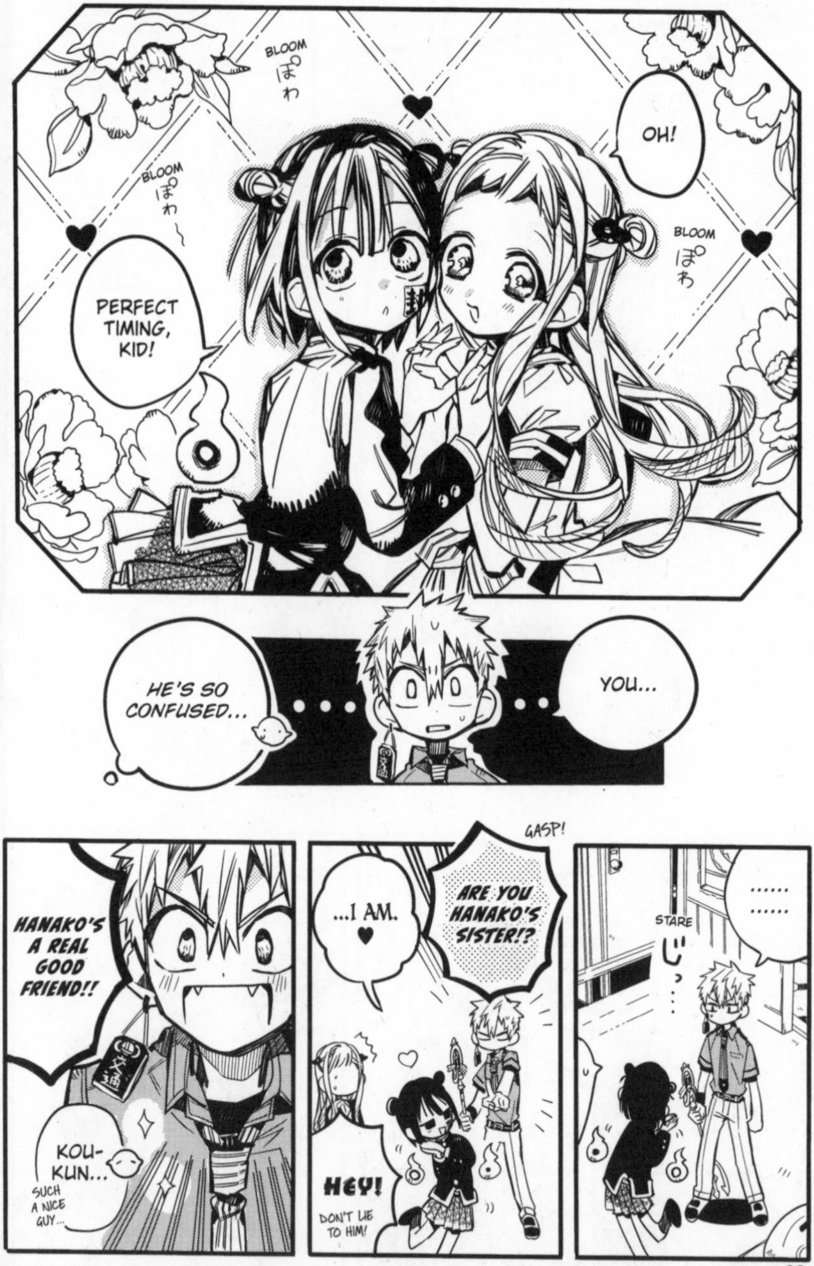
OH!
BLOOM ぽわ
BLOOM ぽわ
BLOOM ぽわ~
PERFECT TIMING, KID!
YOU...
...
...
HE'S SO CONFUSED...
......
......
STARE じっ...
GASP!
ARE YOU HANAKO'S SISTER!?
...I AM. ♥
HEY!
DON'T LIE TO HIM!
HANAKO'S A REAL GOOD FRIEND!!
KOU-KUN...
SUCH A NICE GUY...

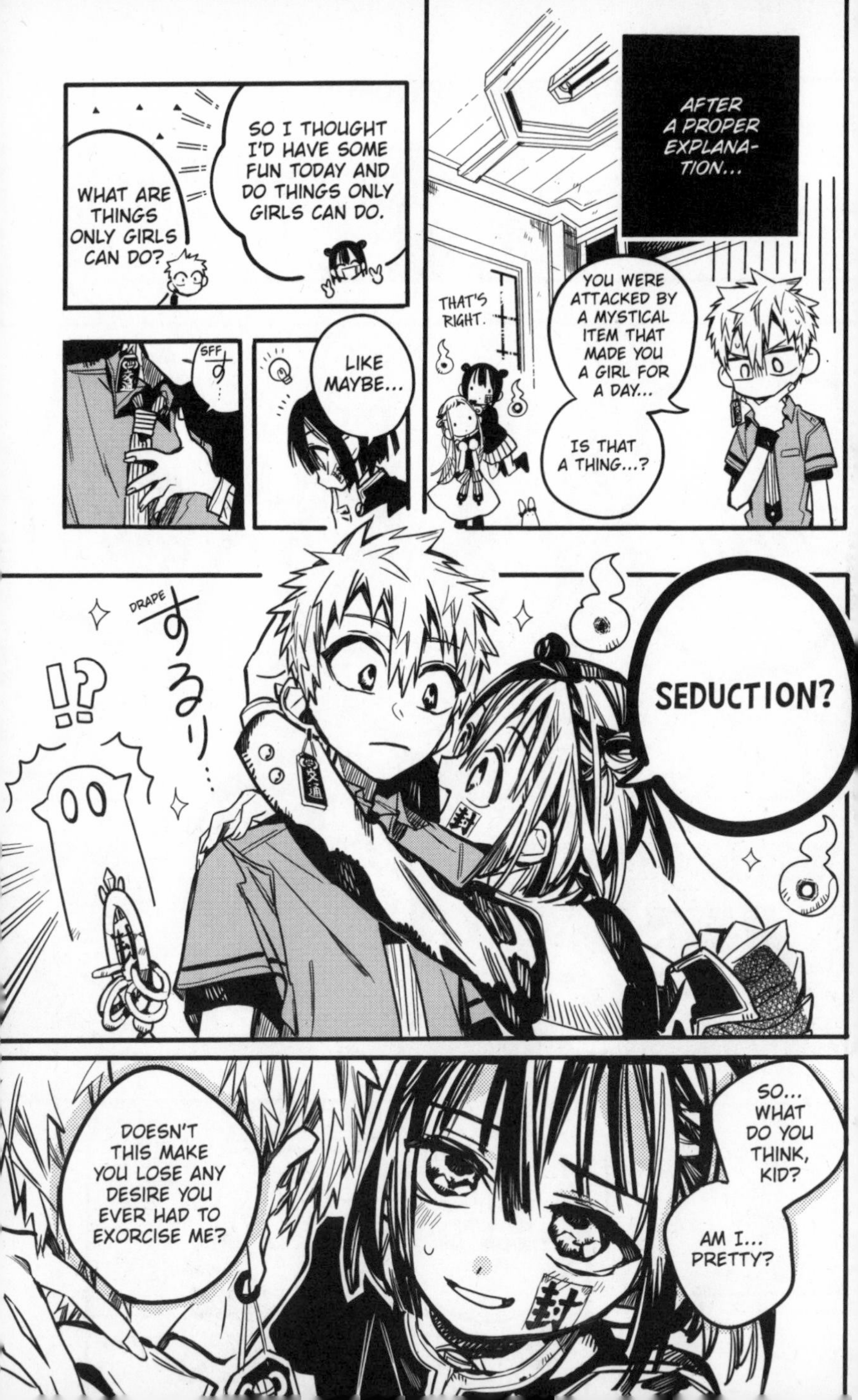
AFTER A PROPER EXPLANATION...
YOU WERE ATTACKED BY A MYSTICAL ITEM THAT MADE YOU A GIRL FOR A DAY...
IS THAT A THING...?
THAT'S RIGHT.
SO I THOUGHT I'D HAVE SOME FUN TODAY AND DO THINGS ONLY GIRLS CAN DO.
WHAT ARE THINGS ONLY GIRLS CAN DO?
LIKE MAYBE...
SFF
SEDUCTION?
DRAPE
!?
SO... WHAT DO YOU THINK, KID?
AM I... PRETTY?
DOESN'T THIS MAKE YOU LOSE ANY DESIRE YOU EVER HAD TO EXORCISE ME?

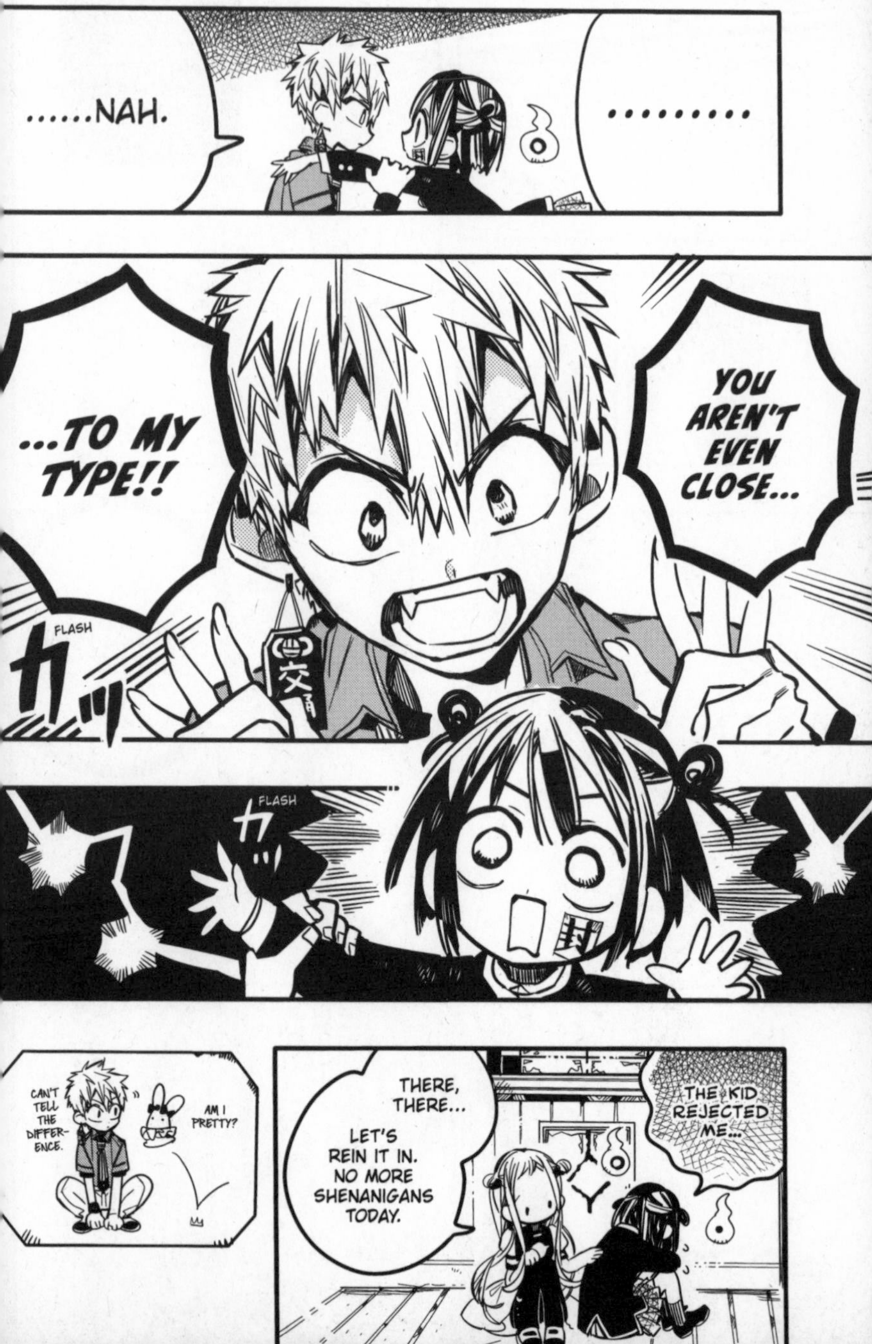
....
......NAH.
YOU AREN'T EVEN CLOSE...
...TO MY TYPE!!
FLASH
カッ
FLASH
カッ
THE KID REJECTED ME...
THERE, THERE...
LET'S REIN IT IN. NO MORE SHENANIGANS TODAY.
AM I PRETTY?
CAN'T TELL THE DIFFERENCE.

After·School
Hanako-Kun

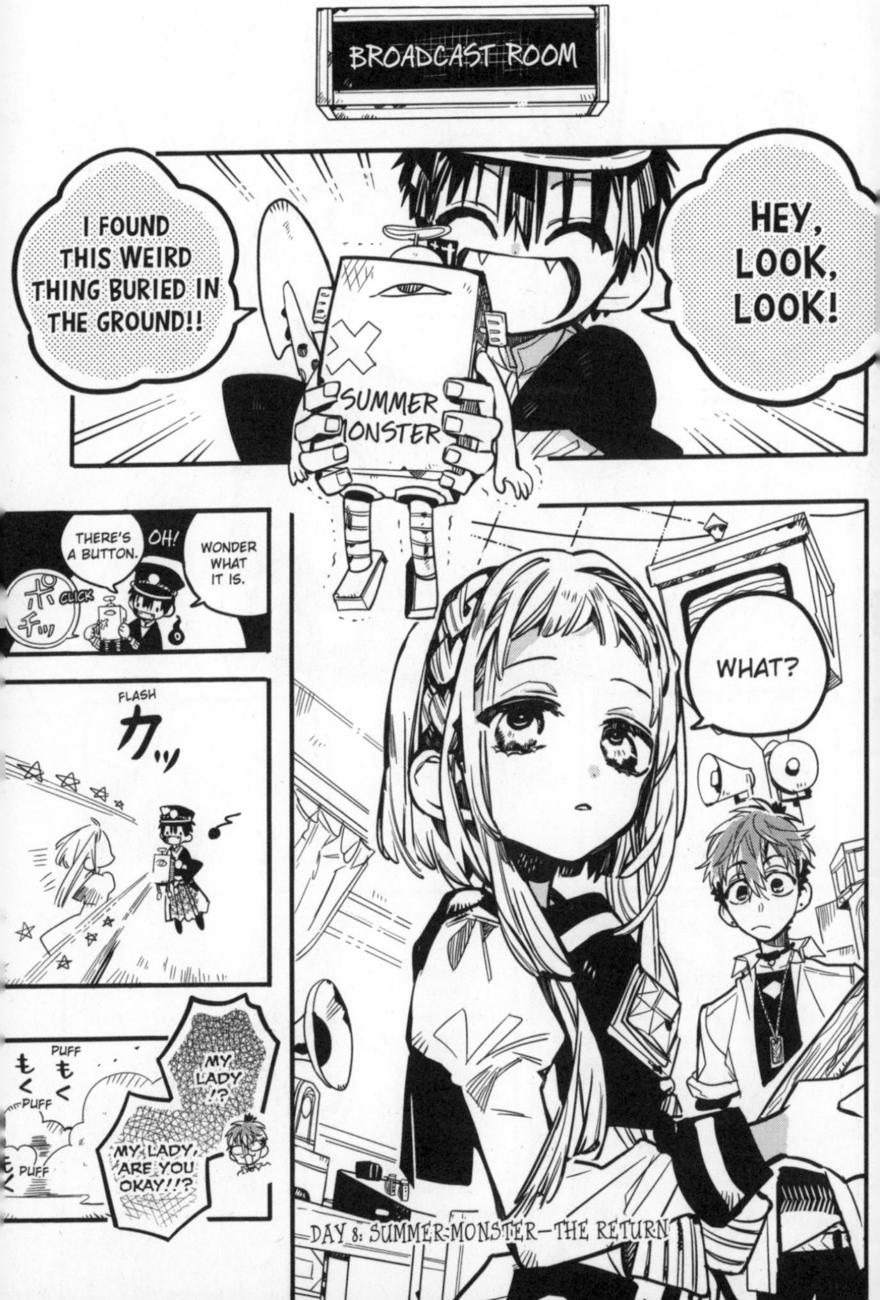

BROADCAST ROOM
HEY, LOOK, LOOK!
I FOUND THIS WEIRD THING BURIED IN THE GROUND!!
SUMMER MONSTER
WHAT?
DAY 8: SUMMER-MONSTER—THE RETURN
WONDER WHAT IT IS.
OH!
THERE'S A BUTTON.
ポチッ
CLICK
カッ
FLASH
MY LADY!?
MY LADY, ARE YOU OKAY!!?
もく
PUFF
もく
PUFF
もく
PUFF

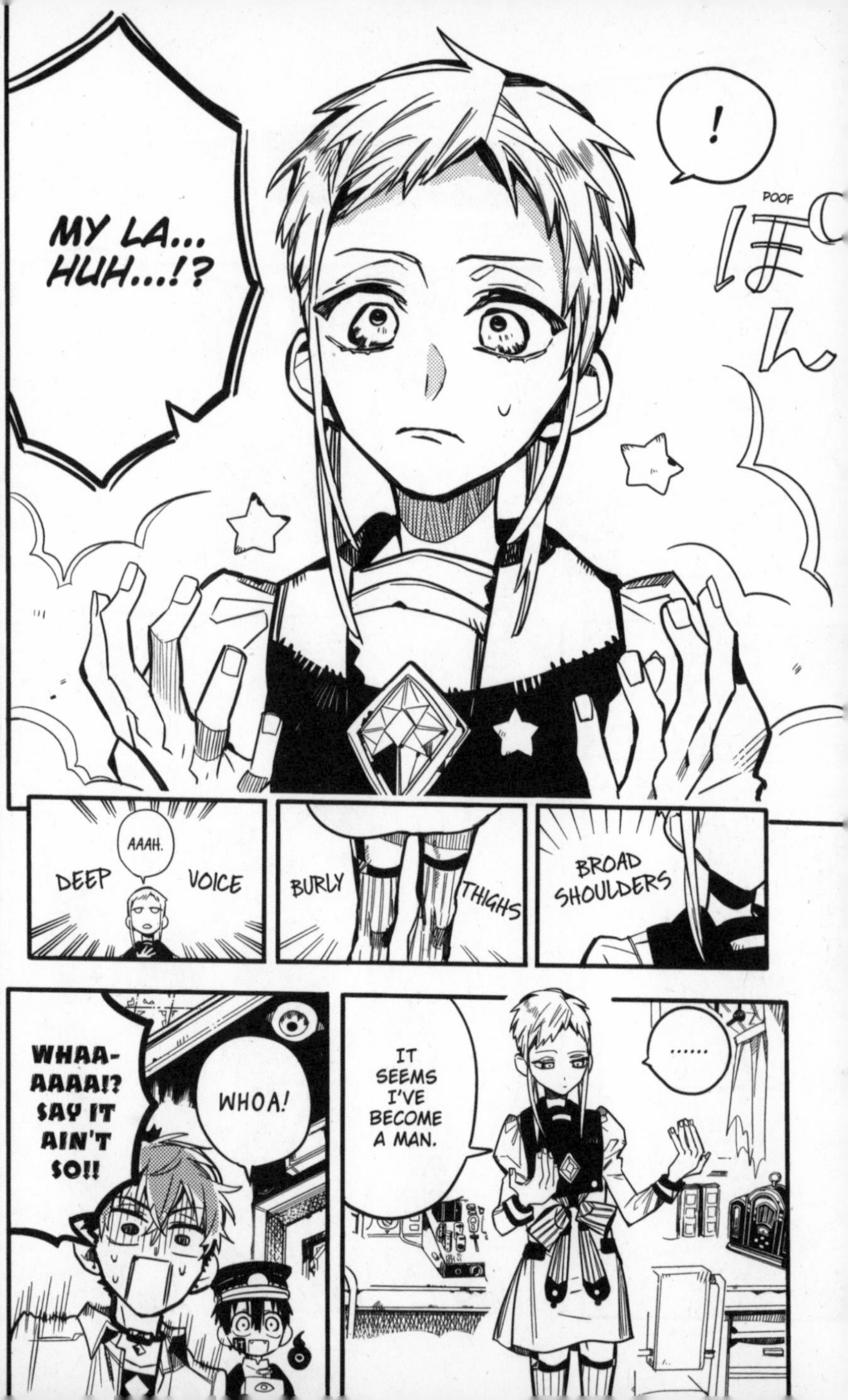
!
POOF
ぽん
MY LA... HUH...!?
BROAD SHOULDERS
BURLY THIGHS
AAAH.
DEEP VOICE
......
IT SEEMS I'VE BECOME A MAN.
WHOA!
WHAA-AAAA!? SAY IT AIN'T SO!!

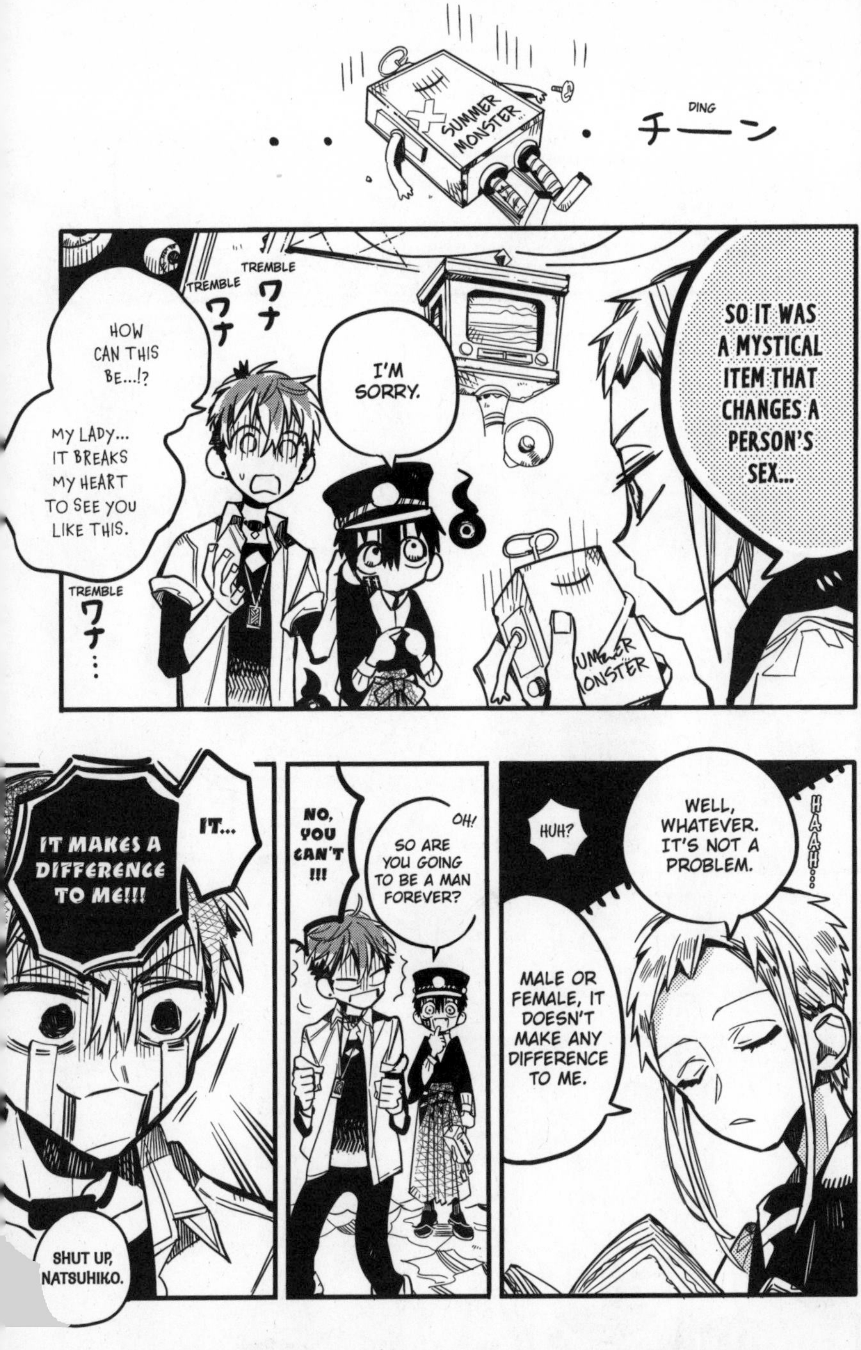
SUMMER MONSTER
. . .
DING
チーン
SO IT WAS A MYSTICAL ITEM THAT CHANGES A PERSON'S SEX...
SUMMER MONSTER
I'M SORRY.
TREMBLE
ワナ
TREMBLE
ワナ
HOW CAN THIS BE...!?
MY LADY... IT BREAKS MY HEART TO SEE YOU LIKE THIS.
TREMBLE
ワナ...
WELL, WHATEVER. IT'S NOT A PROBLEM.
HAAAH...
HUH?
MALE OR FEMALE, IT DOESN'T MAKE ANY DIFFERENCE TO ME.
OH!
SO ARE YOU GOING TO BE A MAN FOREVER?
NO, YOU CAN'T!!!
IT...
IT MAKES A DIFFERENCE TO ME!!!
SHUT UP, NATSUHIKO.

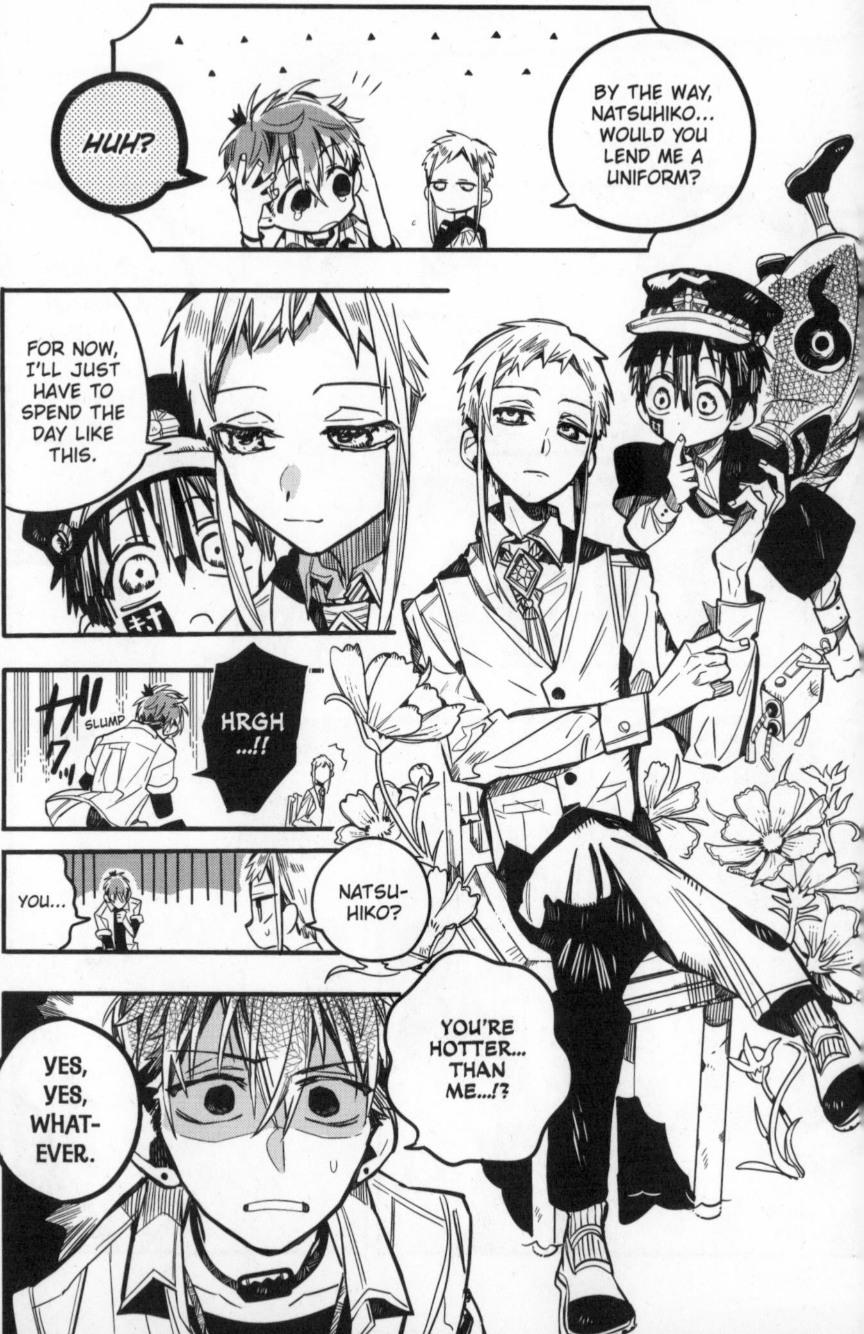
BY THE WAY, NATSUHIKO... WOULD YOU LEND ME A UNIFORM?
HUH?
FOR NOW, I'LL JUST HAVE TO SPEND THE DAY LIKE THIS.
HRGH ...!!
SLUMP
NATSU-HIKO?
YOU...
YOU'RE HOTTER... THAN ME...!?
YES, YES, WHAT-EVER.

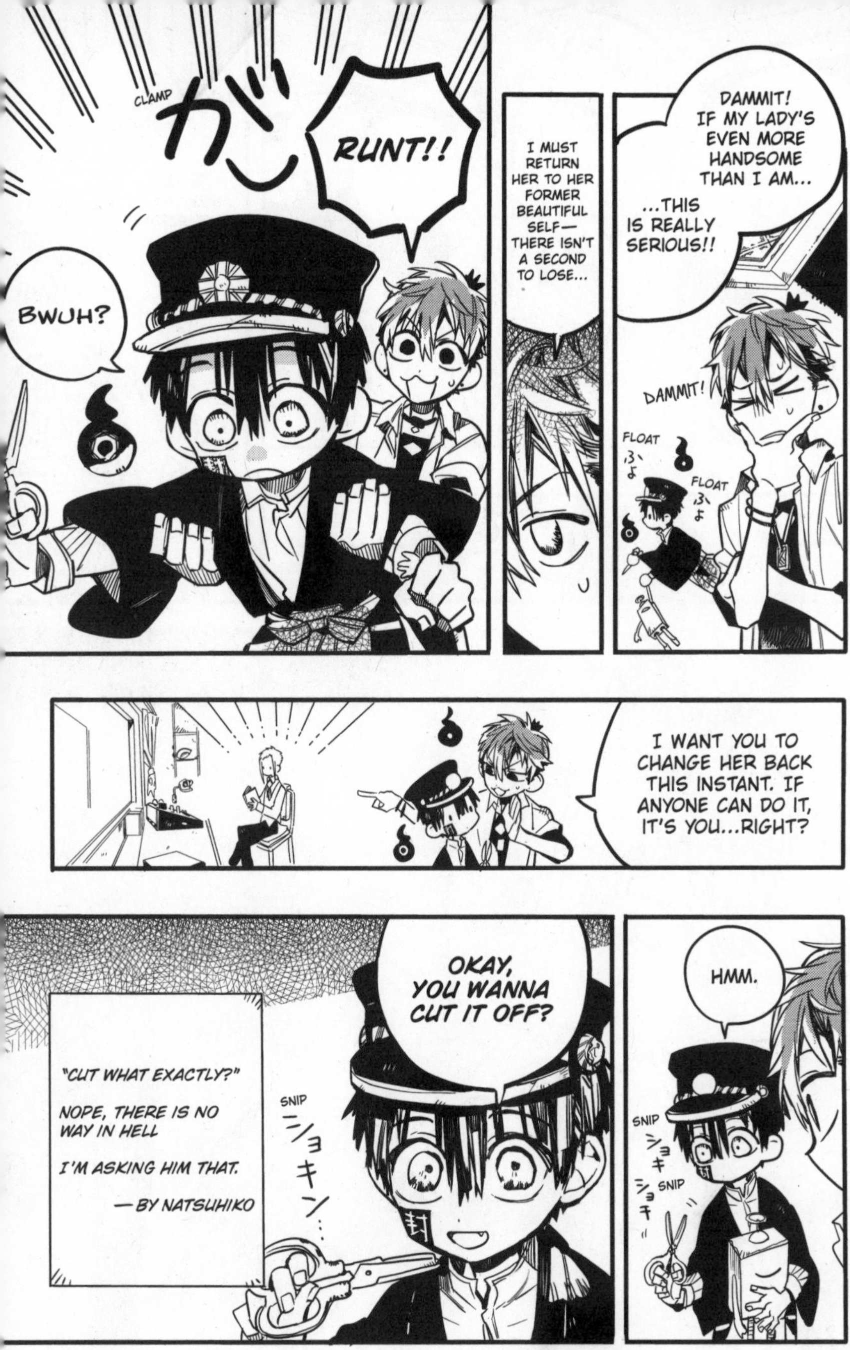
DAMMIT! IF MY LADY'S EVEN MORE HANDSOME THAN I AM...
...THIS IS REALLY SERIOUS!!
DAMMIT!
FLOAT ふよ
FLOAT ふよ
I MUST RETURN HER TO HER FORMER BEAUTIFUL SELF—THERE ISN'T A SECOND TO LOSE...
CLAMP がッ
RUNT!!
BWUH?
I WANT YOU TO CHANGE HER BACK THIS INSTANT. IF ANYONE CAN DO IT, IT'S YOU...RIGHT?
HMM.
SNIP ショキ
SNIP ショキ
OKAY, YOU WANNA CUT IT OFF?
SNIP ショキン...
"CUT WHAT EXACTLY?"
NOPE, THERE IS NO WAY IN HELL
I'M ASKING HIM THAT.
—BY NATSUHIKO

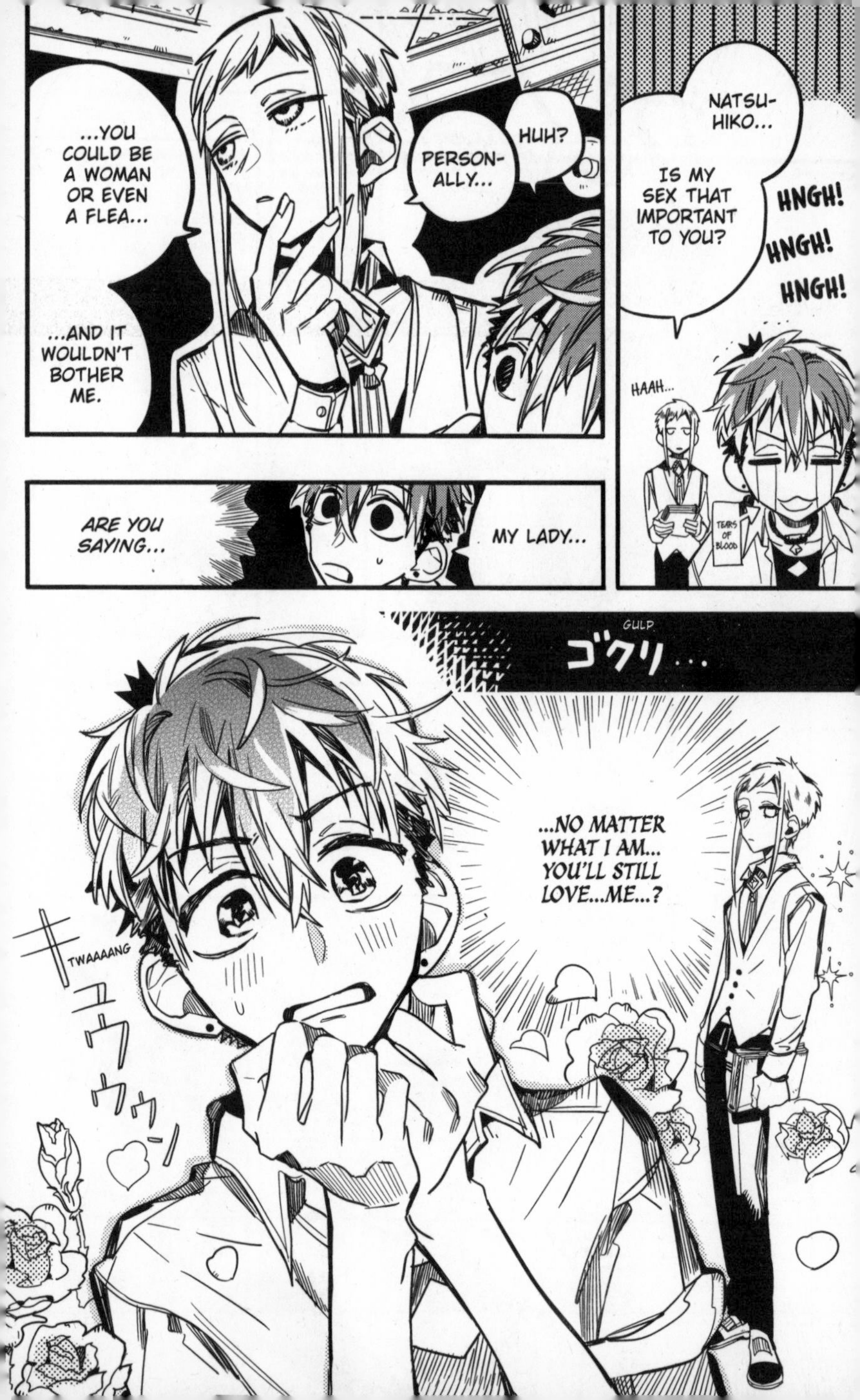
NATSU-HIKO... IS MY SEX THAT IMPORTANT TO YOU?
HNGH!
HNGH!
HNGH!
TEARS OF BLOOD
HAAAH...
HUH?
PERSON-ALLY...
...YOU COULD BE A WOMAN OR EVEN A FLEA...
...AND IT WOULDN'T BOTHER ME.
MY LADY...
ARE YOU SAYING...
ゴクリ...
GULP
...NO MATTER WHAT I AM... YOU'LL STILL LOVE...ME...?
キュウゥゥーン
TWAAAANG

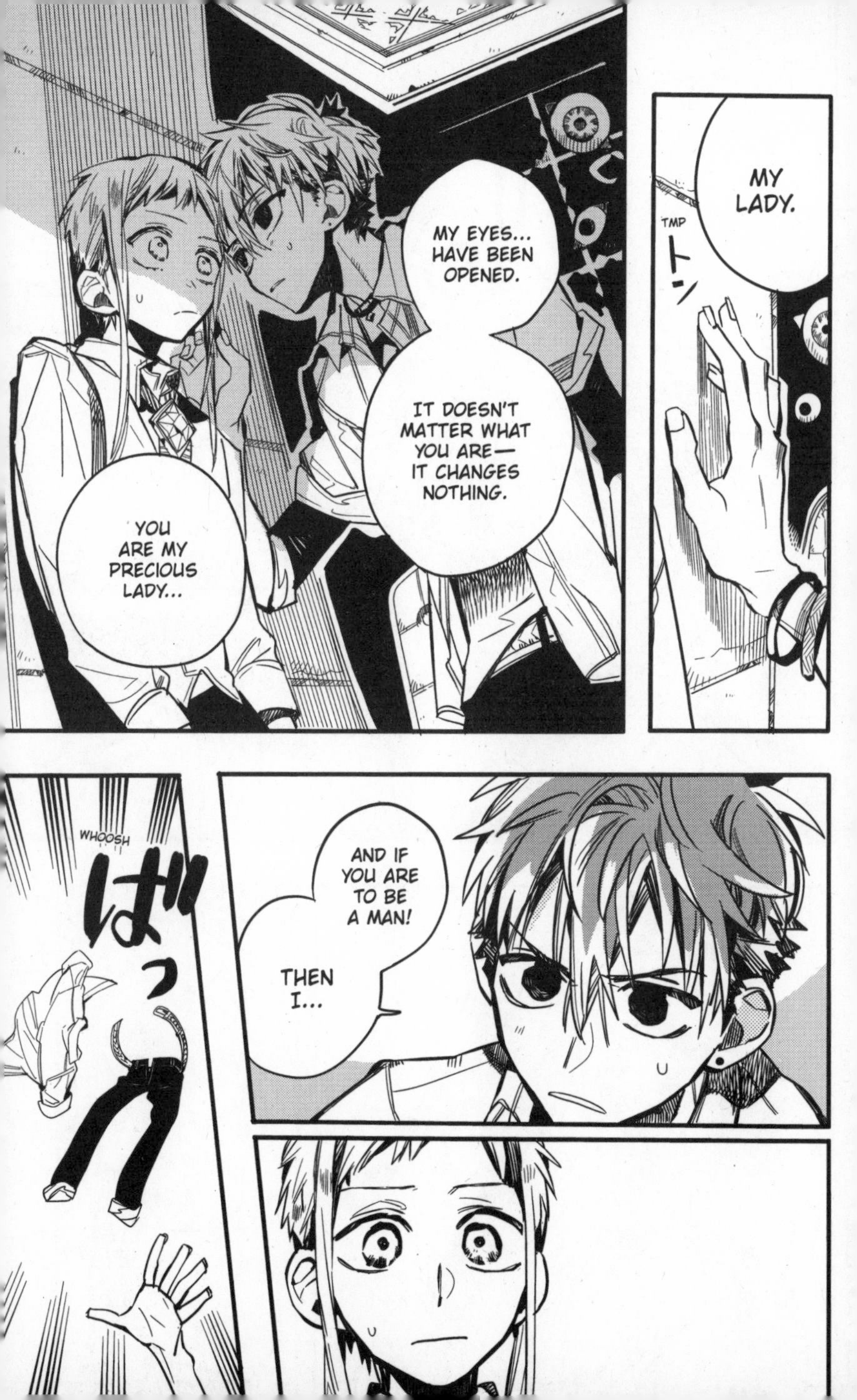
MY LADY.
TMP
MY EYES... HAVE BEEN OPENED.
IT DOESN'T MATTER WHAT YOU ARE— IT CHANGES NOTHING.
YOU ARE MY PRECIOUS LADY...
AND IF YOU ARE TO BE A MAN!
THEN I...
WHOOSH
ばっ

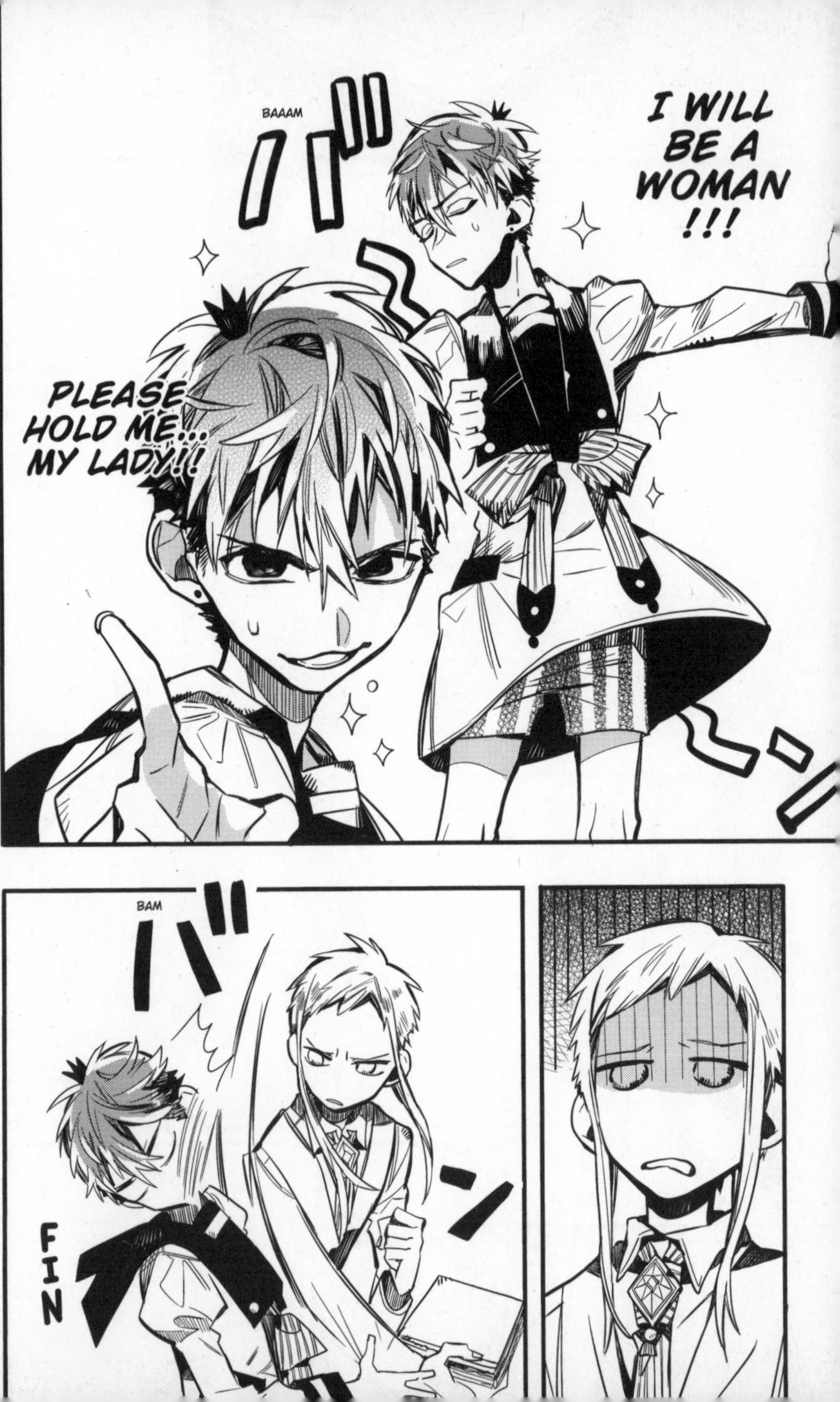
I WILL BE A WOMAN!!!
BAAAM
PLEASE HOLD ME... MY LADY!!
BAM
FIN

After-School Hanako-Kun

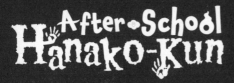

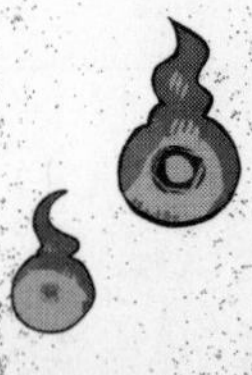

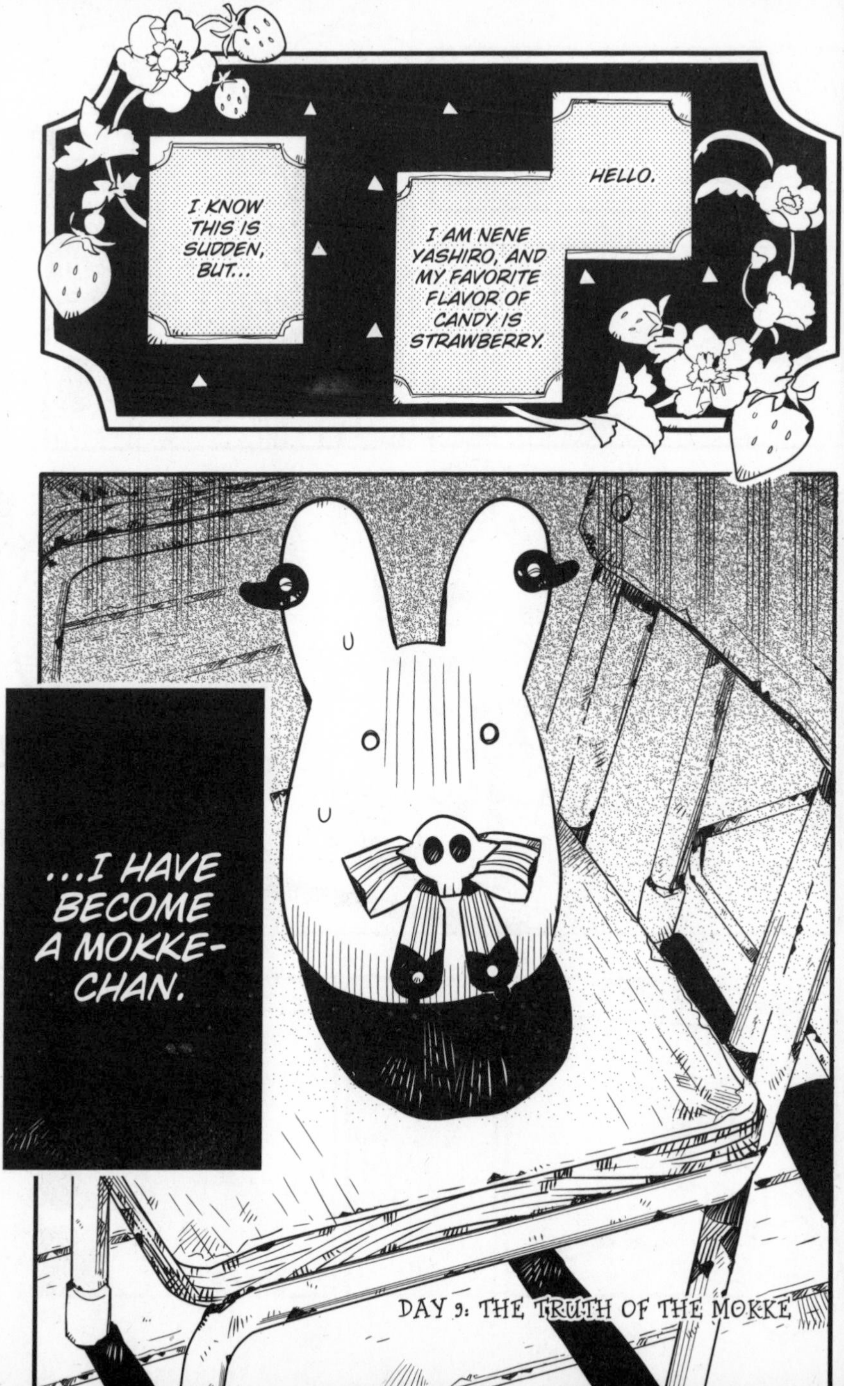
HELLO.
I AM NENE YASHIRO, AND MY FAVORITE FLAVOR OF CANDY IS STRAWBERRY.
I KNOW THIS IS SUDDEN, BUT...
...I HAVE BECOME A MOKKE-CHAN.
DAY 9: THE TRUTH OF THE MOKKE

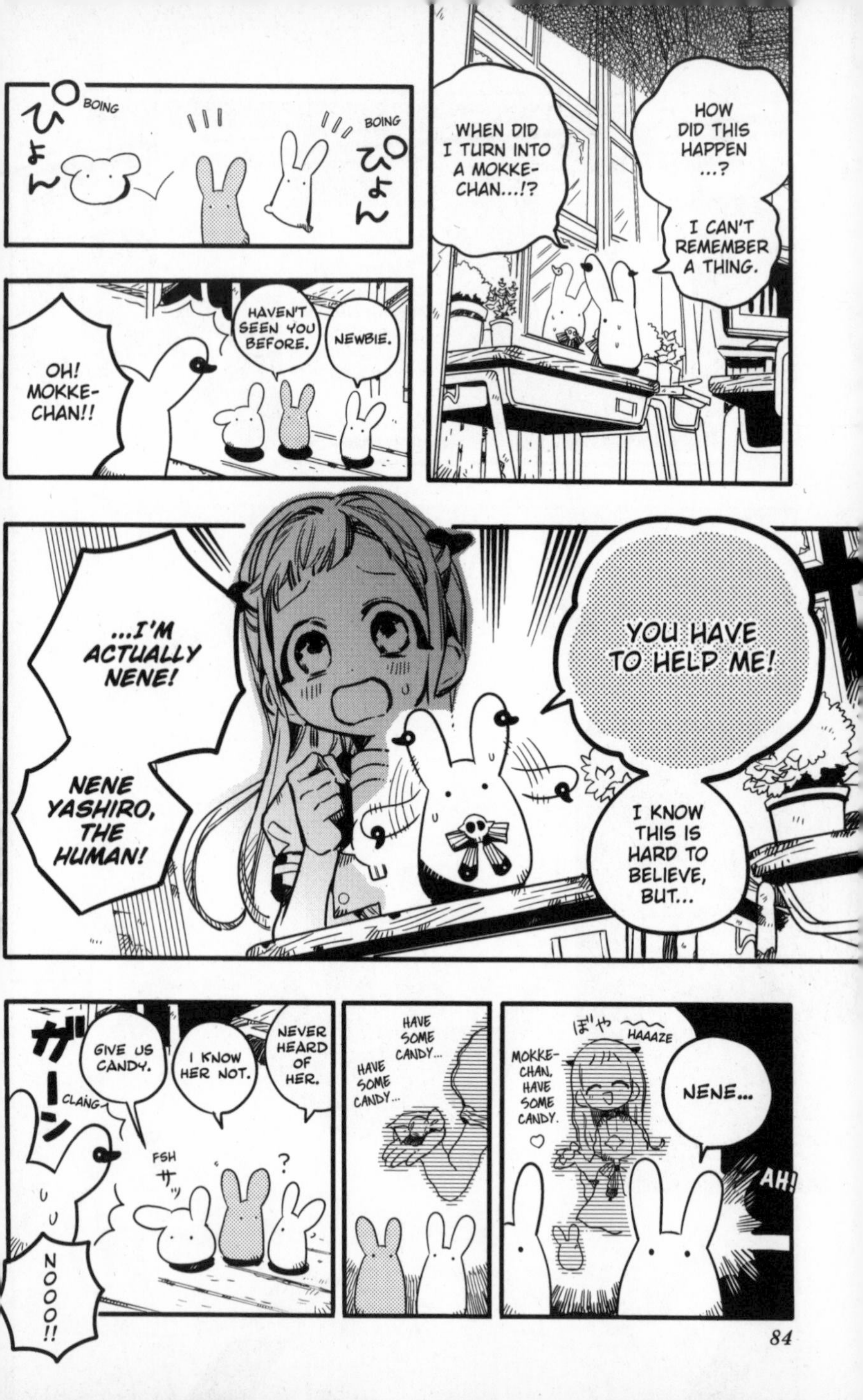
HOW DID THIS HAPPEN ...?
I CAN'T REMEMBER A THING.
WHEN DID I TURN INTO A MOKKE-CHAN...!?
ぴょん〜
BOING
ぴょん〜
BOING
NEWBIE.
HAVEN'T SEEN YOU BEFORE.
OH! MOKKE-CHAN!!
YOU HAVE TO HELP ME!
I KNOW THIS IS HARD TO BELIEVE, BUT...
...I'M ACTUALLY NENE!
NENE YASHIRO, THE HUMAN!
ぼや
HAAAZE
MOKKE-CHAN, HAVE SOME CANDY. ♡
NENE...
AH!
HAVE SOME CANDY...
HAVE SOME CANDY...
NEVER HEARD OF HER.
I KNOW HER NOT.
GIVE US CANDY.
ガーン
CLANG
FSH
サッ
?
NOOOO!!

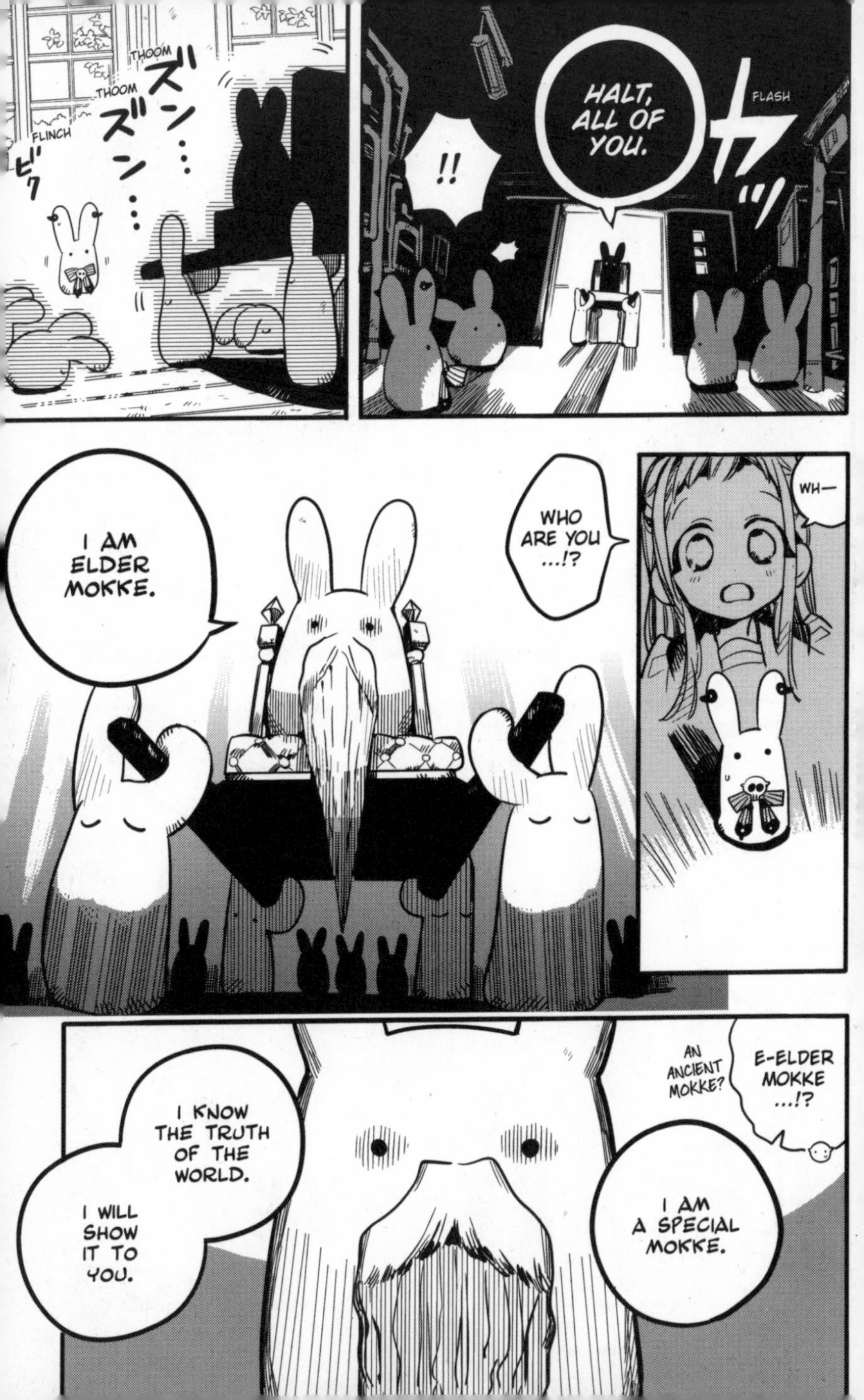

FLASH
カッ
HALT, ALL OF YOU.
!!
THOOM
ズン…
THOOM
ズン…
FLINCH
ビク
WH—
WHO ARE YOU ...!?
I AM ELDER MOKKE.
E-ELDER MOKKE ...!?
AN ANCIENT MOKKE?
I AM A SPECIAL MOKKE.
I KNOW THE TRUTH OF THE WORLD.
I WILL SHOW IT TO YOU.

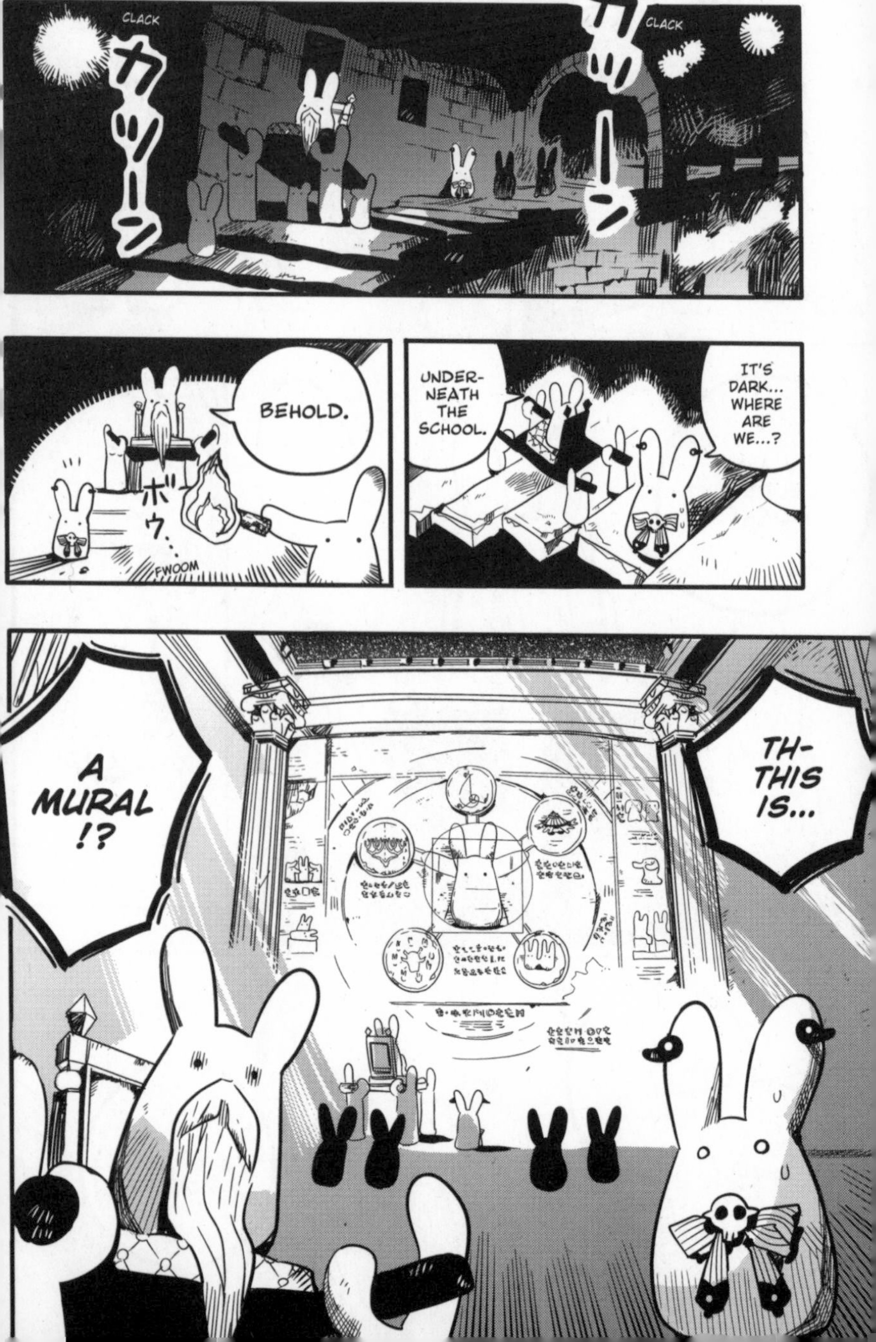
カッーン
CLACK
カッーン
CLACK
IT'S DARK... WHERE ARE WE...?
UNDER-NEATH THE SCHOOL.
BEHOLD.
ボウ...
FWOOM
TH-THIS IS...
A MURAL!?

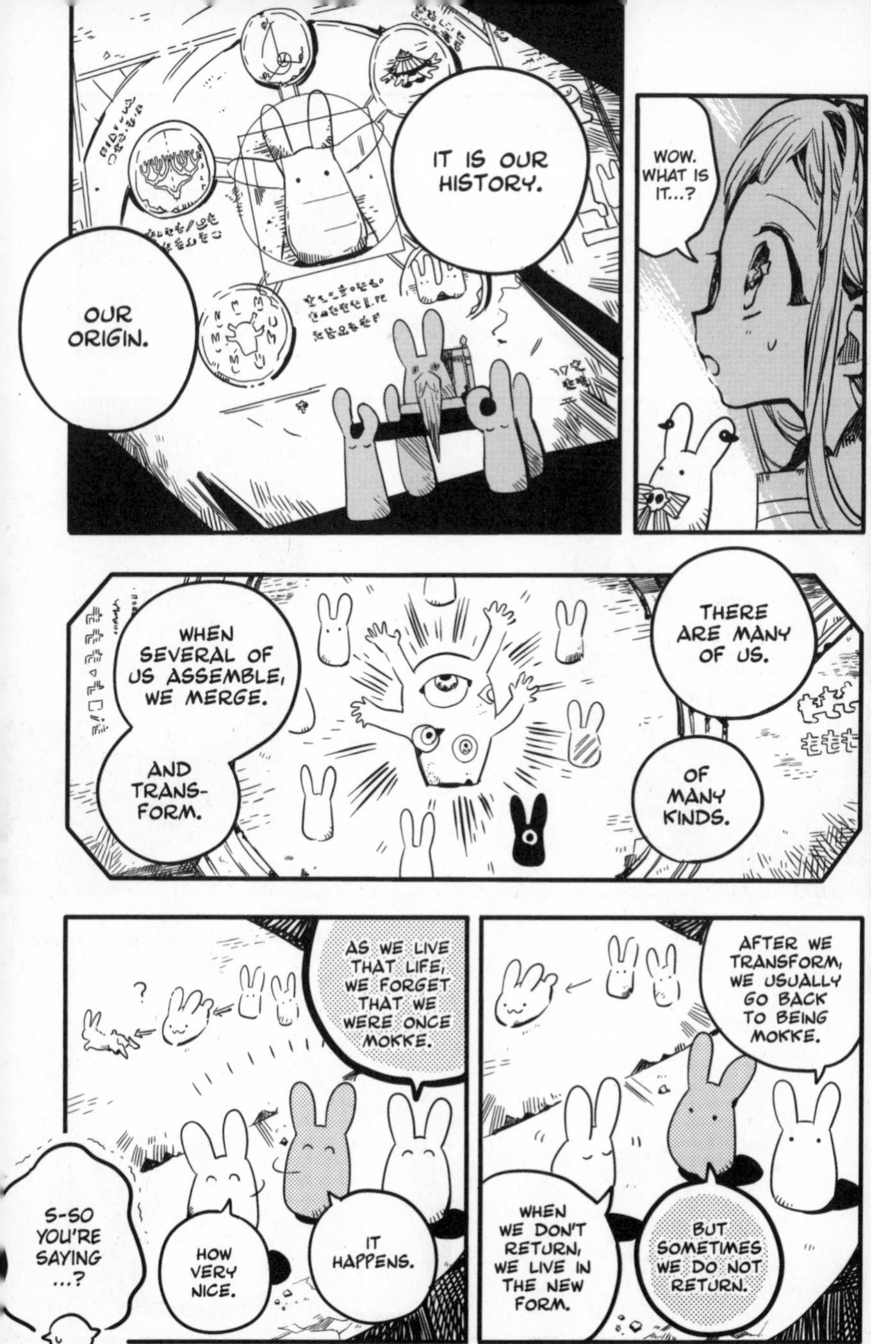
WOW. WHAT IS IT...?
IT IS OUR HISTORY.
OUR ORIGIN.
THERE ARE MANY OF US.
OF MANY KINDS.
WHEN SEVERAL OF US ASSEMBLE, WE MERGE.
AND TRANSFORM.
AFTER WE TRANSFORM, WE USUALLY GO BACK TO BEING MOKKE.
BUT SOMETIMES WE DO NOT RETURN.
WHEN WE DON'T RETURN, WE LIVE IN THE NEW FORM.
AS WE LIVE THAT LIFE, WE FORGET THAT WE WERE ONCE MOKKE.
IT HAPPENS.
HOW VERY NICE.
S-SO YOU'RE SAYING ...?

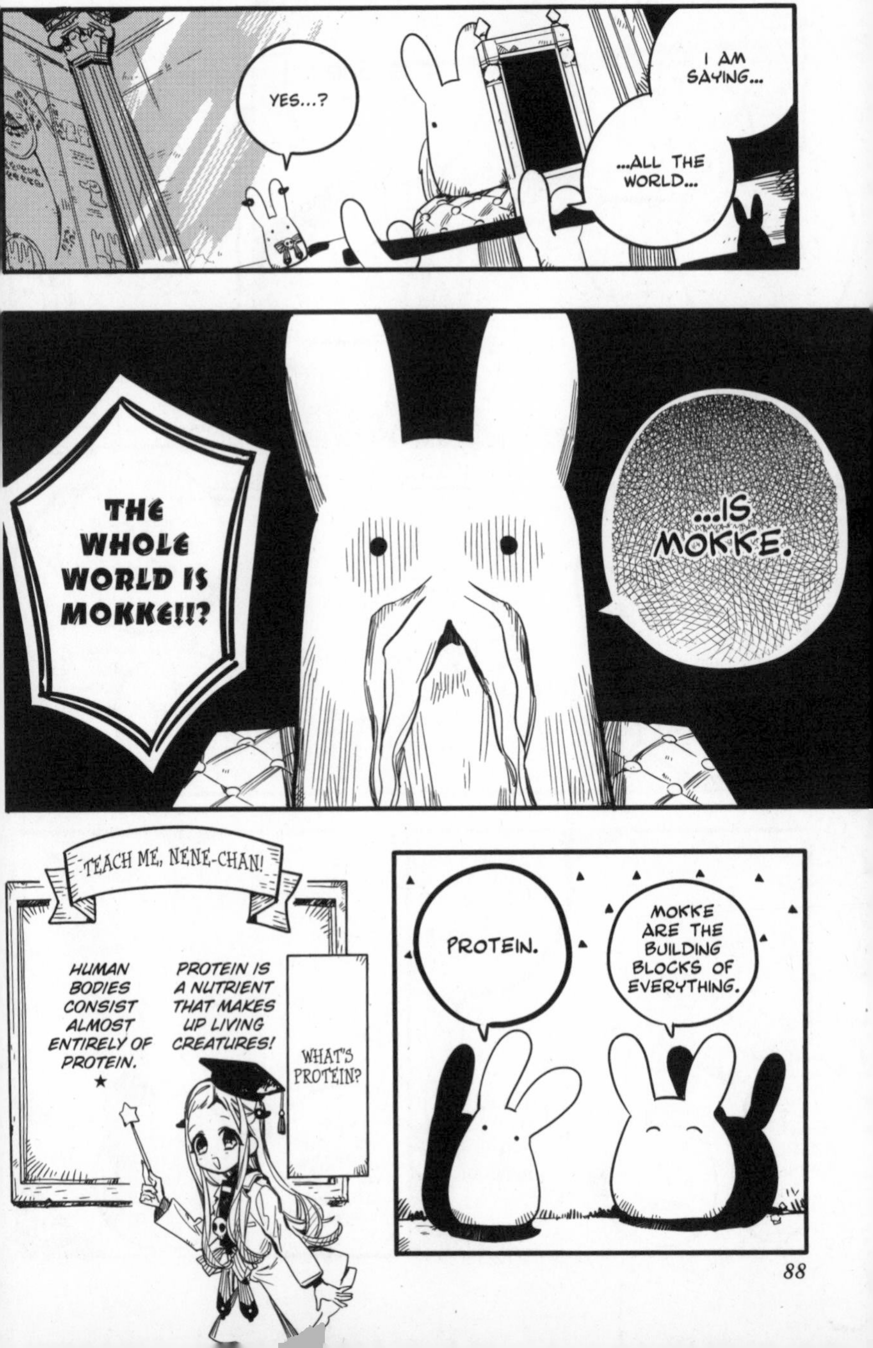
I AM SAYING...
...ALL THE WORLD...
YES...?
...IS MOKKE.
THE WHOLE WORLD IS MOKKE!!?
MOKKE ARE THE BUILDING BLOCKS OF EVERYTHING.
PROTEIN.
TEACH ME, NENE-CHAN!
WHAT'S PROTEIN?
PROTEIN IS A NUTRIENT THAT MAKES UP LIVING CREATURES!
HUMAN BODIES CONSIST ALMOST ENTIRELY OF PROTEIN. ★

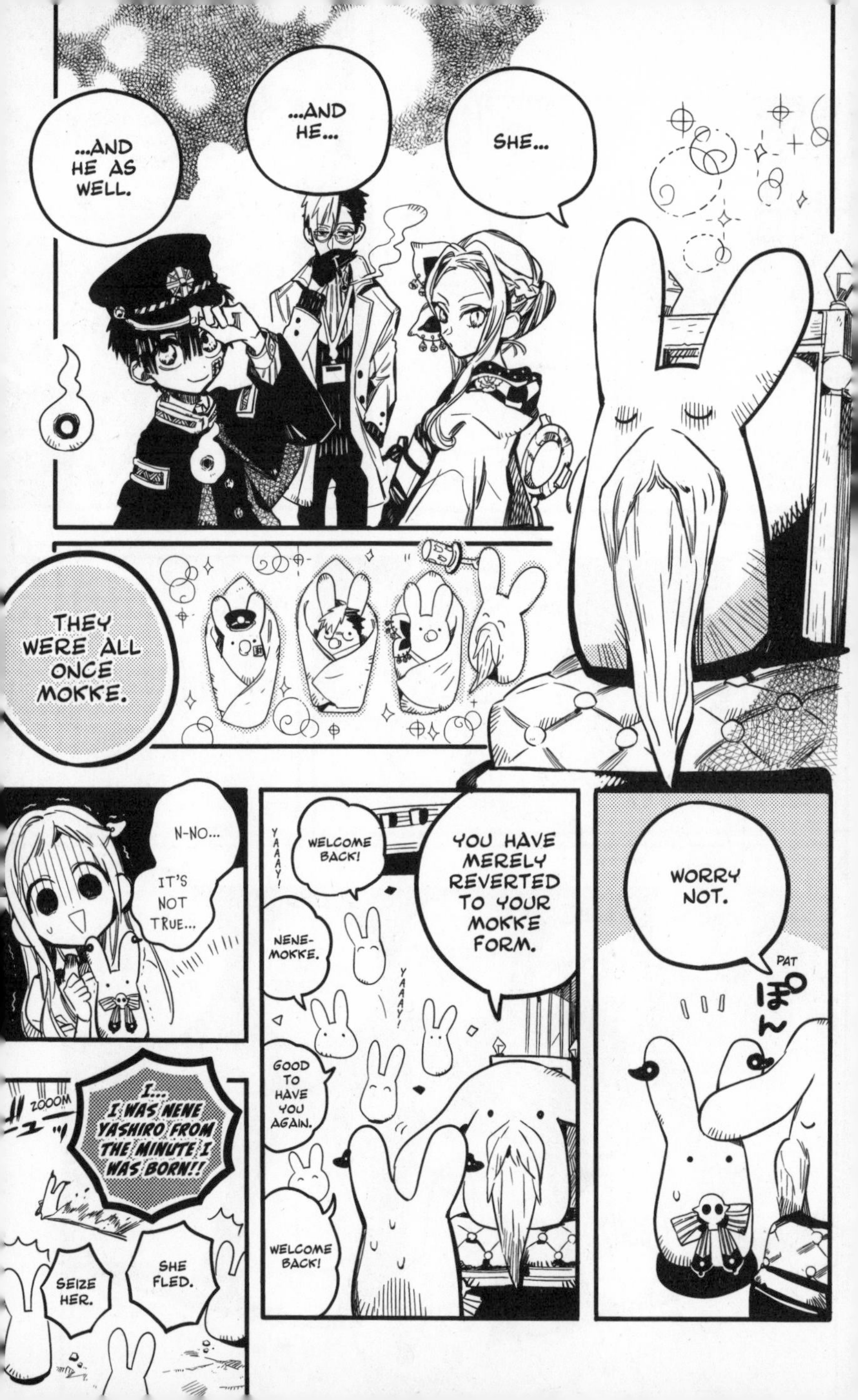
SHE...
...AND HE...
...AND HE AS WELL.
THEY WERE ALL ONCE MOKKE.
WORRY NOT.
PAT
ぽん
YOU HAVE MERELY REVERTED TO YOUR MOKKE FORM.
WELCOME BACK!
YAAAY!
NENE-MOKKE.
YAAAY!
GOOD TO HAVE YOU AGAIN.
WELCOME BACK!
N-NO...
IT'S NOT TRUE...
I... I WAS NENE YASHIRO FROM THE MINUTE I WAS BORN!!
ZOOOM
SHE FLED.
SEIZE HER.

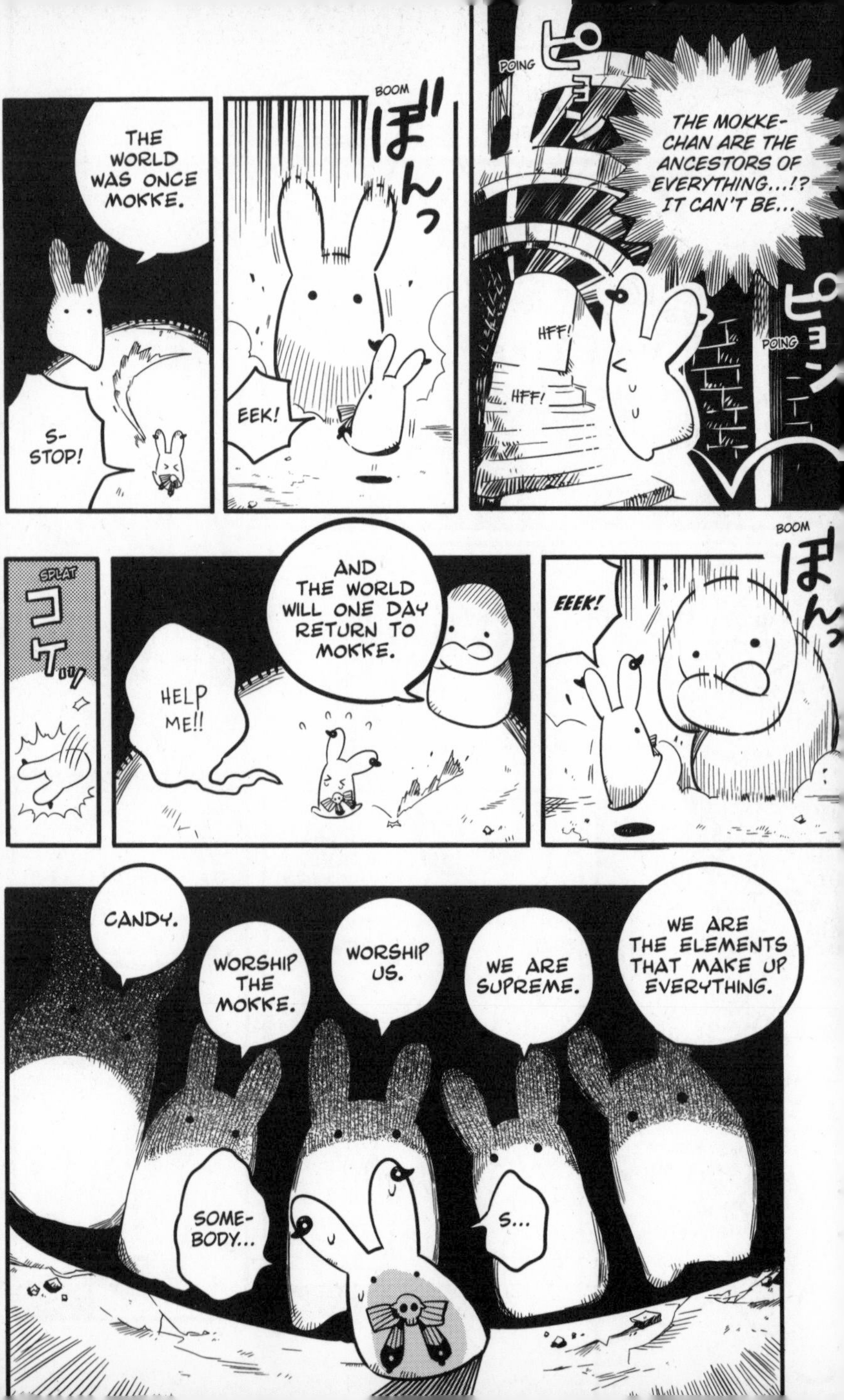
POING
ピョ
THE MOKKE-CHAN ARE THE ANCESTORS OF EVERYTHING...!? IT CAN'T BE...
HFF!
HFF!
POING
ピョン
BOOM
ぼんっ
EEK!
THE WORLD WAS ONCE MOKKE.
S-STOP!
BOOM
ぼんっ
EEEK!
AND THE WORLD WILL ONE DAY RETURN TO MOKKE.
HELP ME!!
SPLAT
コケッ
WE ARE THE ELEMENTS THAT MAKE UP EVERYTHING.
WE ARE SUPREME.
WORSHIP US.
WORSHIP THE MOKKE.
CANDY.
S...
SOME-BODY...

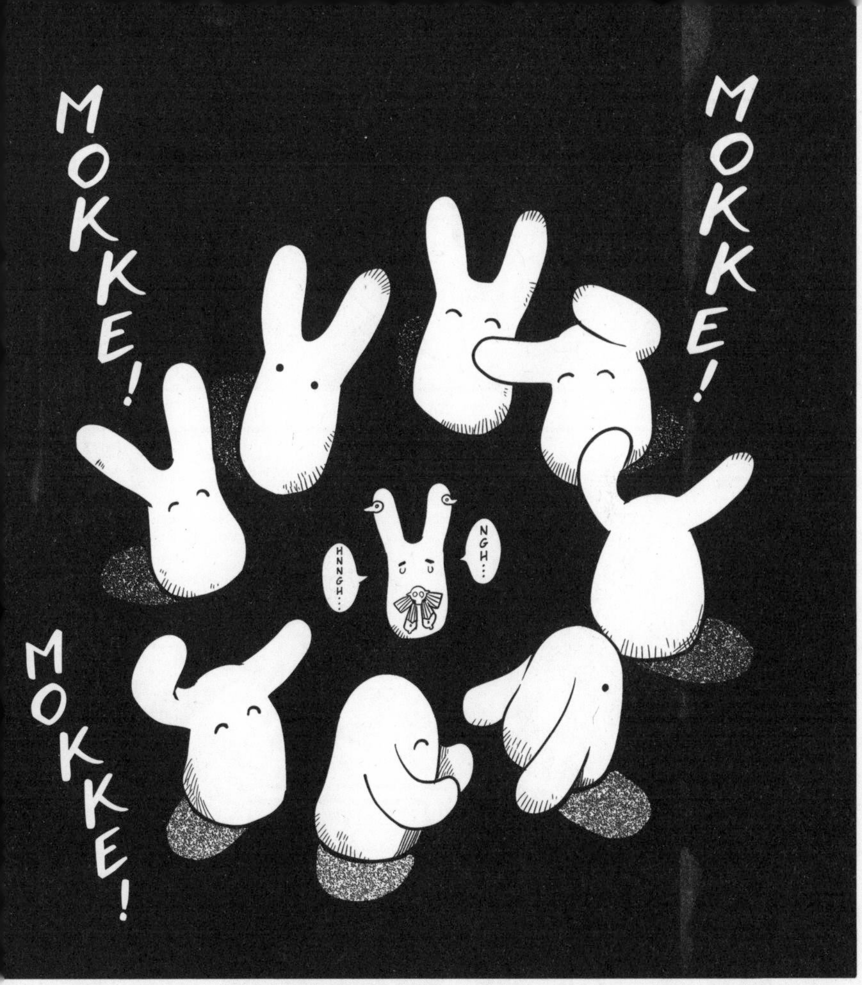
MOKKE!
MOKKE!
NGH...
HNNGH...
MOKKE!
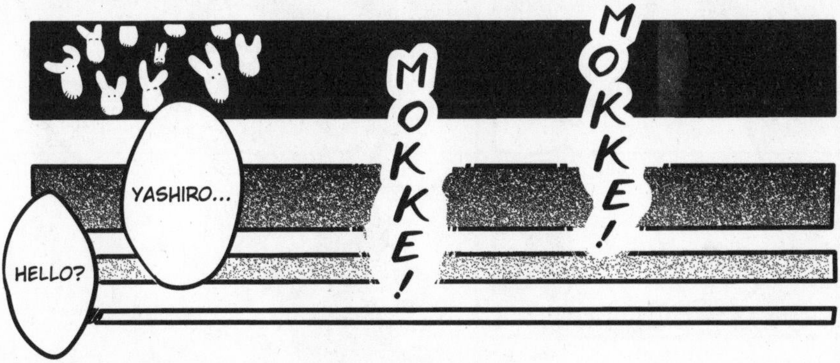
MOKKE!
MOKKE!
YASHIRO...
HELLO?

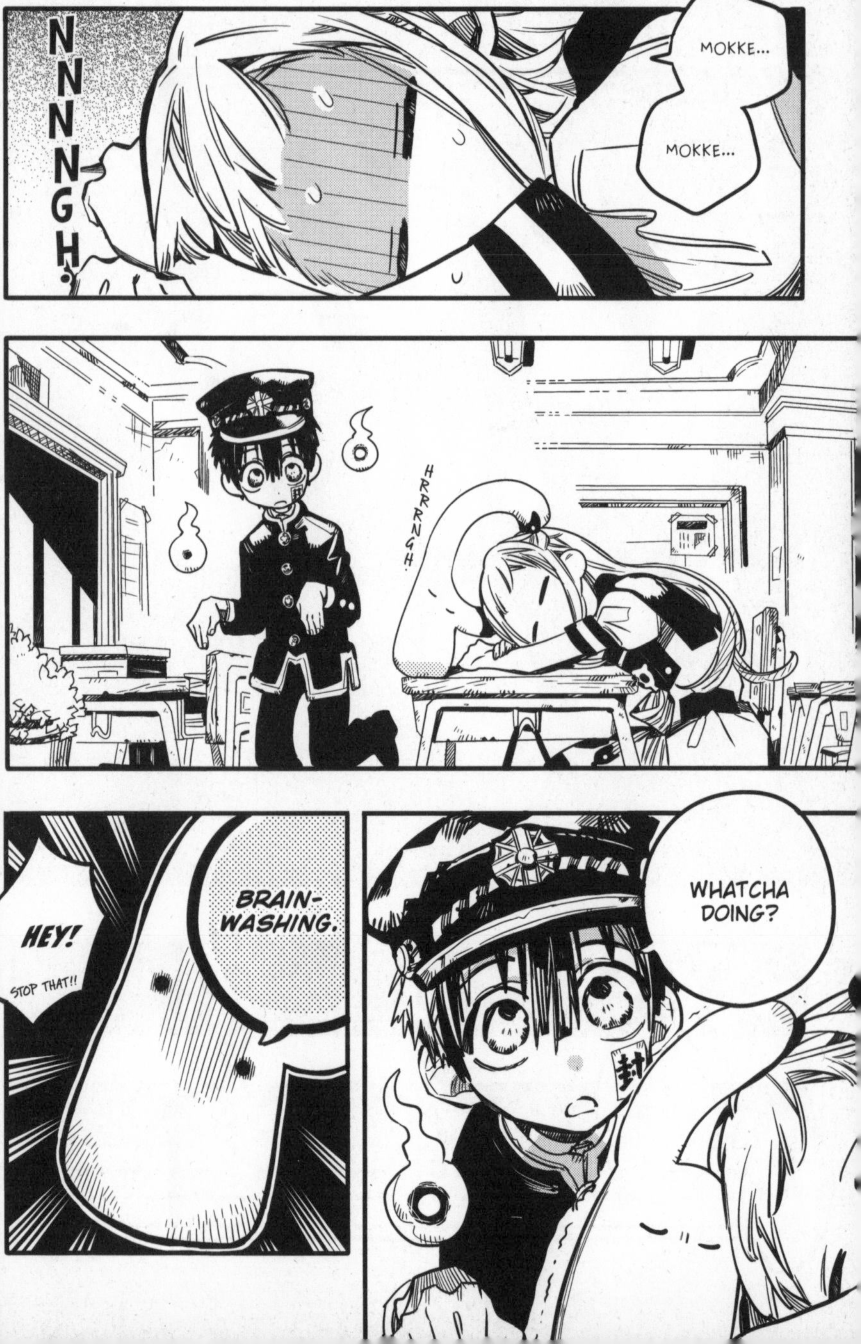
MOKKE...
MOKKE...
NNNNGH!
HRRRNGH
WHATCHA DOING?
BRAIN-WASHING.
HEY!
STOP THAT!!

After-School
Hanako-Kun

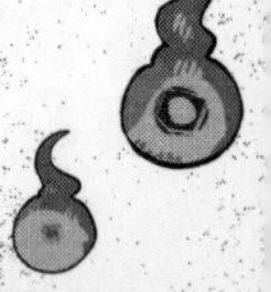

DAY 10: THE HIGH SCHOOL SPOOK

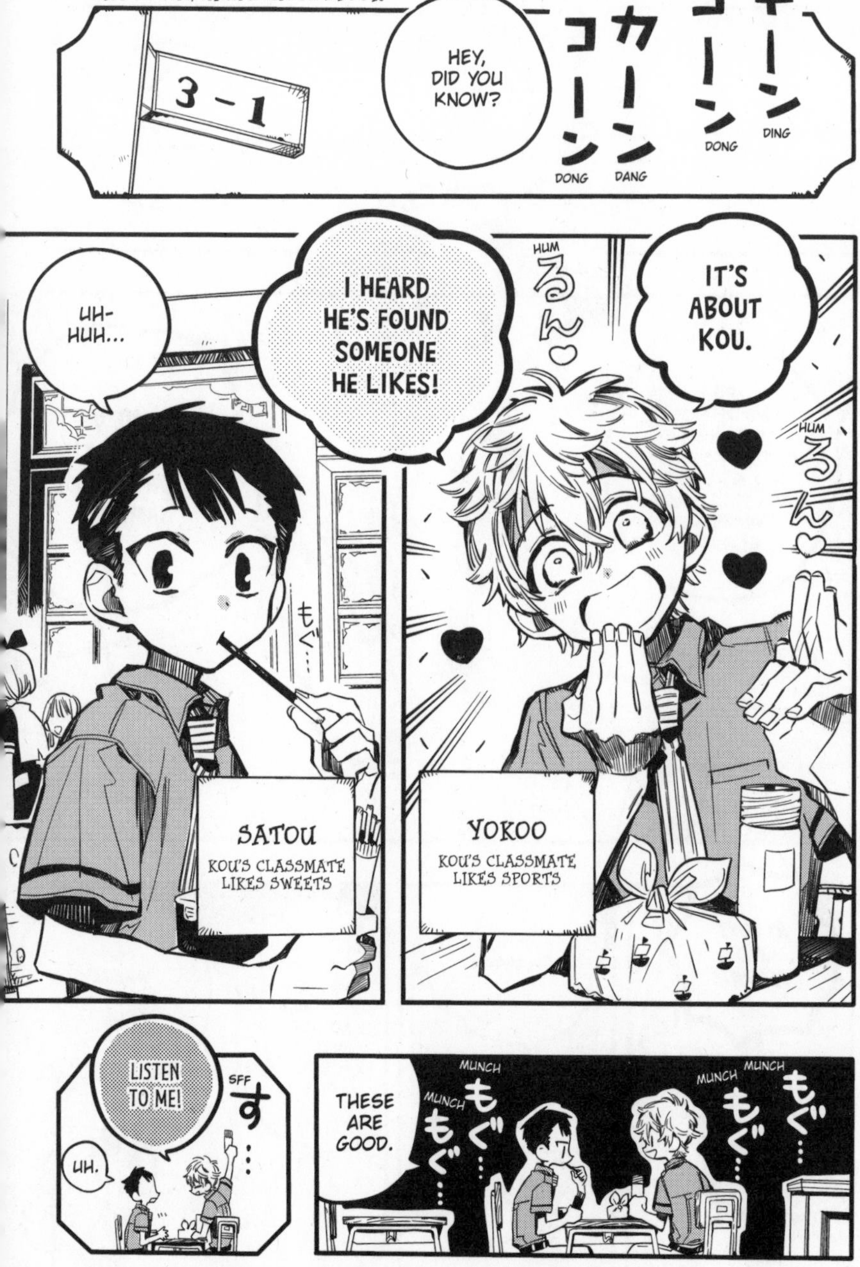
キーン DING
コーン DONG
カーン DANG
コーン DONG
HEY, DID YOU KNOW?
3 - 1
IT'S ABOUT KOU.
HUM るん♡
HUM るん♡
YOKOO
KOU'S CLASSMATE
LIKES SPORTS
I HEARD HE'S FOUND SOMEONE HE LIKES!
UH-HUH...
もぐ…
SATOU
KOU'S CLASSMATE
LIKES SWEETS
MUNCH もぐ…
MUNCH もぐ…
THESE ARE GOOD.
MUNCH もぐ
MUNCH もぐ…
LISTEN TO ME!
SFF す…
UH.

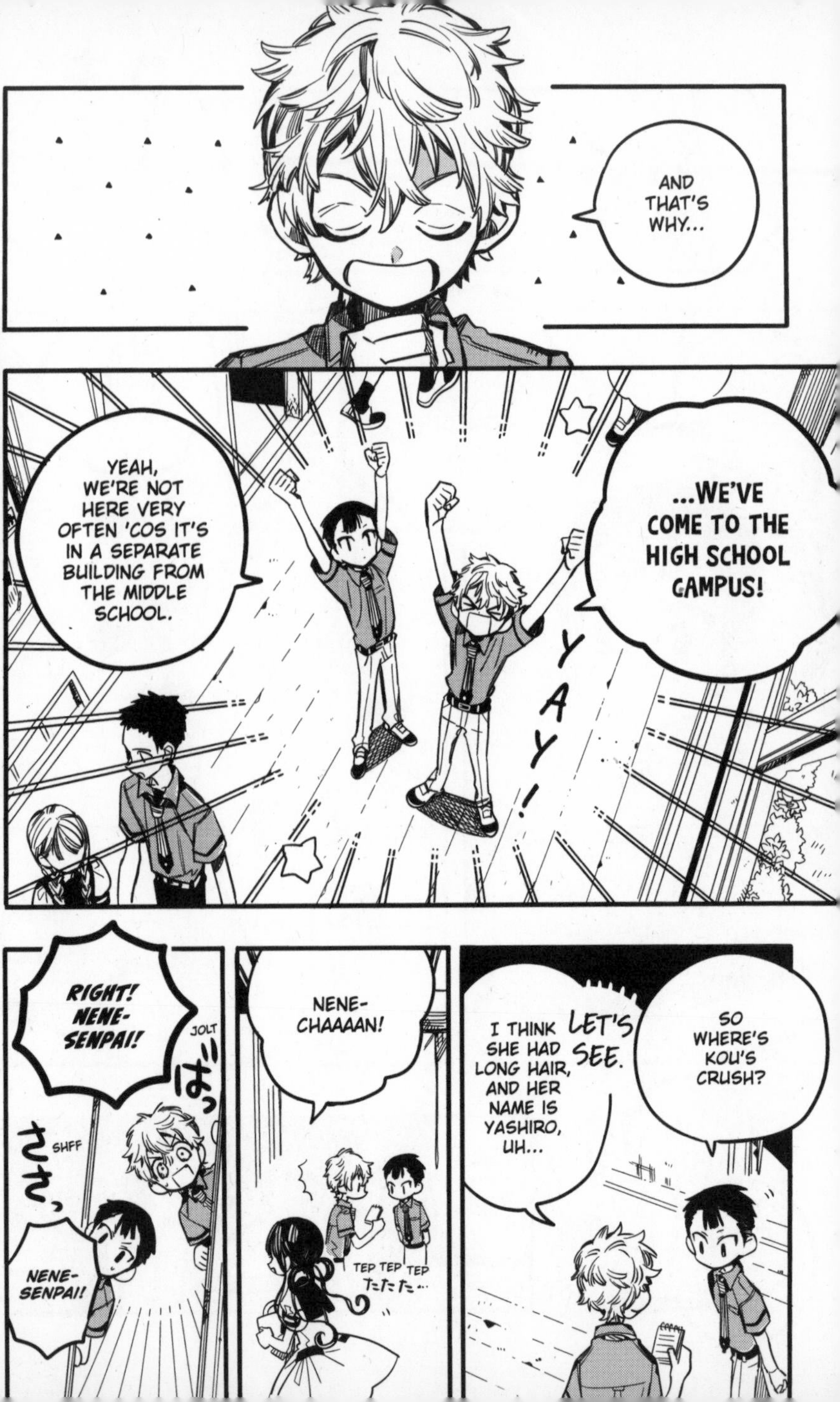
AND THAT'S WHY...
...WE'VE COME TO THE HIGH SCHOOL CAMPUS!
YAY!
YEAH, WE'RE NOT HERE VERY OFTEN 'COS IT'S IN A SEPARATE BUILDING FROM THE MIDDLE SCHOOL.
SO WHERE'S KOU'S CRUSH?
LET'S SEE.
I THINK SHE HAD LONG HAIR, AND HER NAME IS YASHIRO, UH...
NENE-CHAAAAN!
TEP TEP TEP
たたた…
RIGHT! NENE-SENPAI!
JOLT
ばっ
SHFF
ささっ
NENE-SENPAI!

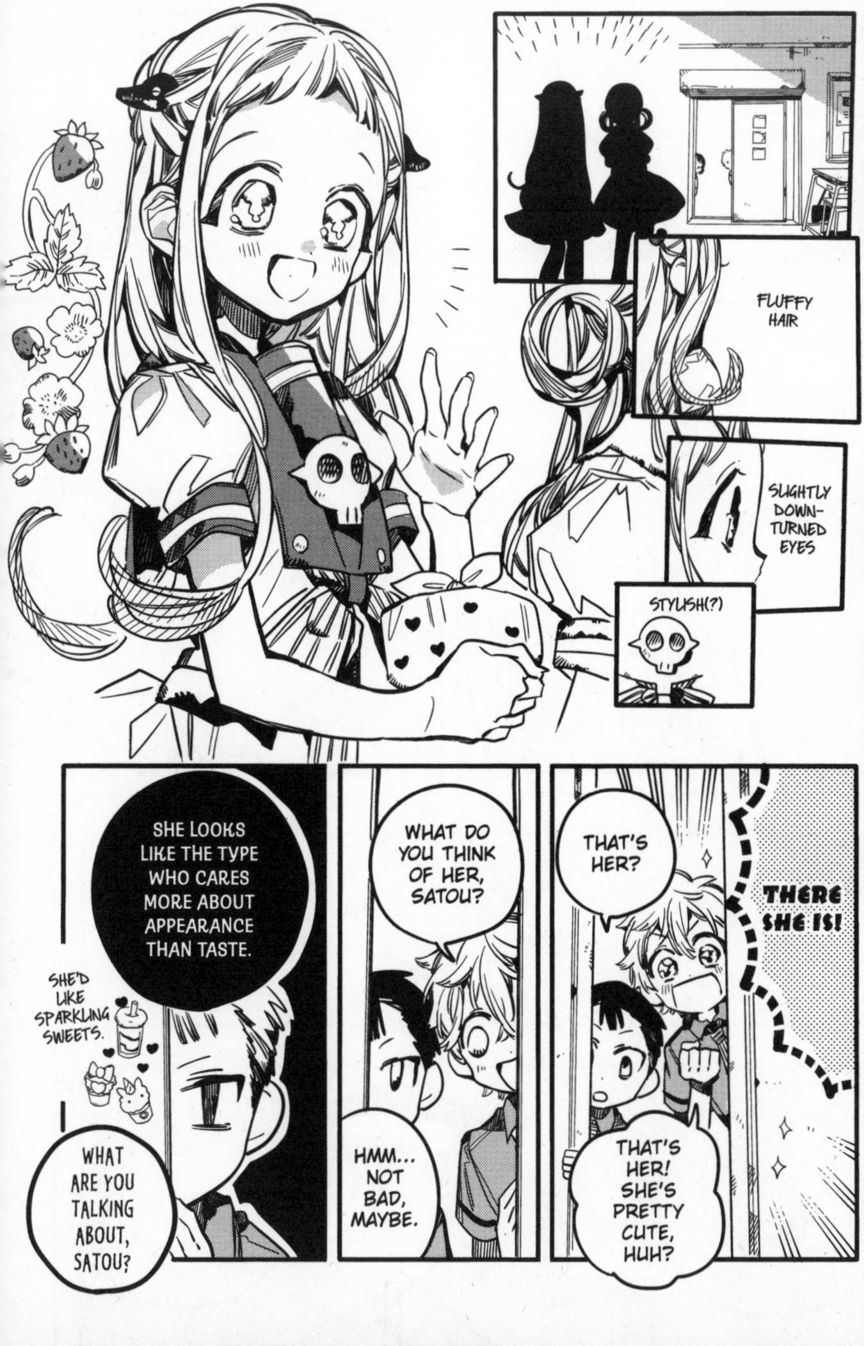
FLUFFY HAIR
SLIGHTLY DOWN-TURNED EYES
STYLISH(?)
THERE SHE IS!
THAT'S HER?
THAT'S HER! SHE'S PRETTY CUTE, HUH?
WHAT DO YOU THINK OF HER, SATOU?
HMM... NOT BAD, MAYBE.
SHE LOOKS LIKE THE TYPE WHO CARES MORE ABOUT APPEARANCE THAN TASTE.
SHE'D LIKE SPARKLING SWEETS.
WHAT ARE YOU TALKING ABOUT, SATOU?

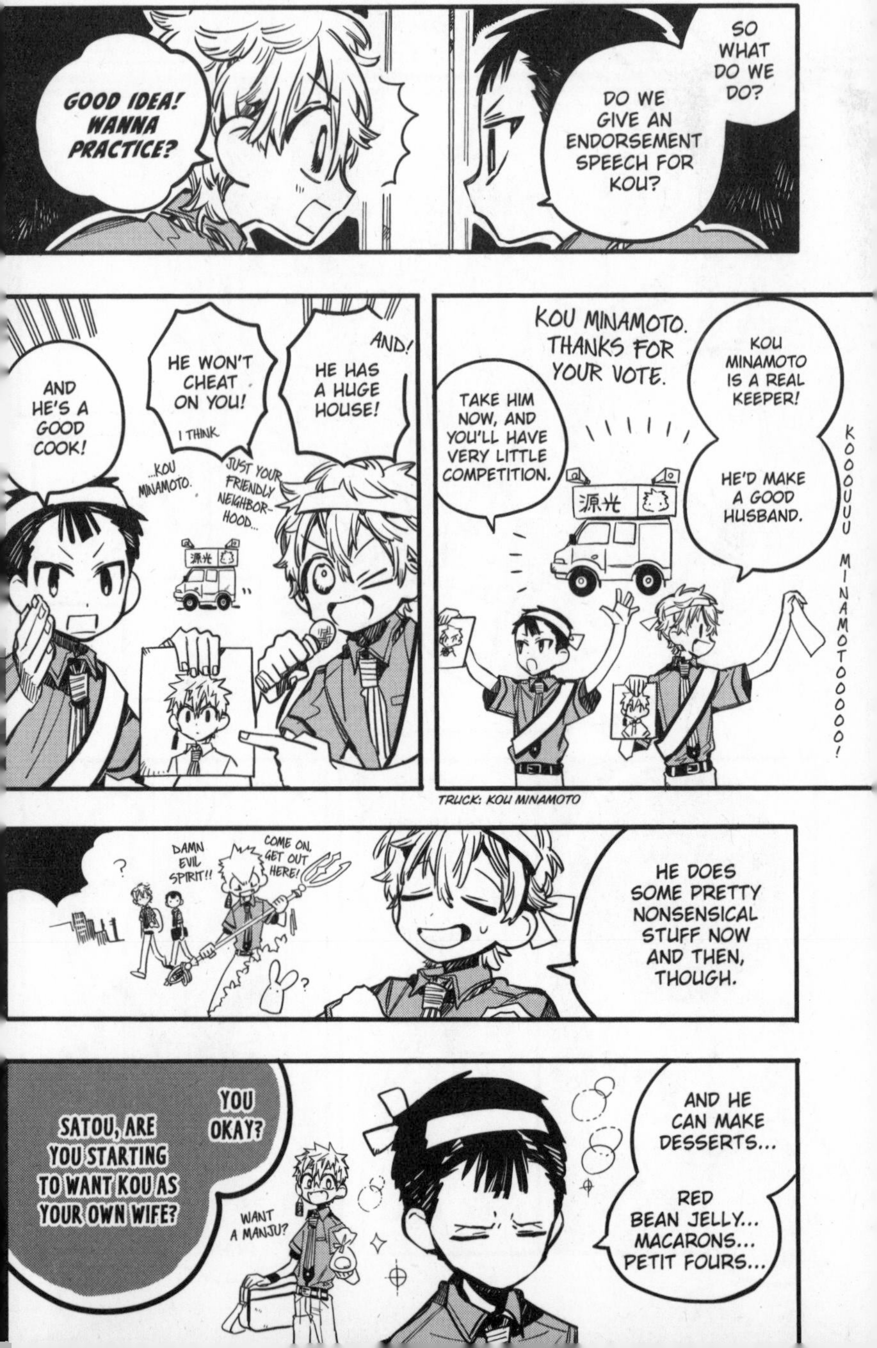
SO WHAT DO WE DO?
DO WE GIVE AN ENDORSEMENT SPEECH FOR KOU?
GOOD IDEA! WANNA PRACTICE?
KOU MINAMOTO IS A REAL KEEPER!
HE'D MAKE A GOOD HUSBAND.
KOU MINAMOTO. THANKS FOR YOUR VOTE.
TAKE HIM NOW, AND YOU'LL HAVE VERY LITTLE COMPETITION.
KOOOUUU MINAMOTOOOOOO!
AND!
HE HAS A HUGE HOUSE!
HE WON'T CHEAT ON YOU!
I THINK.
JUST YOUR FRIENDLY NEIGHBORHOOD...
...KOU MINAMOTO.
AND HE'S A GOOD COOK!
TRUCK: KOU MINAMOTO
HE DOES SOME PRETTY NONSENSICAL STUFF NOW AND THEN, THOUGH.
COME ON, GET OUT HERE!
DAMN EVIL SPIRIT!!
AND HE CAN MAKE DESSERTS...
RED BEAN JELLY... MACARONS... PETIT FOURS...
WANT A MANJU?
YOU OKAY?
SATOU, ARE YOU STARTING TO WANT KOU AS YOUR OWN WIFE?

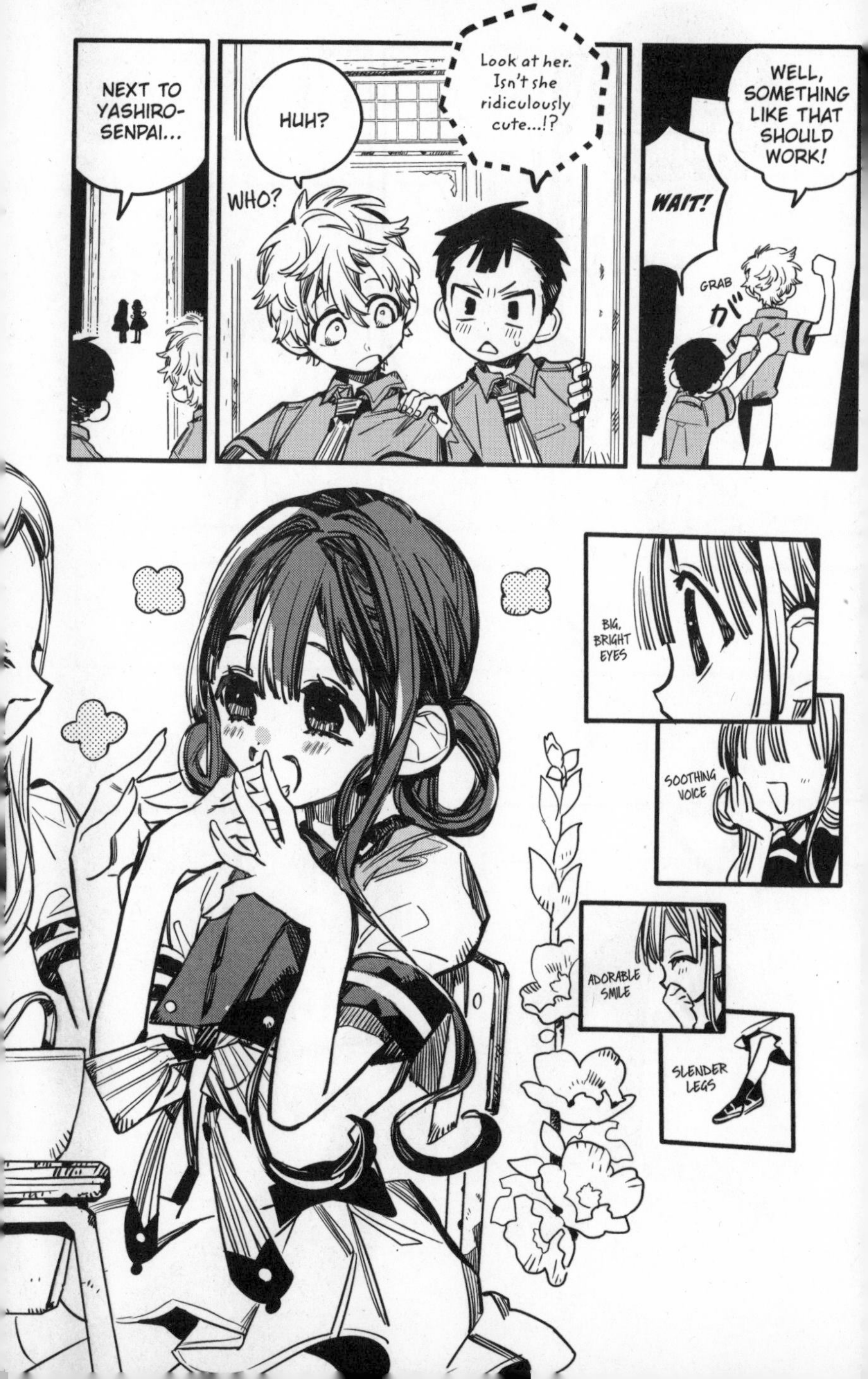
WELL, SOMETHING LIKE THAT SHOULD WORK!
WAIT!
GRAB
が
Look at her. Isn't she ridiculously cute...!?
HUH?
WHO?
NEXT TO YASHIRO-SENPAI...
BIG, BRIGHT EYES
SOOTHING VOICE
ADORABLE SMILE
SLENDER LEGS

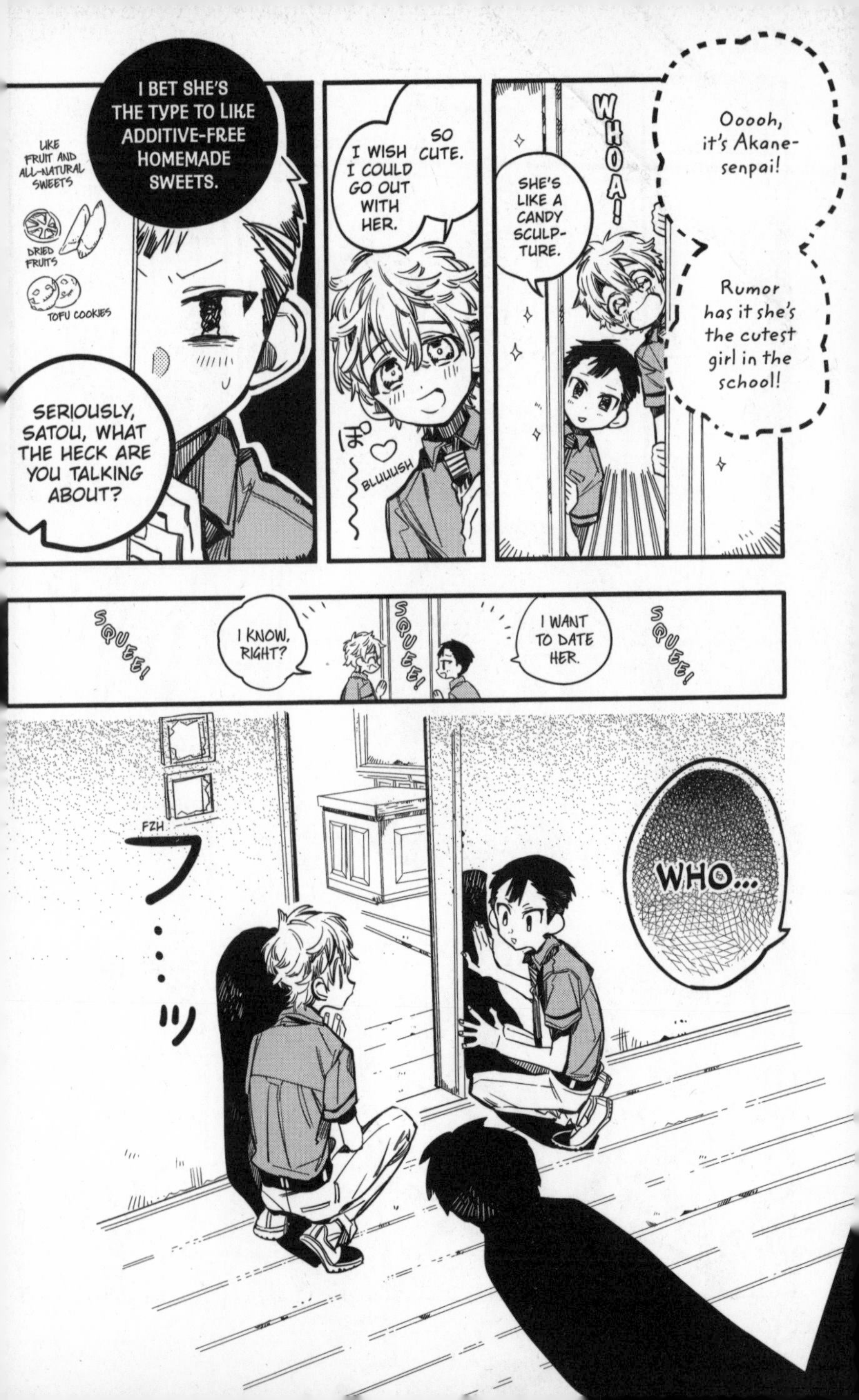
Ooooh, it's Akane-senpai!
Rumor has it she's the cutest girl in the school!
WHOA!
SHE'S LIKE A CANDY SCULPTURE.
SO CUTE.
I WISH I COULD GO OUT WITH HER.
ぽ♡
BLUUUSH
I BET SHE'S THE TYPE TO LIKE ADDITIVE-FREE HOMEMADE SWEETS.
LIKE FRUIT AND ALL-NATURAL SWEETS
DRIED FRUITS
TOFU COOKIES
SERIOUSLY, SATOU, WHAT THE HECK ARE YOU TALKING ABOUT?
SQUEE!
I WANT TO DATE HER.
SQUEE!
I KNOW, RIGHT?
SQUEE!
WHO...
FZH
フ…ッ

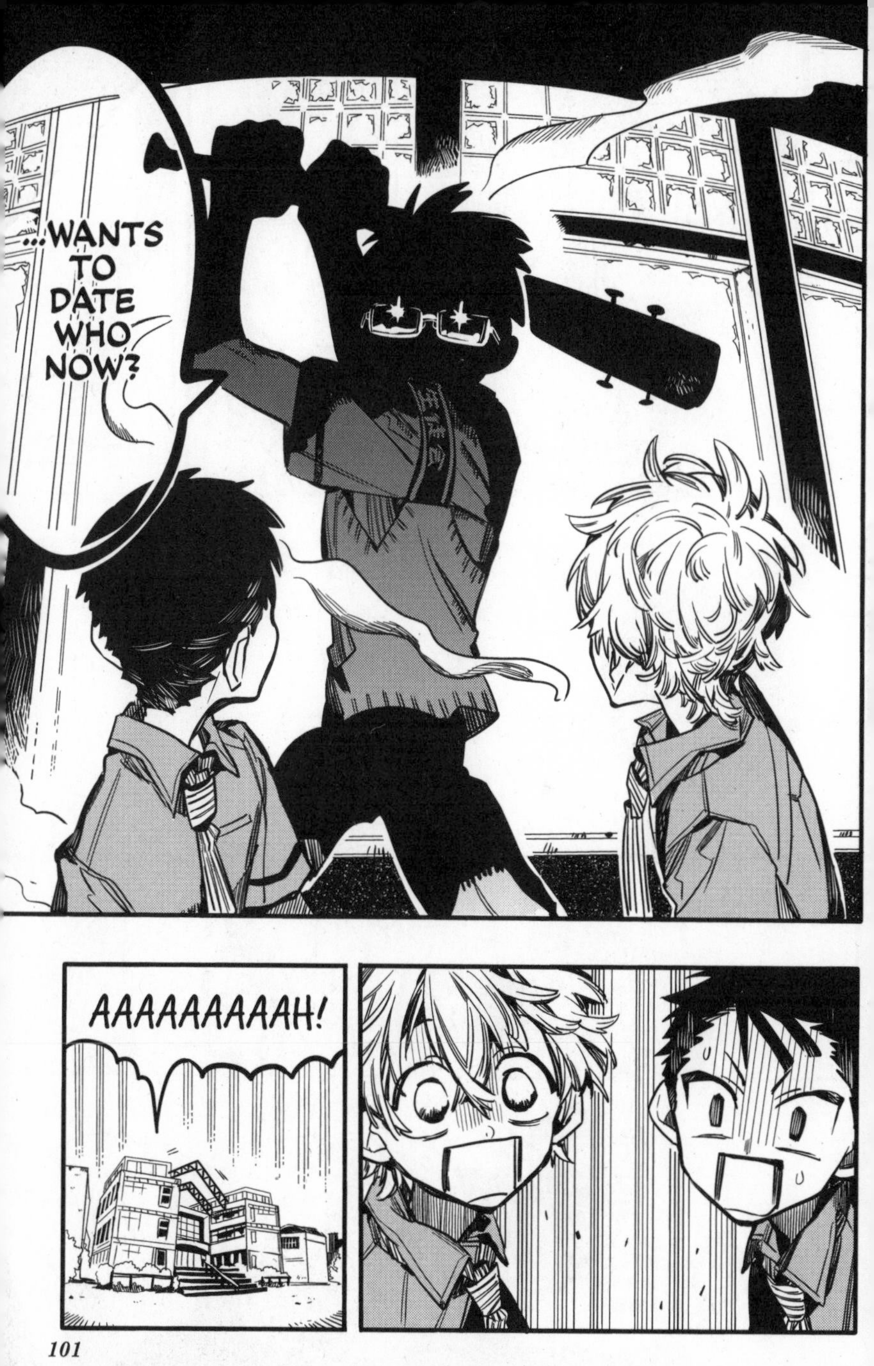
...WANTS TO DATE WHO NOW?
AAAAAAAAAH!

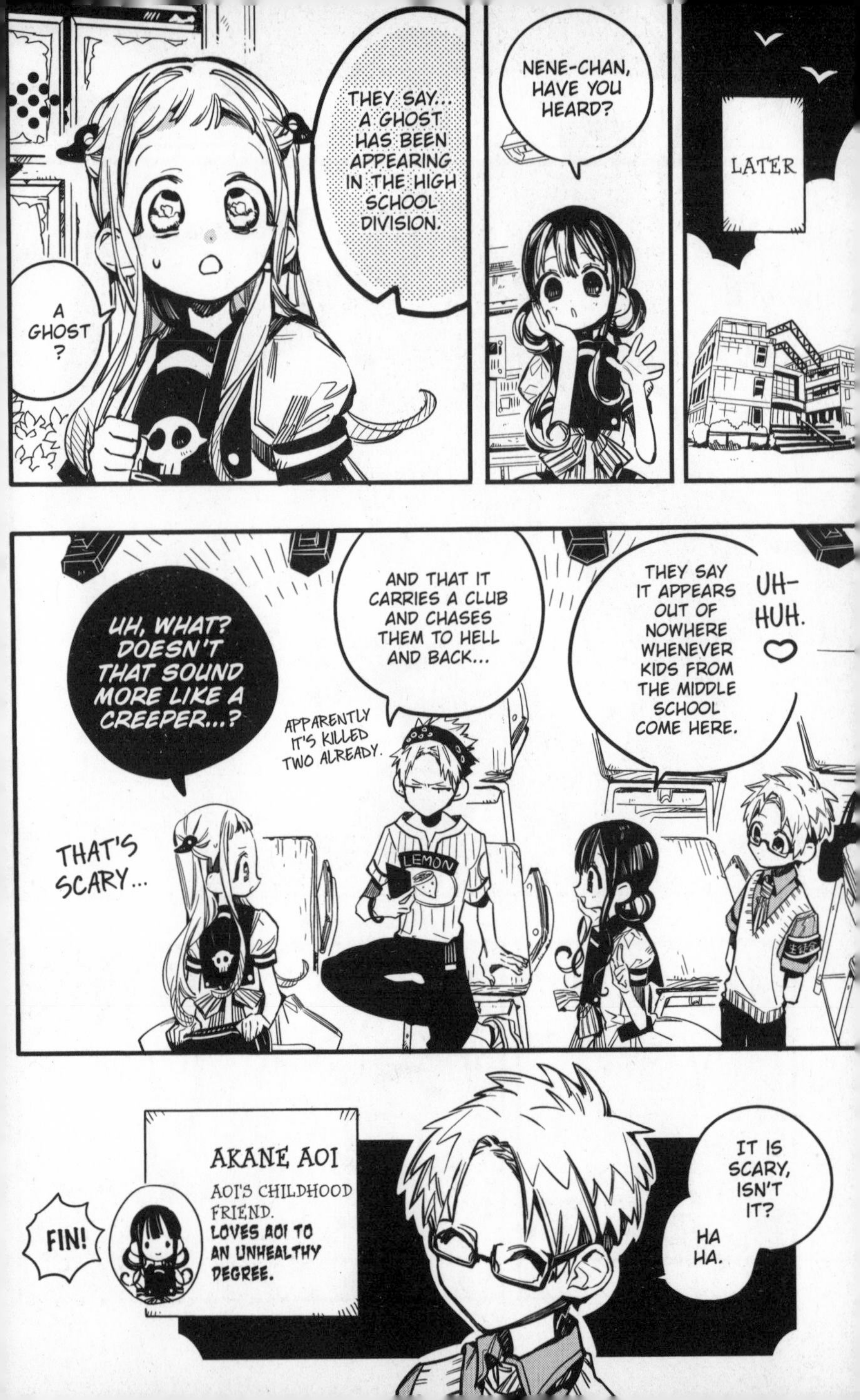
LATER
NENE-CHAN, HAVE YOU HEARD?
THEY SAY... A GHOST HAS BEEN APPEARING IN THE HIGH SCHOOL DIVISION.
A GHOST?
UH-HUH. ♡
THEY SAY IT APPEARS OUT OF NOWHERE WHENEVER KIDS FROM THE MIDDLE SCHOOL COME HERE.
AND THAT IT CARRIES A CLUB AND CHASES THEM TO HELL AND BACK...
APPARENTLY IT'S KILLED TWO ALREADY.
LEMON
UH, WHAT? DOESN'T THAT SOUND MORE LIKE A CREEPER...?
THAT'S SCARY...
IT IS SCARY, ISN'T IT?
HA HA.
AKANE AOI
AOI'S CHILDHOOD FRIEND.
LOVES AOI TO AN UNHEALTHY DEGREE.
FIN!

After-School
Hanako-Kun

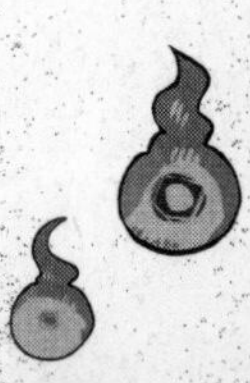

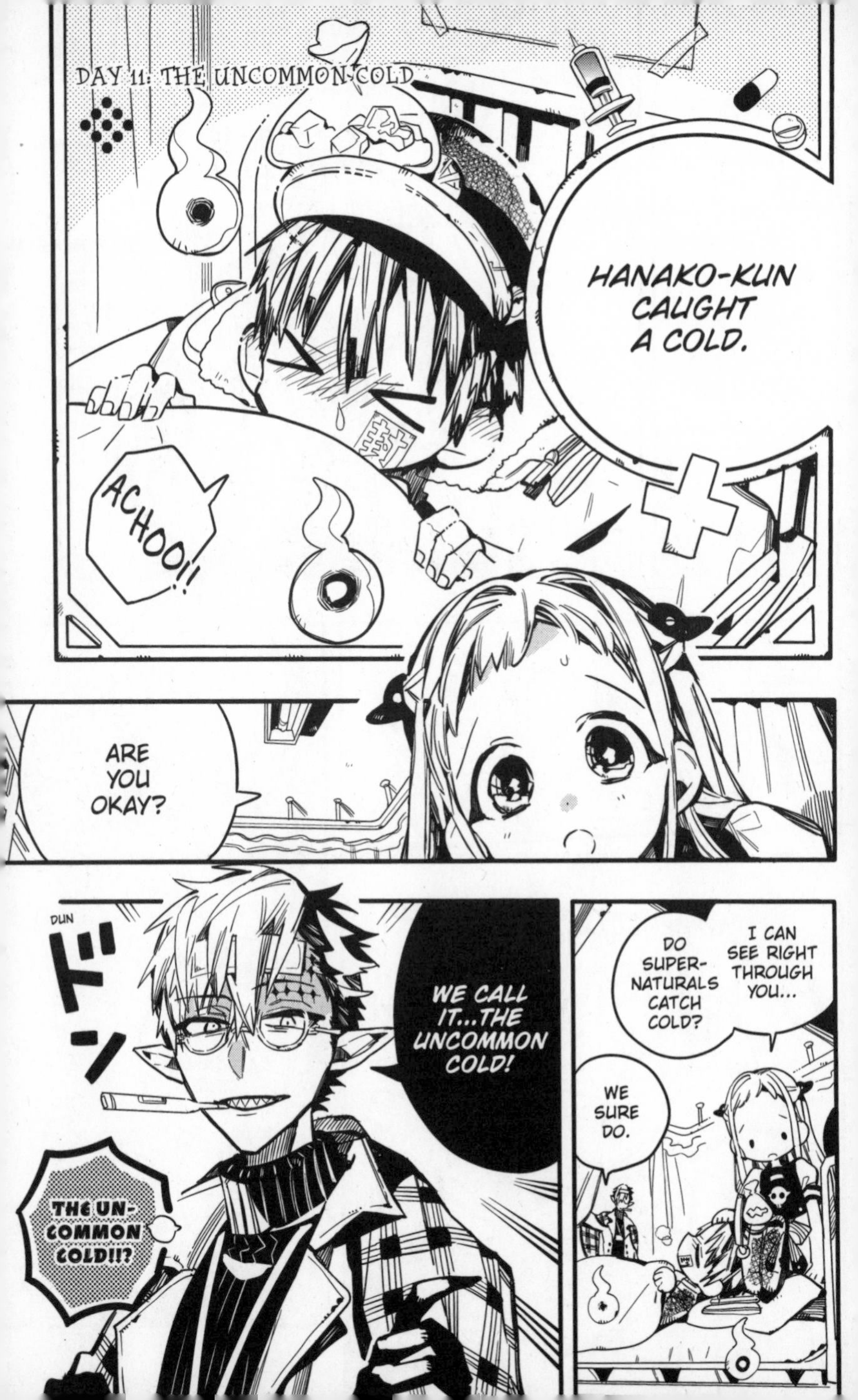
DAY 11: THE UNCOMMON COLD
HANAKO-KUN CAUGHT A COLD.
ACHOO!!
ARE YOU OKAY?
I CAN SEE RIGHT THROUGH YOU...
DO SUPER-NATURALS CATCH COLD?
WE SURE DO.
WE CALL IT...THE UNCOMMON COLD!
DUN
THE UN-COMMON COLD!!?

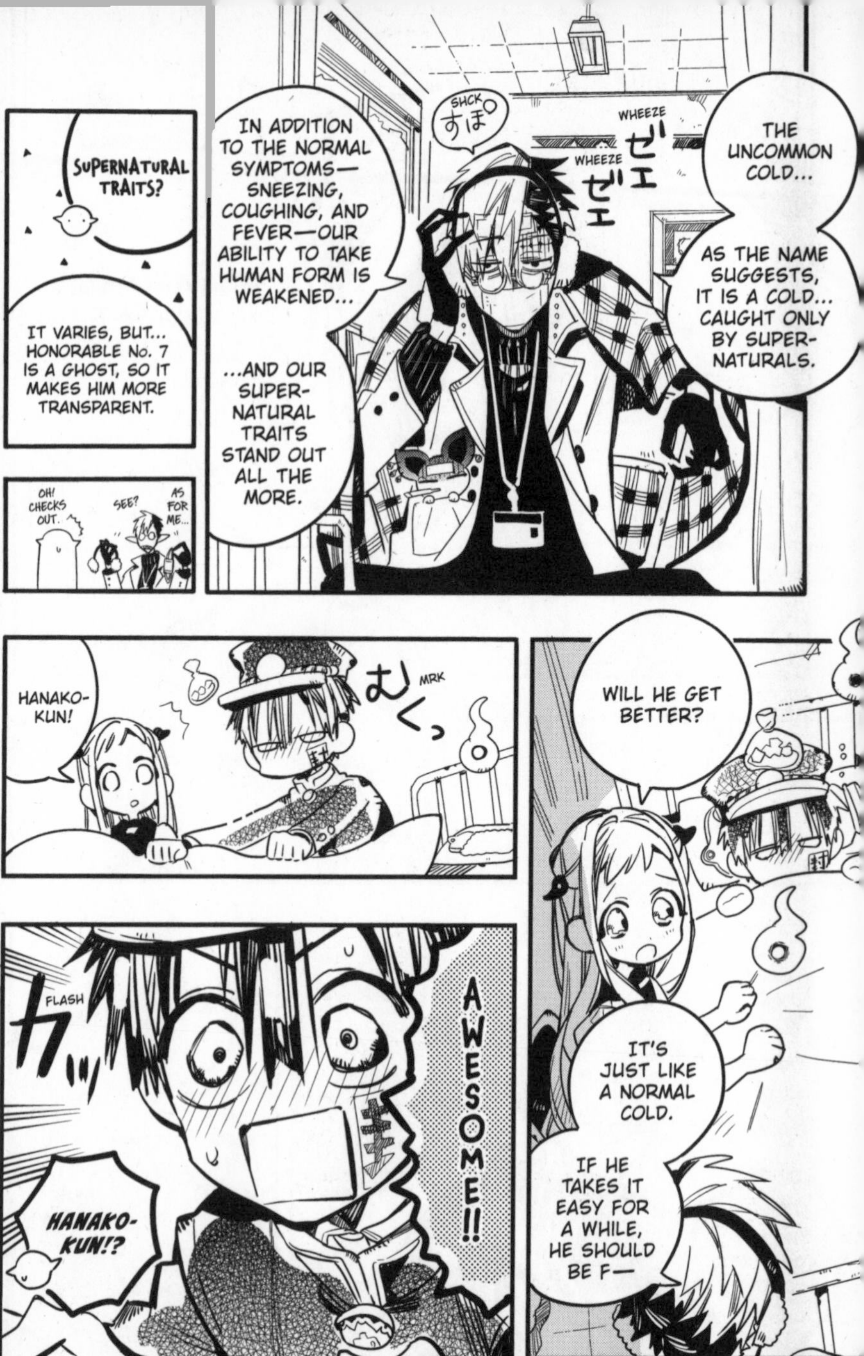

SHCK
すぽ
WHEEZE
ゼエ
WHEEZE
ゼエ
THE UNCOMMON COLD...
AS THE NAME SUGGESTS, IT IS A COLD... CAUGHT ONLY BY SUPER-NATURALS.
IN ADDITION TO THE NORMAL SYMPTOMS—SNEEZING, COUGHING, AND FEVER—OUR ABILITY TO TAKE HUMAN FORM IS WEAKENED...
...AND OUR SUPER-NATURAL TRAITS STAND OUT ALL THE MORE.
SUPERNATURAL TRAITS?
IT VARIES, BUT... HONORABLE No. 7 IS A GHOST, SO IT MAKES HIM MORE TRANSPARENT.
AS FOR ME...
SEE?
OH! CHECKS OUT.
WILL HE GET BETTER?
IT'S JUST LIKE A NORMAL COLD.
IF HE TAKES IT EASY FOR A WHILE, HE SHOULD BE F—
HANAKO-KUN!
MRK
むくっ
FLASH
カッ
AWESOME!!
HANAKO-KUN!?

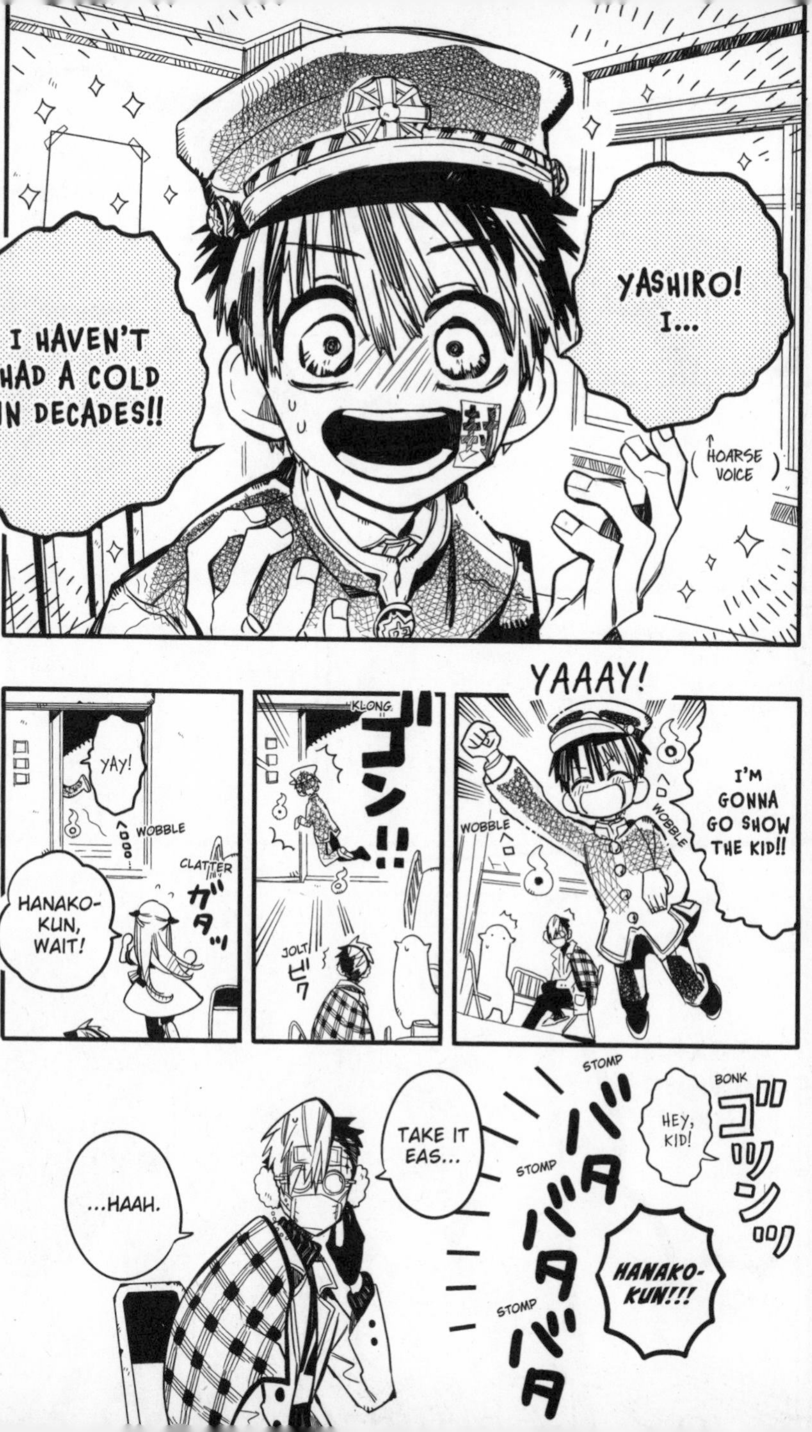
YASHIRO! I...
(↑HOARSE VOICE)
I HAVEN'T HAD A COLD IN DECADES!!
YAAAY!
I'M GONNA GO SHOW THE KID!!
WOBBLE
WOBBLE
KLONG.
ゴン!!
JOLT
ビク
YAY!
WOBBLE
CLATTER
ガタッ
HANAKO-KUN, WAIT!
BONK
ゴッ
ツン
HEY, KID!
HANAKO-KUN!!!
STOMP
STOMP
STOMP
バタバタバタ
TAKE IT EAS...
...HAAH.

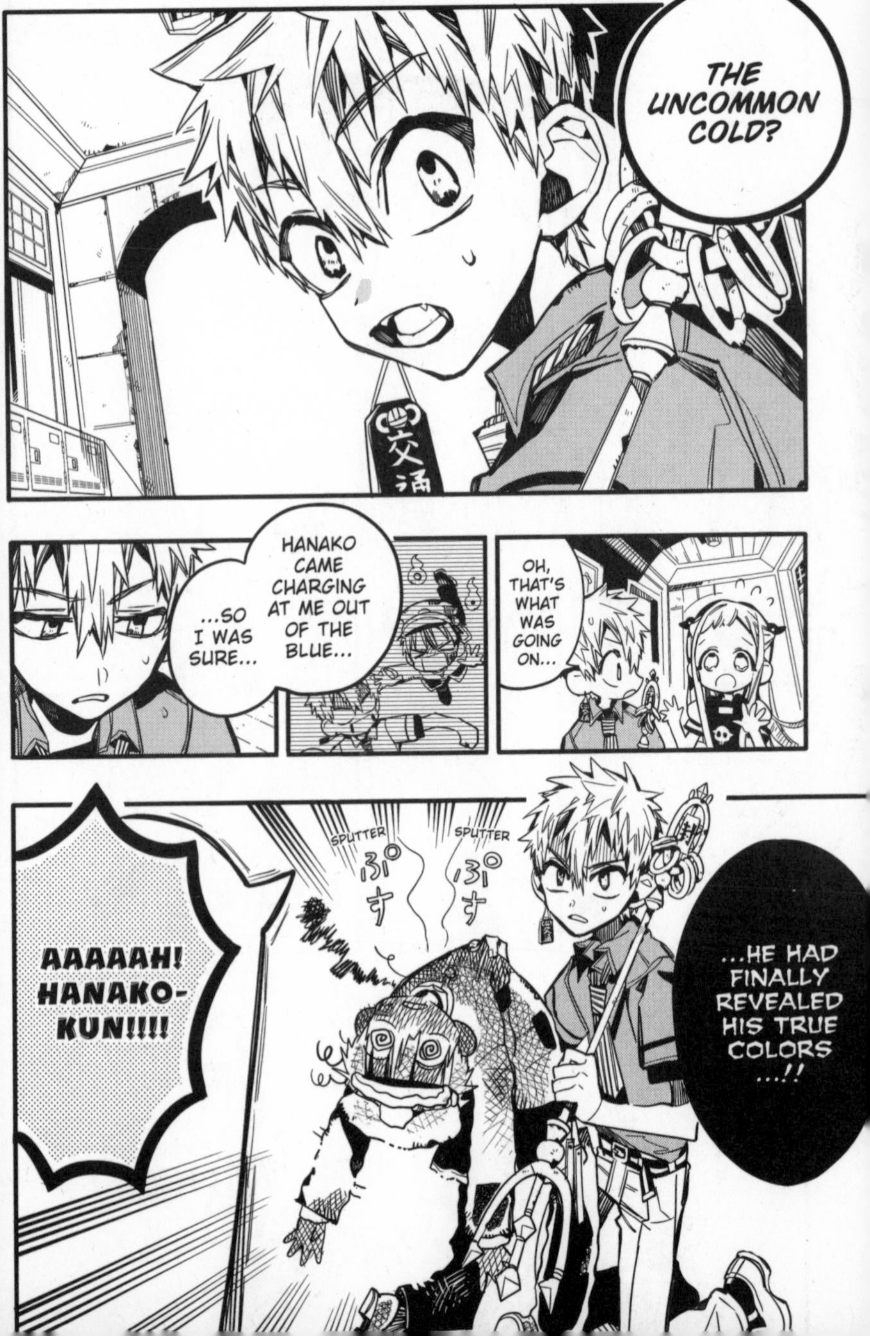
THE UNCOMMON COLD?
OH, THAT'S WHAT WAS GOING ON...
HANAKO CAME CHARGING AT ME OUT OF THE BLUE...
...SO I WAS SURE...
...HE HAD FINALLY REVEALED HIS TRUE COLORS ...!!
SPUTTER
ぷす
SPUTTER
ぷす
AAAAAH! HANAKO-KUN!!!!

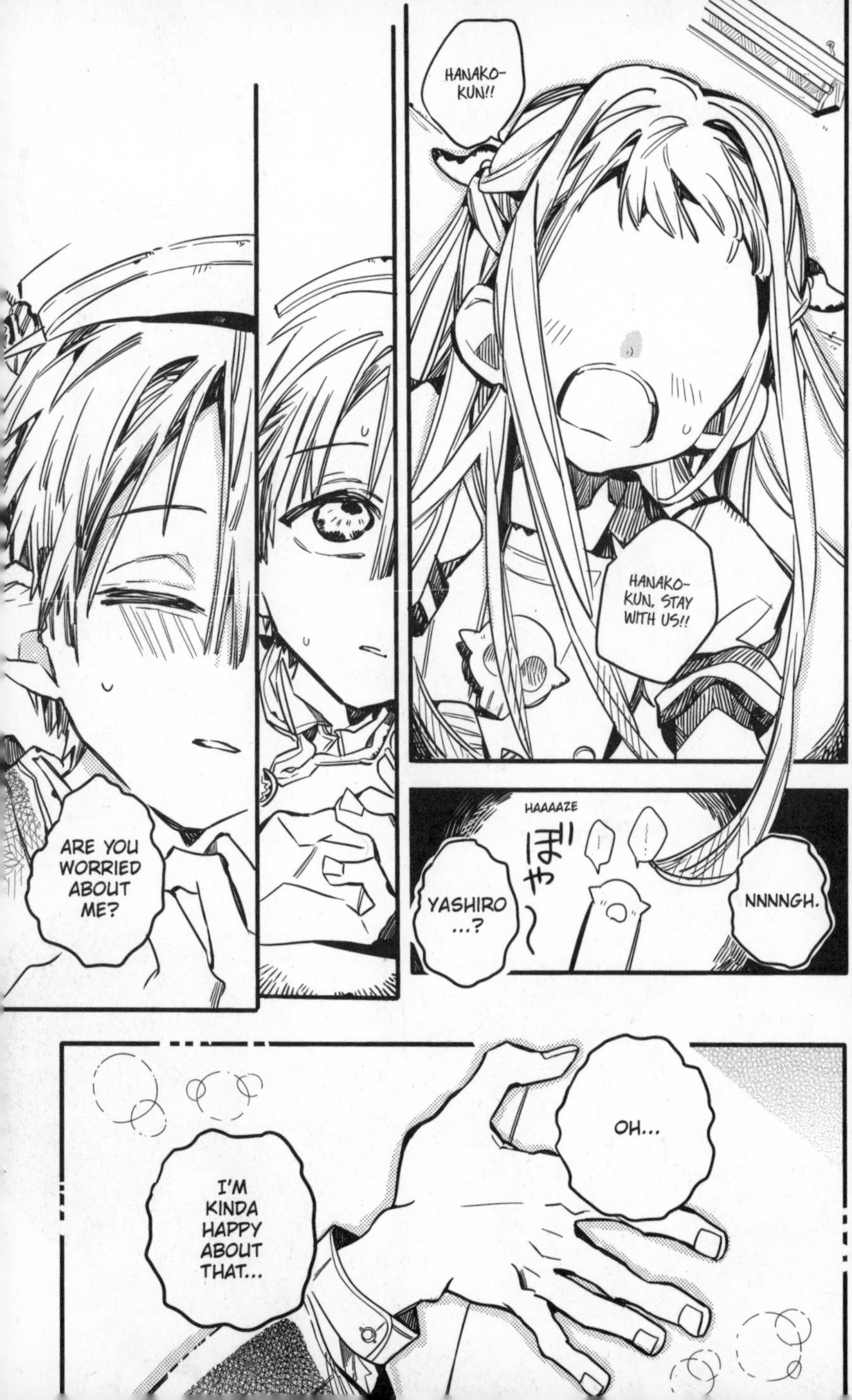
HANAKO-KUN!!
HANAKO-KUN, STAY WITH US!!
NNNNGH.
HAAAAZE
ぼや〜
YASHIRO ...?
ARE YOU WORRIED ABOUT ME?
OH...
I'M KINDA HAPPY ABOUT THAT...

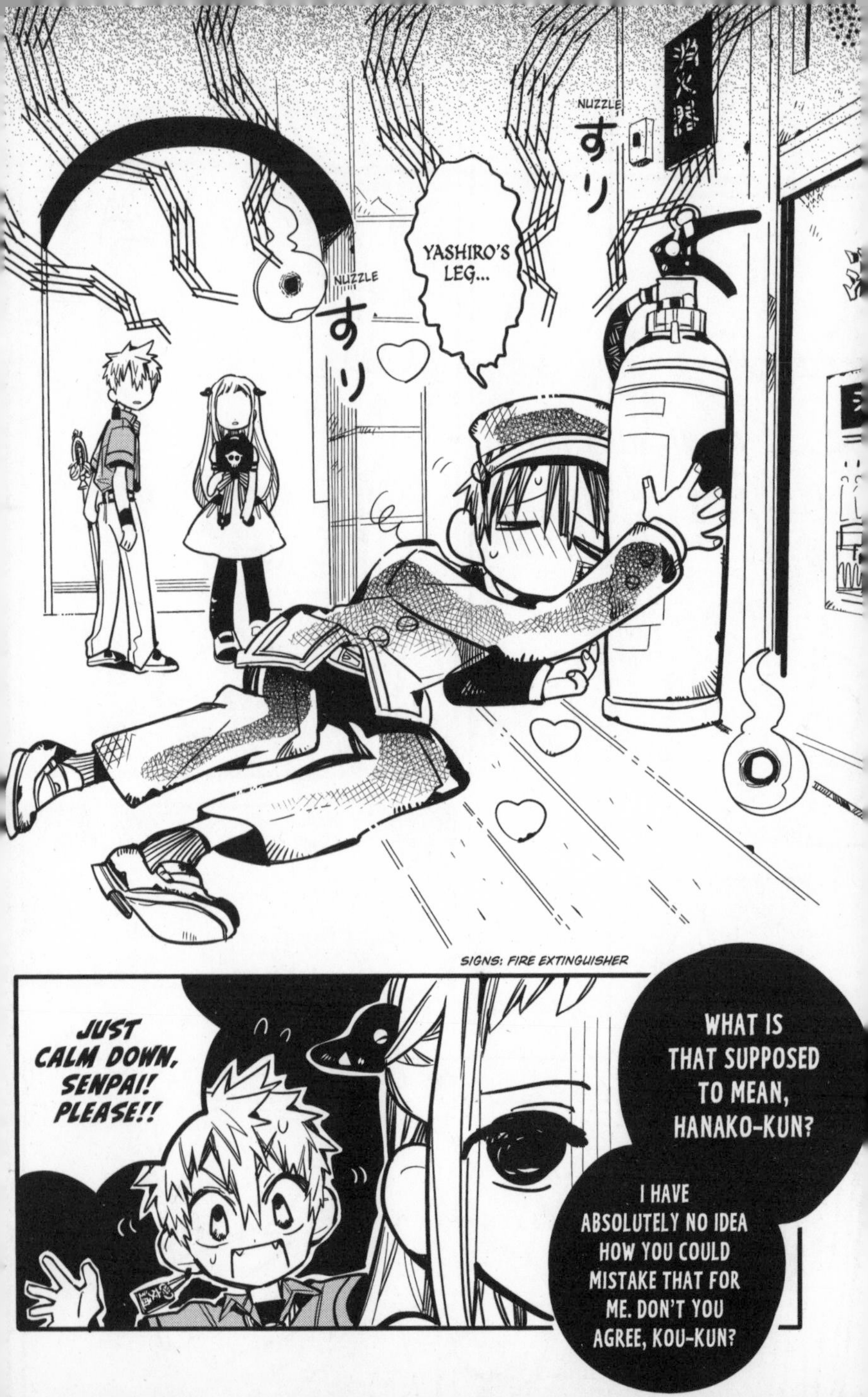
NUZZLE
すり
YASHIRO'S LEG...
NUZZLE
すり
SIGNS: FIRE EXTINGUISHER
WHAT IS THAT SUPPOSED TO MEAN, HANAKO-KUN?
I HAVE ABSOLUTELY NO IDEA HOW YOU COULD MISTAKE THAT FOR ME. DON'T YOU AGREE, KOU-KUN?
JUST CALM DOWN, SENPAI! PLEASE!!

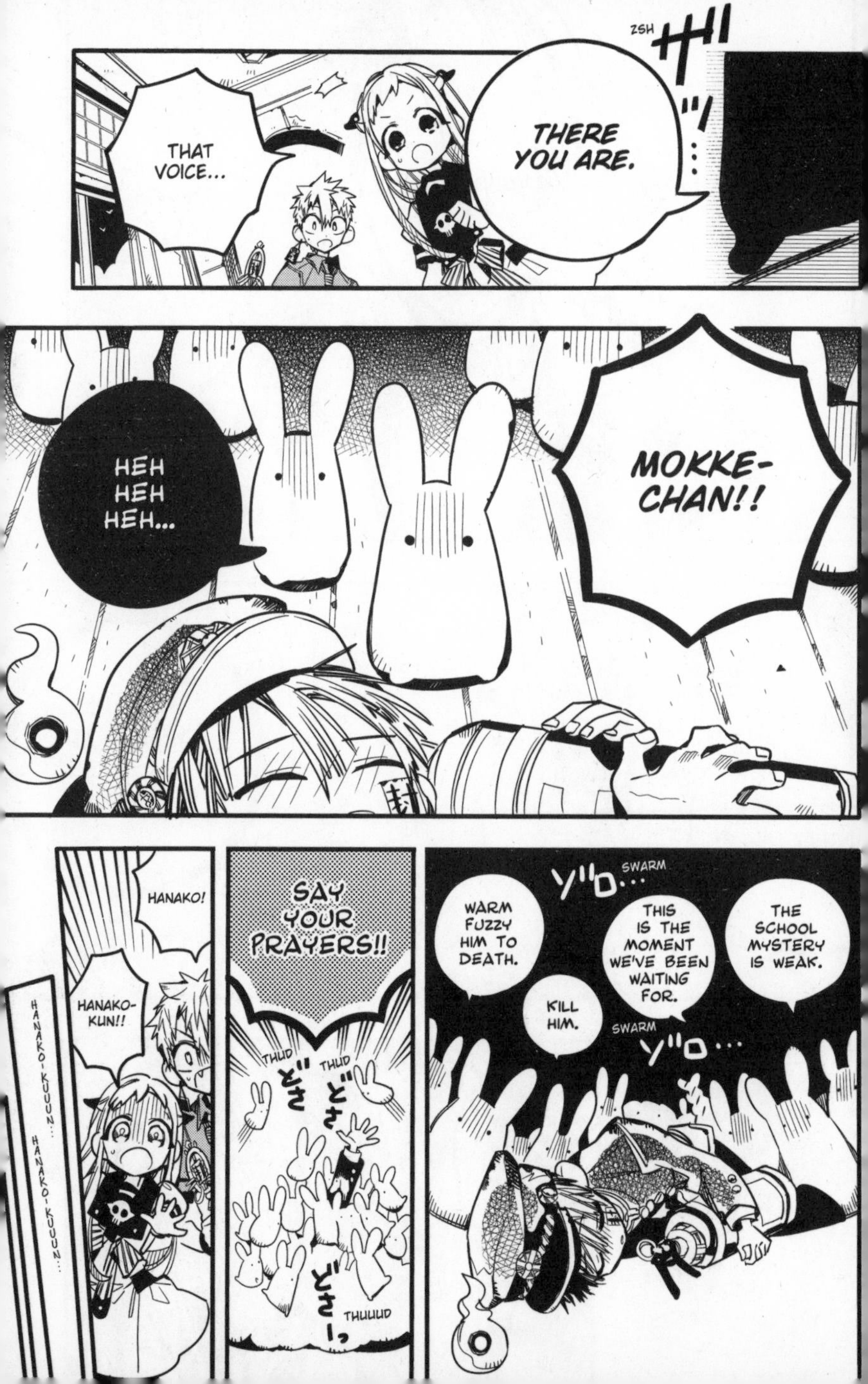

ZSH
THERE YOU ARE.
THAT VOICE...
MOKKE-CHAN!!
HEH HEH HEH...
SWARM
THE SCHOOL MYSTERY IS WEAK.
THIS IS THE MOMENT WE'VE BEEN WAITING FOR.
WARM FUZZY HIM TO DEATH.
KILL HIM.
SWARM
SAY YOUR PRAYERS!!
THUD
THUD
THUUUD
HANAKO!
HANAKO-KUN!!
HANAKO-KUUUN... HANAKO-KUUUN...

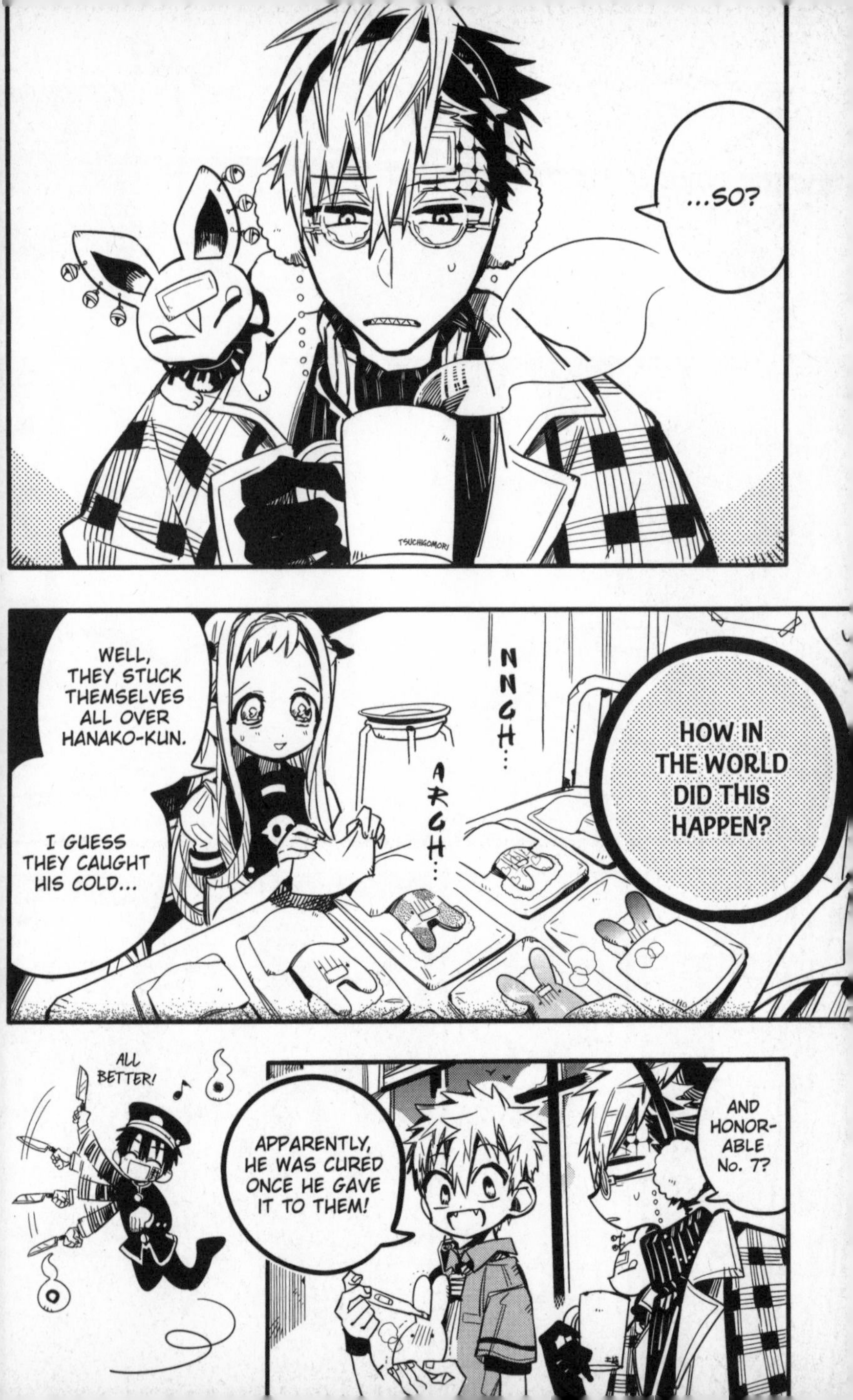
...SO?
TSUCHIGOMORI
HOW IN THE WORLD DID THIS HAPPEN?
NNGH...
ARGH...
WELL, THEY STUCK THEMSELVES ALL OVER HANAKO-KUN.
I GUESS THEY CAUGHT HIS COLD...
AND HONOR-ABLE No. 7?
APPARENTLY, HE WAS CURED ONCE HE GAVE IT TO THEM!
ALL BETTER!

After-School Hanako-Kun

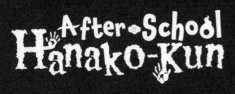

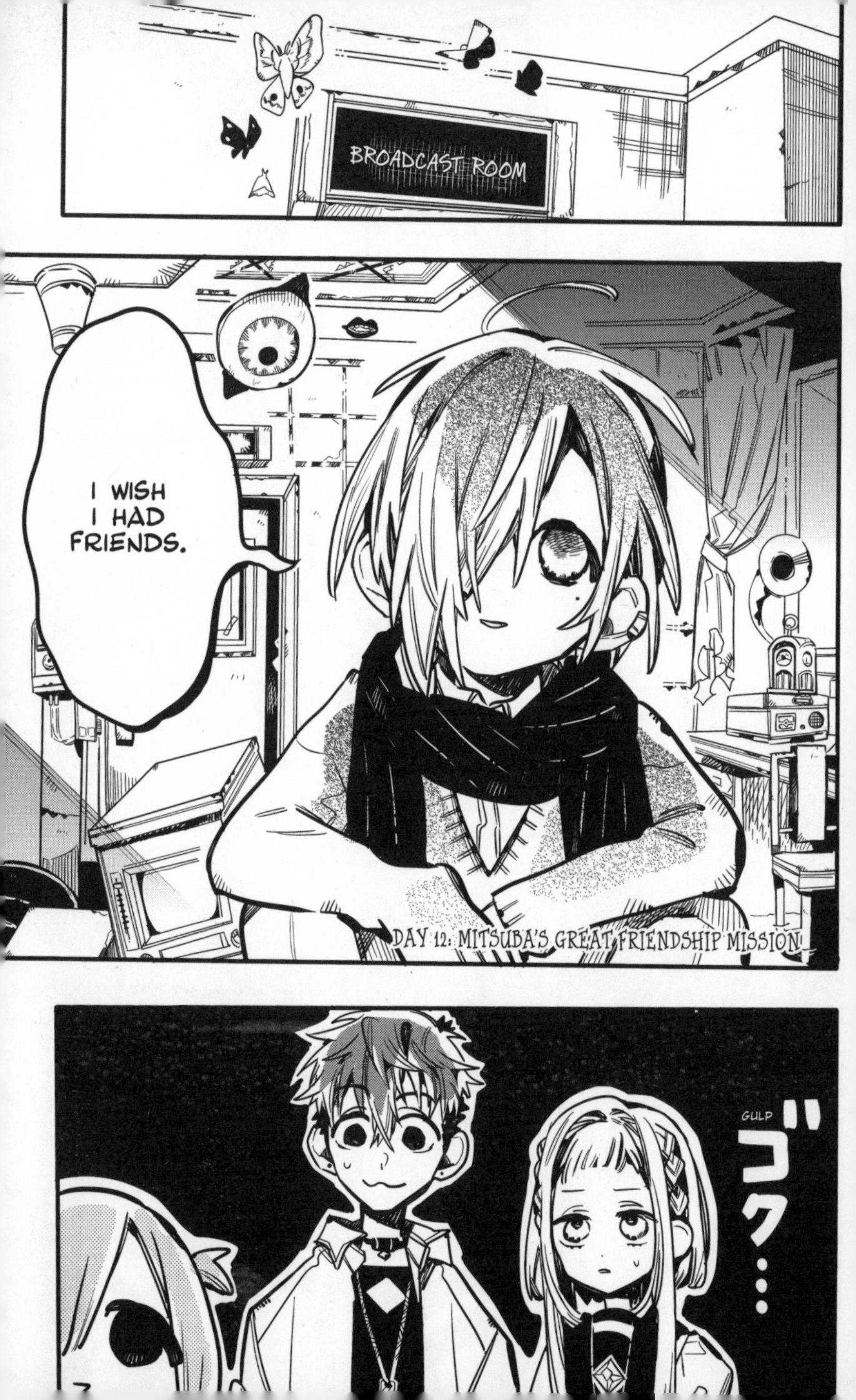
BROADCAST ROOM
I WISH I HAD FRIENDS.
DAY 12: MITSUBA'S GREAT FRIENDSHIP MISSION
GULP
ゴク…

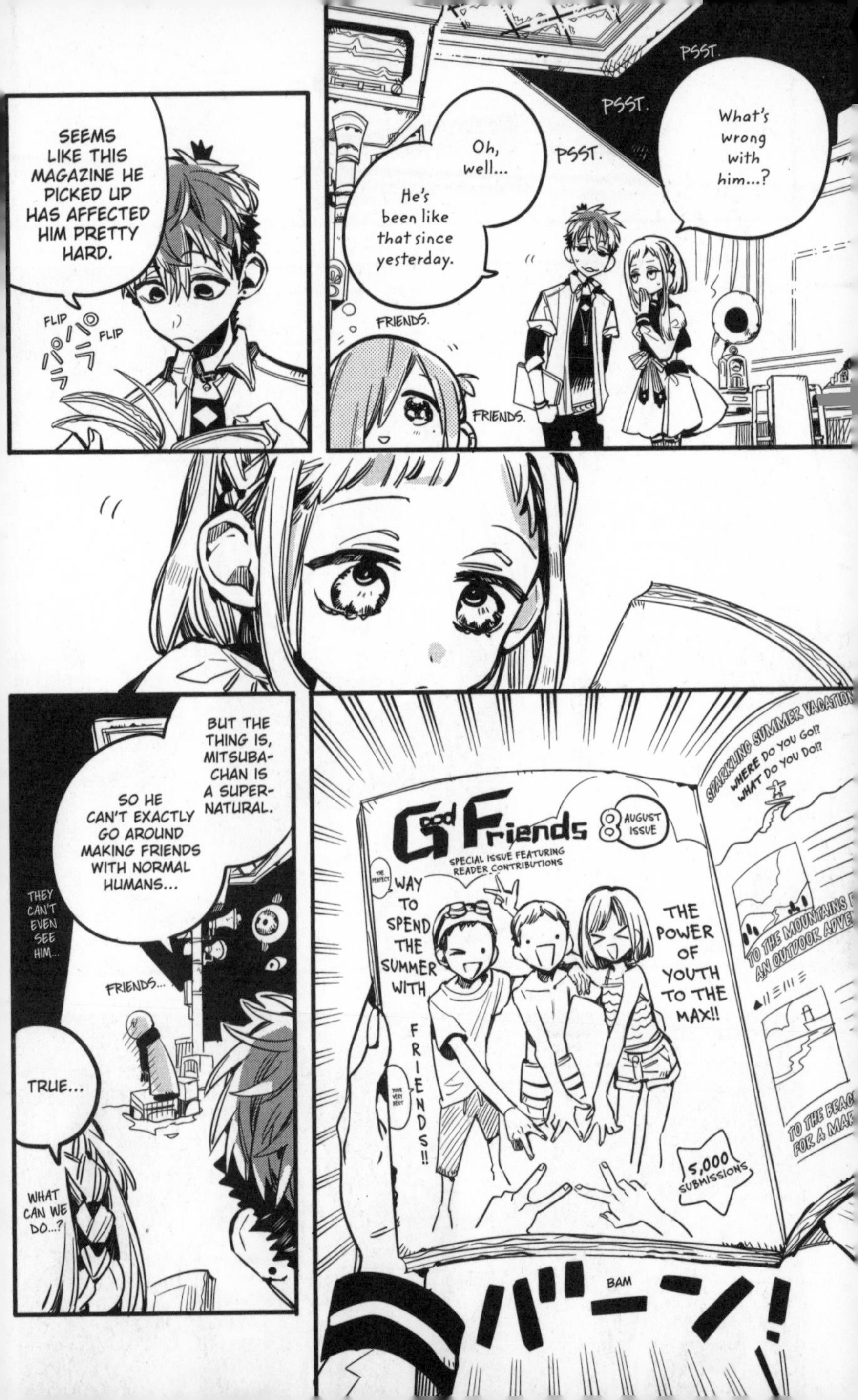
PSST.
PSST.
PSST.
What's wrong with him...?
Oh, well...
He's been like that since yesterday.
FRIENDS.
FRIENDS.
SEEMS LIKE THIS MAGAZINE HE PICKED UP HAS AFFECTED HIM PRETTY HARD.
パラ
FLIP
パラ
FLIP
WHERE DO YOU GO!? WHAT DO YOU DO!?
Good Friends 8
AUGUST ISSUE
SPECIAL ISSUE FEATURING READER CONTRIBUTIONS
THE PERFECT WAY TO SPEND THE SUMMER WITH FRIENDS!!
YOUR VERY BEST
THE POWER OF YOUTH TO THE MAX!!
5,000 SUBMISSIONS
BAM
バーン!
BUT THE THING IS, MITSUBA-CHAN IS A SUPERNATURAL.
SO HE CAN'T EXACTLY GO AROUND MAKING FRIENDS WITH NORMAL HUMANS...
THEY CAN'T EVEN SEE HIM...
FRIENDS...
TRUE...
WHAT CAN WE DO...?

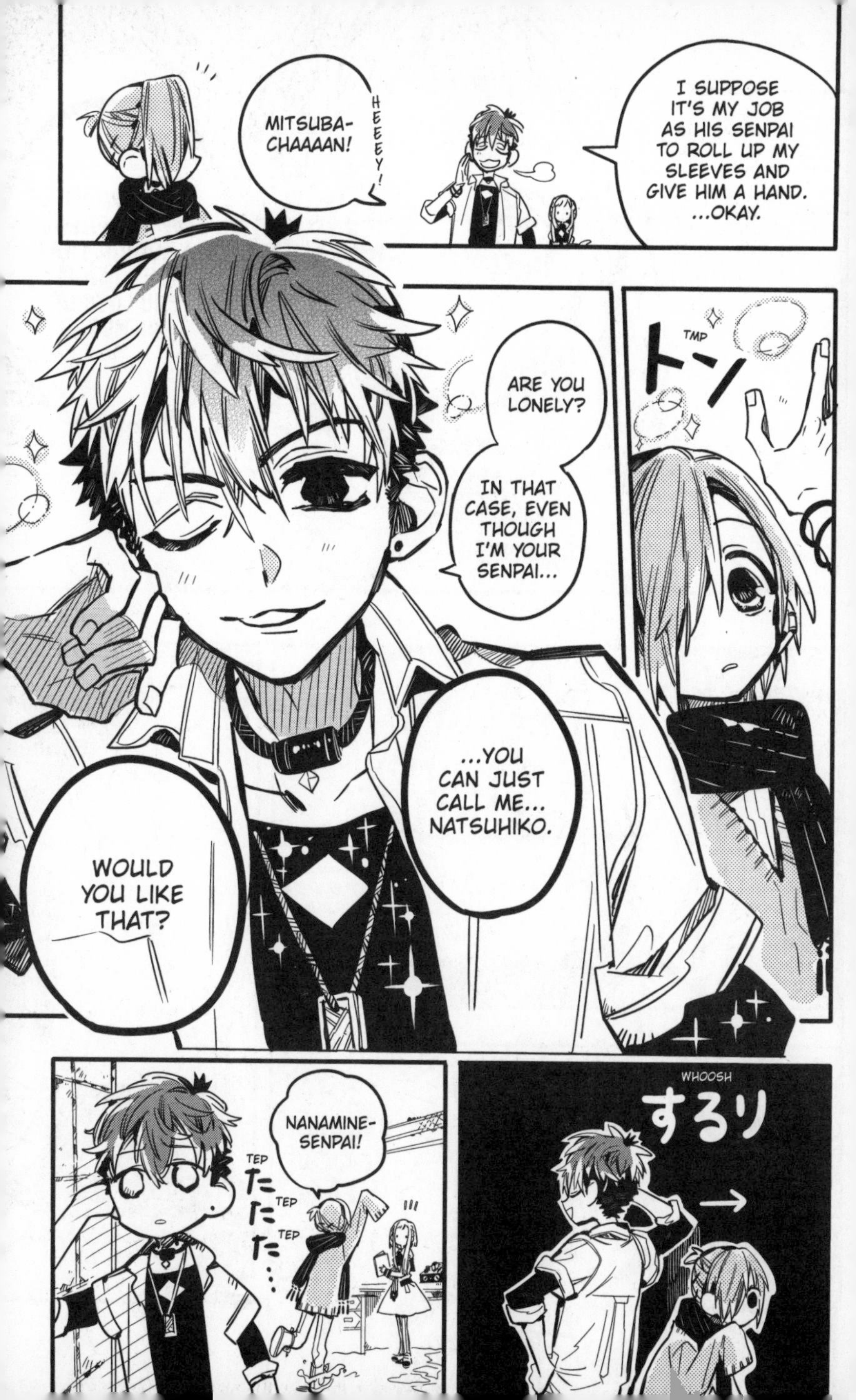
I SUPPOSE IT'S MY JOB AS HIS SENPAI TO ROLL UP MY SLEEVES AND GIVE HIM A HAND. ...OKAY.
HEEEY!
MITSUBA-CHAAAAN!
TMP
トン
ARE YOU LONELY?
IN THAT CASE, EVEN THOUGH I'M YOUR SENPAI...
...YOU CAN JUST CALL ME... NATSUHIKO.
WOULD YOU LIKE THAT?
WHOOSH
するり
NANAMINE-SENPAI!
TEP TEP TEP
たたた…

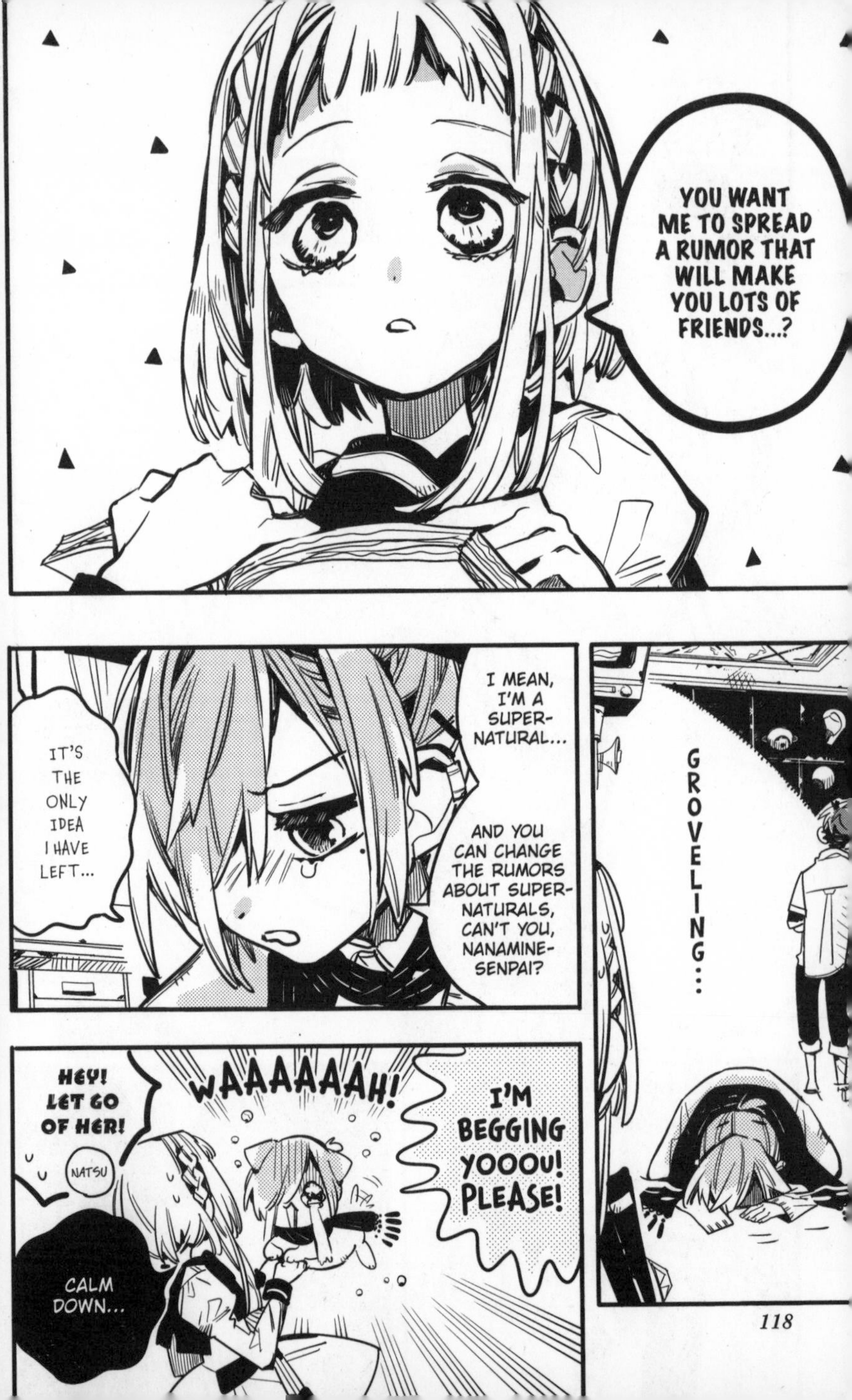
YOU WANT ME TO SPREAD A RUMOR THAT WILL MAKE YOU LOTS OF FRIENDS...?
GROVELING...
I MEAN, I'M A SUPER-NATURAL...
AND YOU CAN CHANGE THE RUMORS ABOUT SUPER-NATURALS, CAN'T YOU, NANAMINE-SENPAI?
IT'S THE ONLY IDEA I HAVE LEFT...
I'M BEGGING YOOOU! PLEASE!
WAAAAAAAH!
HEY! LET GO OF HER!
NATSU
CALM DOWN...

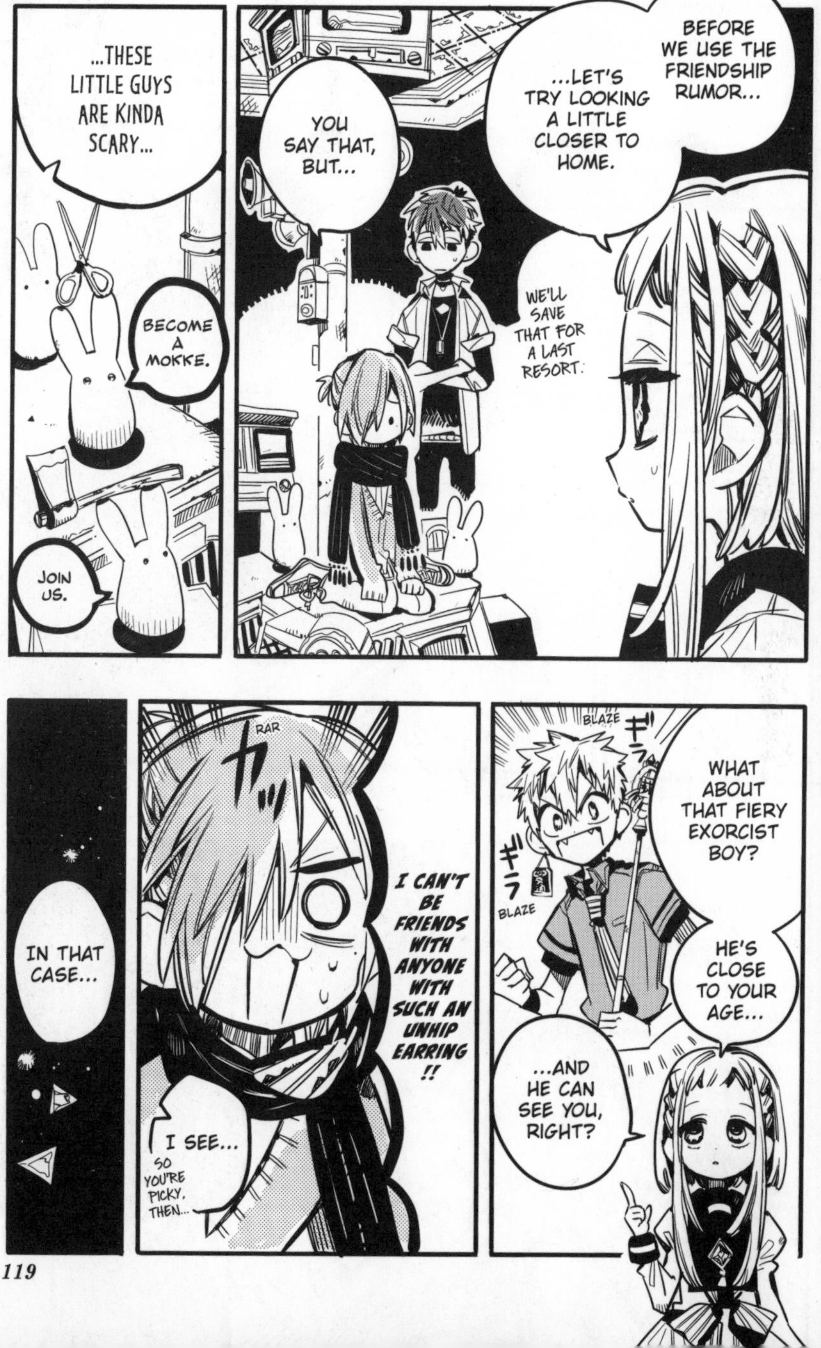
BEFORE WE USE THE FRIENDSHIP RUMOR...
...LET'S TRY LOOKING A LITTLE CLOSER TO HOME.
WE'LL SAVE THAT FOR A LAST RESORT.
YOU SAY THAT, BUT...
...THESE LITTLE GUYS ARE KINDA SCARY...
BECOME A MOKKE.
JOIN US.
BLAZE
BLAZE
WHAT ABOUT THAT FIERY EXORCIST BOY?
HE'S CLOSE TO YOUR AGE...
...AND HE CAN SEE YOU, RIGHT?
RAR
I CAN'T BE FRIENDS WITH ANYONE WITH SUCH AN UNHIP EARRING!!
I SEE...
SO YOU'RE PICKY, THEN...
IN THAT CASE...

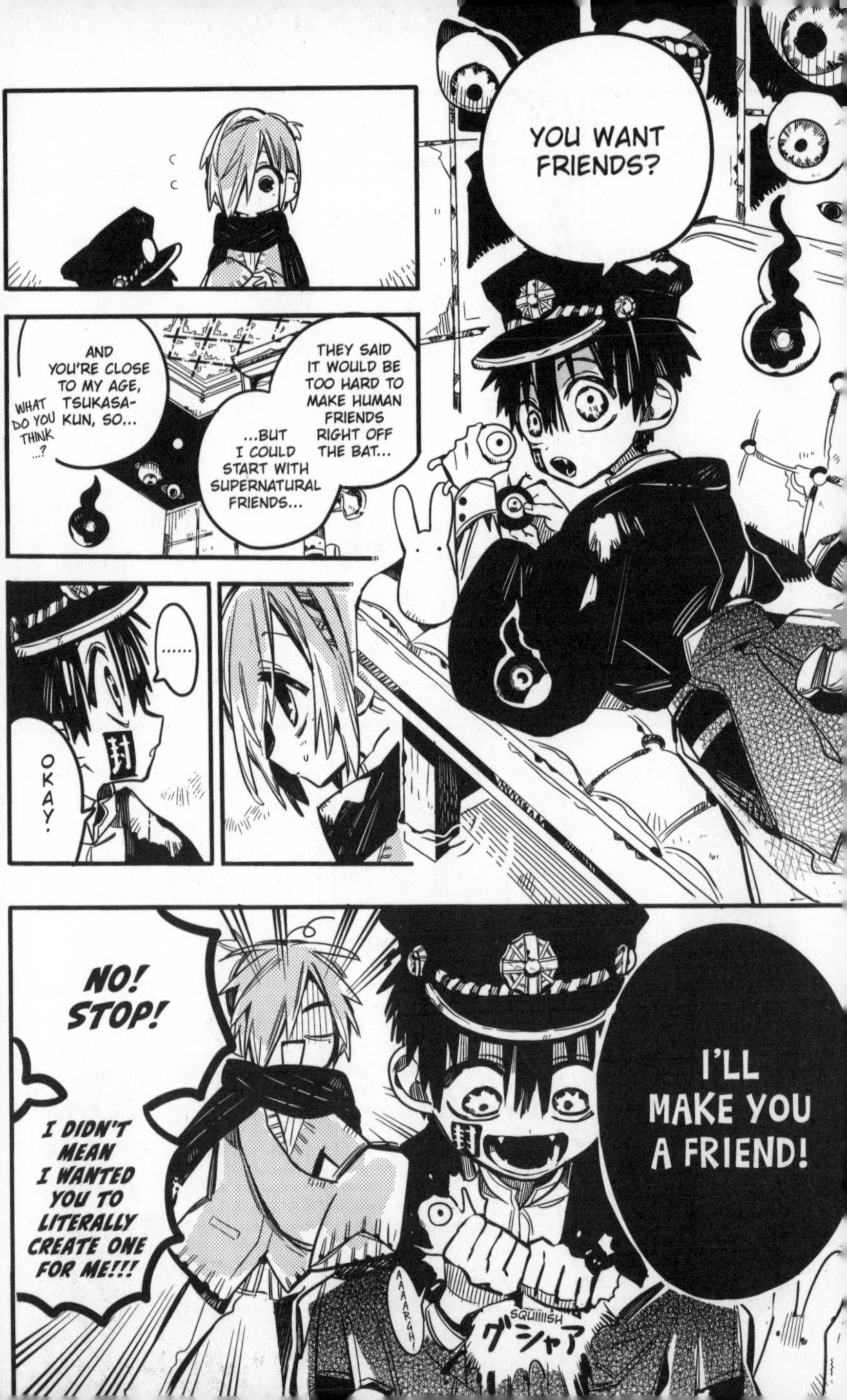
YOU WANT FRIENDS?
THEY SAID IT WOULD BE TOO HARD TO MAKE HUMAN FRIENDS RIGHT OFF THE BAT...
...BUT I COULD START WITH SUPERNATURAL FRIENDS...
AND YOU'RE CLOSE TO MY AGE, TSUKASA-KUN, SO...
WHAT DO YOU THINK ...?
......
OKAY.
I'LL MAKE YOU A FRIEND!
SQUIIISH
グシャア
AAAARGH!
NO! STOP!
I DIDN'T MEAN I WANTED YOU TO LITERALLY CREATE ONE FOR ME!!!

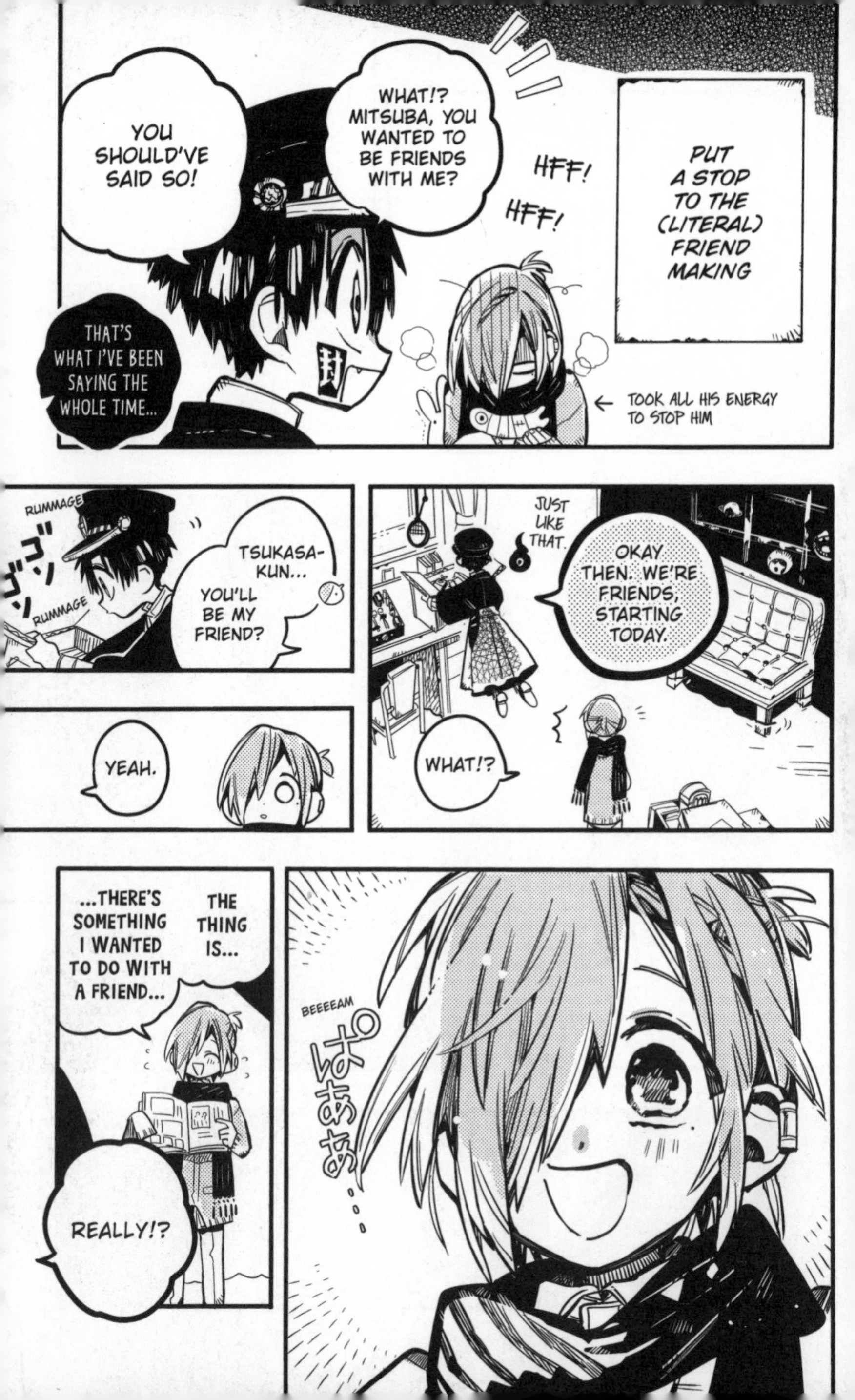
PUT A STOP TO THE (LITERAL) FRIEND MAKING
HFF!
HFF!
WHAT!? MITSUBA, YOU WANTED TO BE FRIENDS WITH ME?
YOU SHOULD'VE SAID SO!
← TOOK ALL HIS ENERGY TO STOP HIM
THAT'S WHAT I'VE BEEN SAYING THE WHOLE TIME...
JUST LIKE THAT.
OKAY THEN. WE'RE FRIENDS, STARTING TODAY.
WHAT!?
RUMMAGE
ゴソゴソ
RUMMAGE
TSUKASA-KUN... YOU'LL BE MY FRIEND?
YEAH.
BEEEEAM
ぱあああ
THE THING IS...
...THERE'S SOMETHING I WANTED TO DO WITH A FRIEND...
REALLY!?

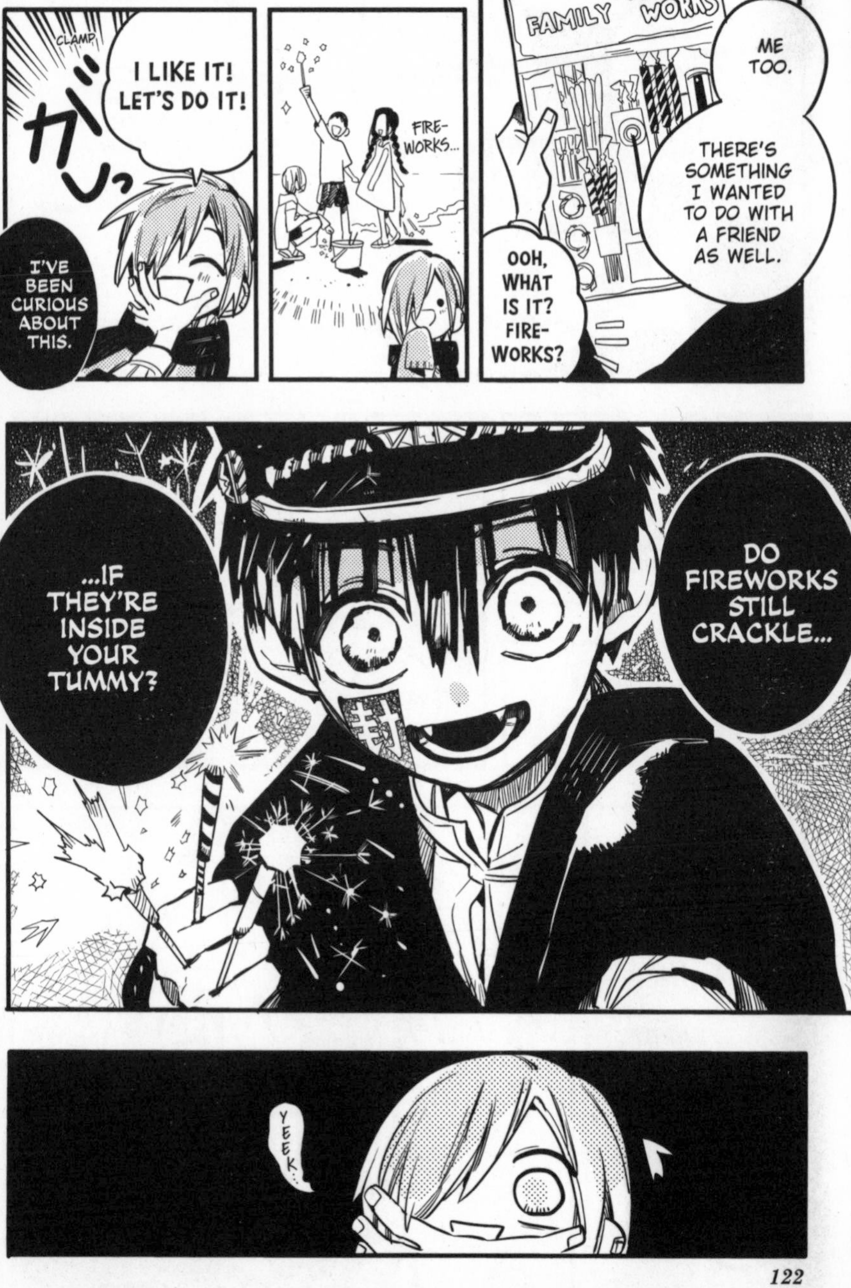
FAMILY FIRE-WORKS
ME TOO.
THERE'S SOMETHING I WANTED TO DO WITH A FRIEND AS WELL.
OOH, WHAT IS IT? FIRE-WORKS?
FIRE-WORKS...
I LIKE IT! LET'S DO IT!
CLAMP
I'VE BEEN CURIOUS ABOUT THIS.
DO FIREWORKS STILL CRACKLE...
...IF THEY'RE INSIDE YOUR TUMMY?
YEEK...

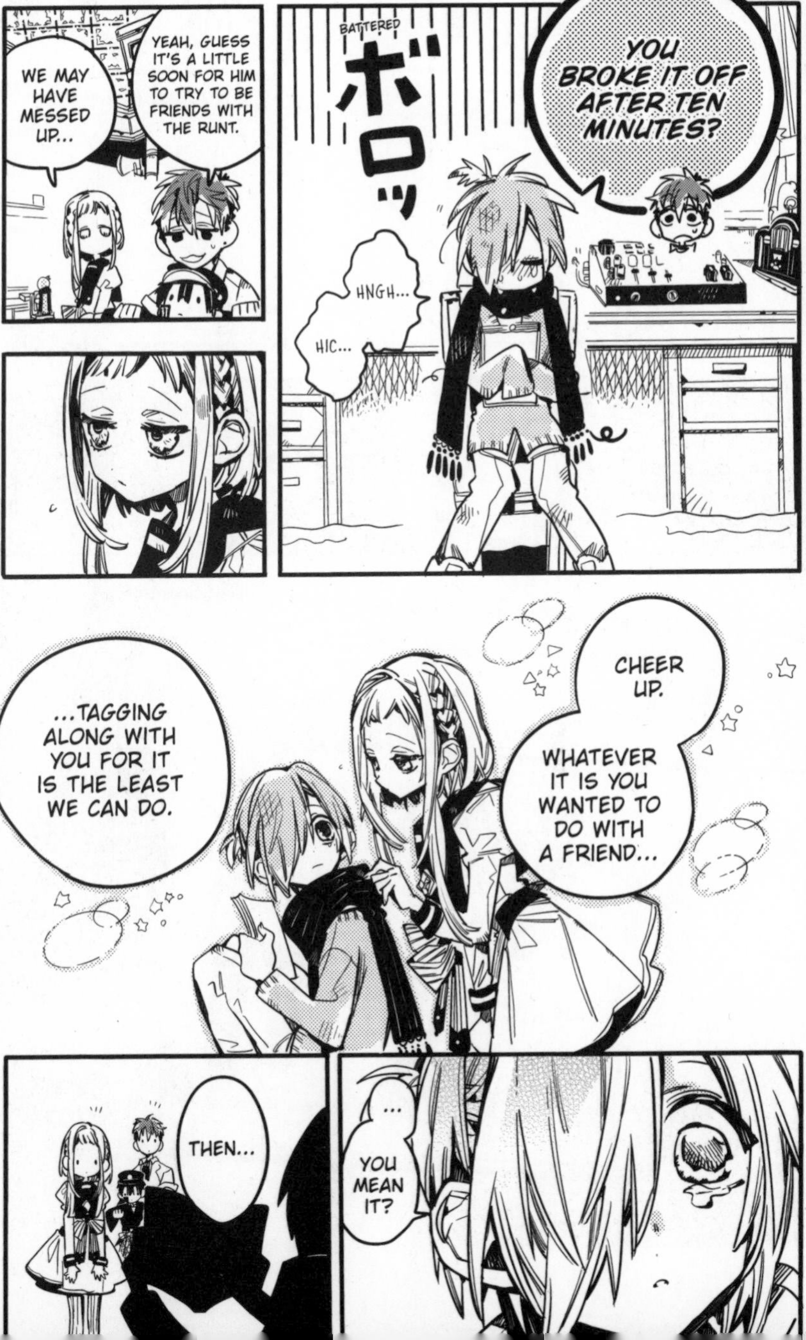
YOU BROKE IT OFF AFTER TEN MINUTES?
BATTERED
ボロッ
HNGH...
HIC...
YEAH, GUESS IT'S A LITTLE SOON FOR HIM TO TRY TO BE FRIENDS WITH THE RUNT.
WE MAY HAVE MESSED UP...
CHEER UP.
WHATEVER IT IS YOU WANTED TO DO WITH A FRIEND...
...TAGGING ALONG WITH YOU FOR IT IS THE LEAST WE CAN DO.
...
YOU MEAN IT?
THEN...

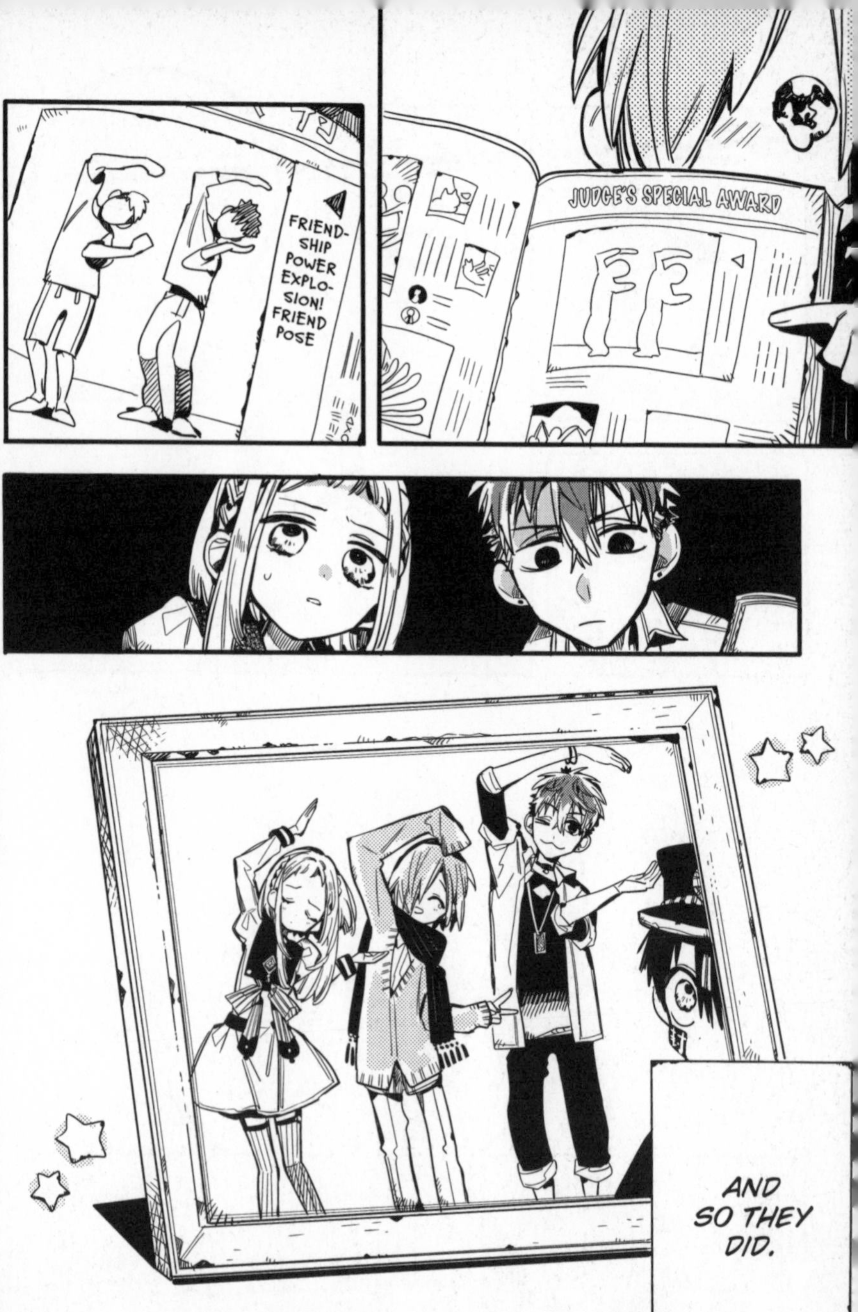
JUDGE'S SPECIAL AWARD
FRIEND-SHIP POWER EXPLO-SION! FRIEND POSE
AND SO THEY DID.

After-School
Hanako-Kun

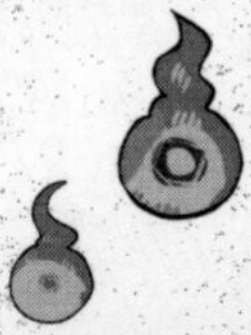

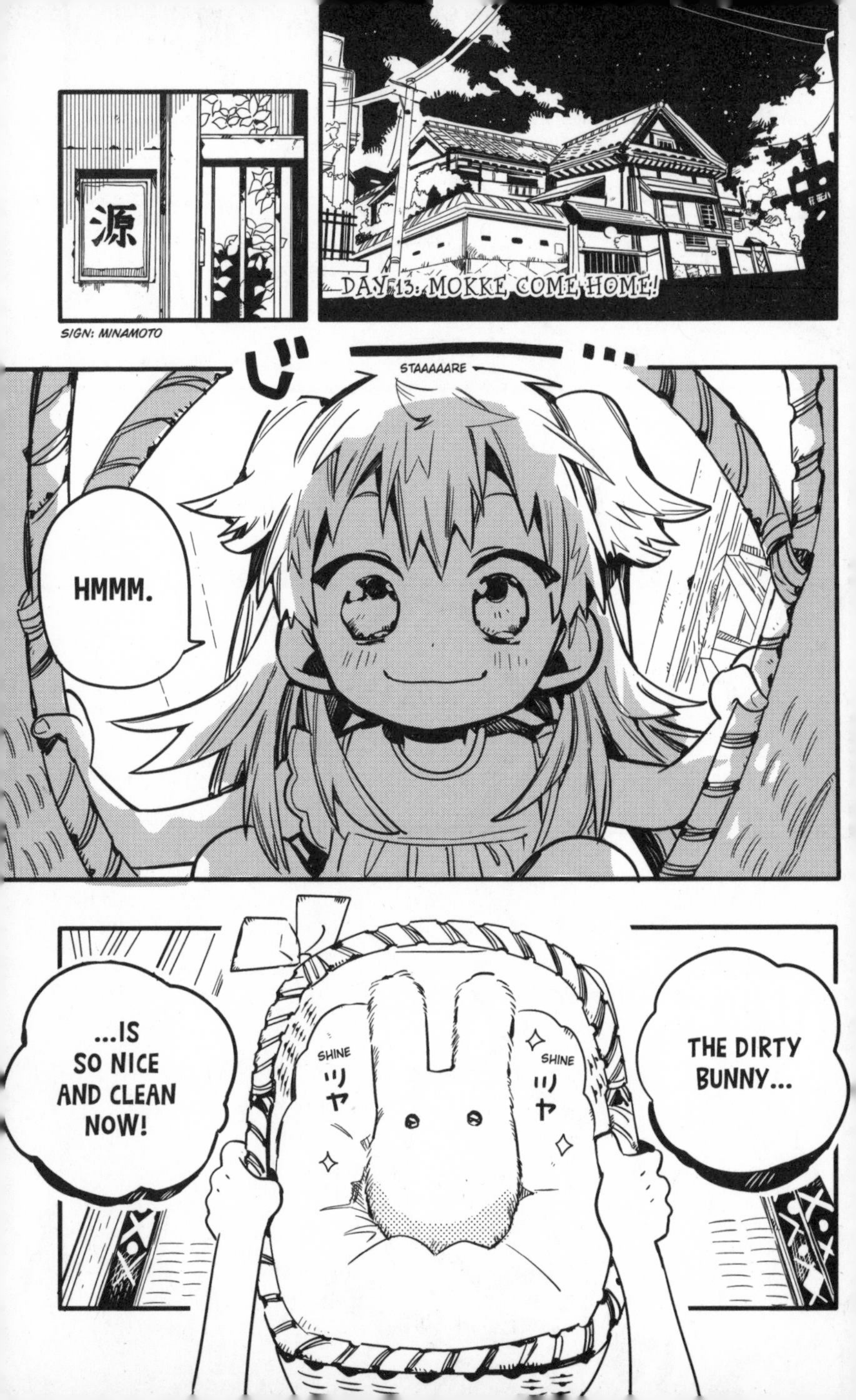
DAY 13: MOKKE, COME HOME!
源
SIGN: MINAMOTO
じー…
STAAAAARE
HMMM.
THE DIRTY BUNNY...
...IS SO NICE AND CLEAN NOW!
SHINE
ツヤ
SHINE
ツヤ

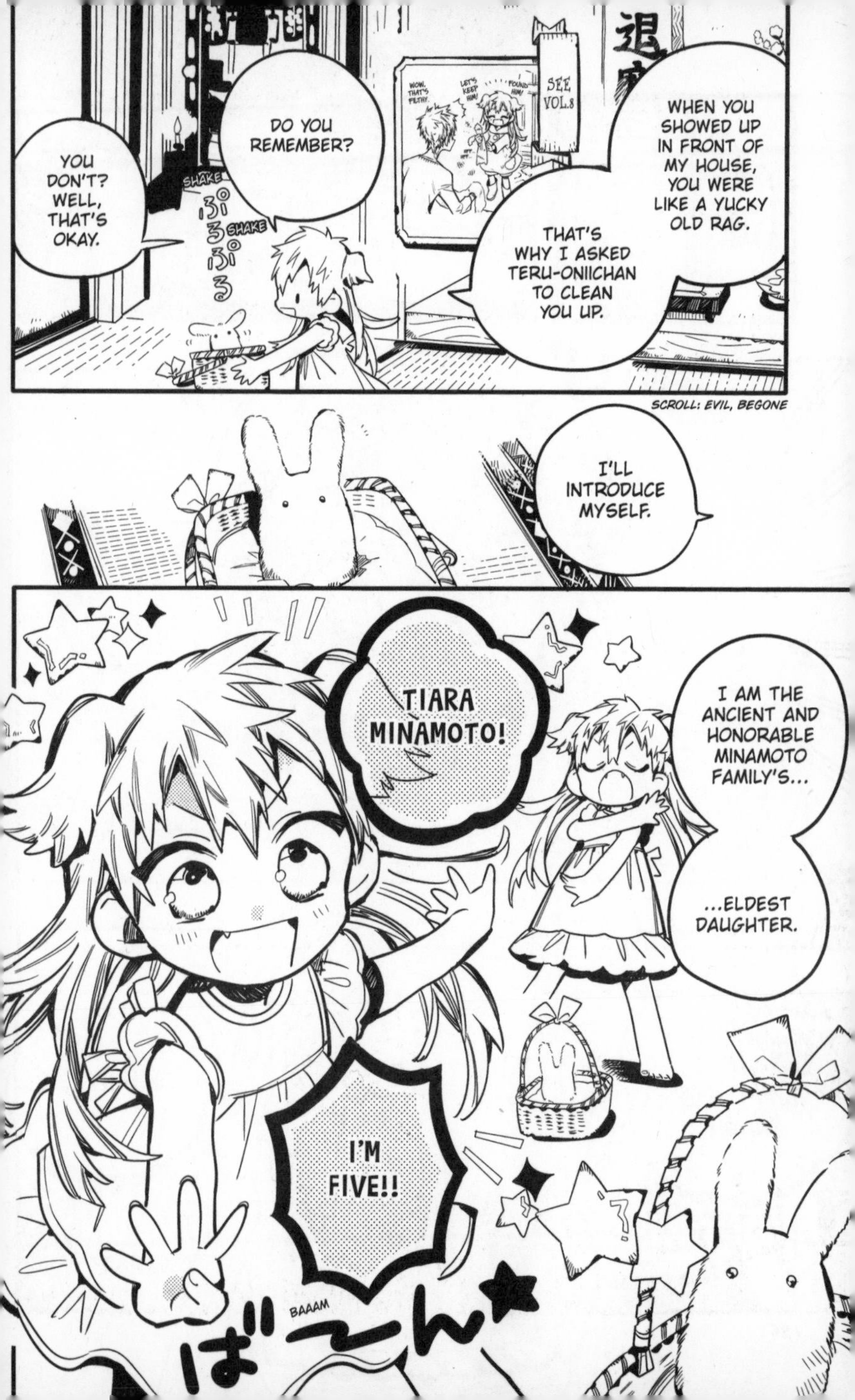
SEE VOL.8
I FOUND HIM!
LET'S KEEP HIM!
WOW, THAT'S FILTHY.
WHEN YOU SHOWED UP IN FRONT OF MY HOUSE, YOU WERE LIKE A YUCKY OLD RAG.
THAT'S WHY I ASKED TERU-ONIICHAN TO CLEAN YOU UP.
DO YOU REMEMBER?
SHAKE
SHAKE
YOU DON'T? WELL, THAT'S OKAY.
SCROLL: EVIL, BEGONE
I'LL INTRODUCE MYSELF.
I AM THE ANCIENT AND HONORABLE MINAMOTO FAMILY'S...
...ELDEST DAUGHTER.
TIARA MINAMOTO!
I'M FIVE!!
BAAAM

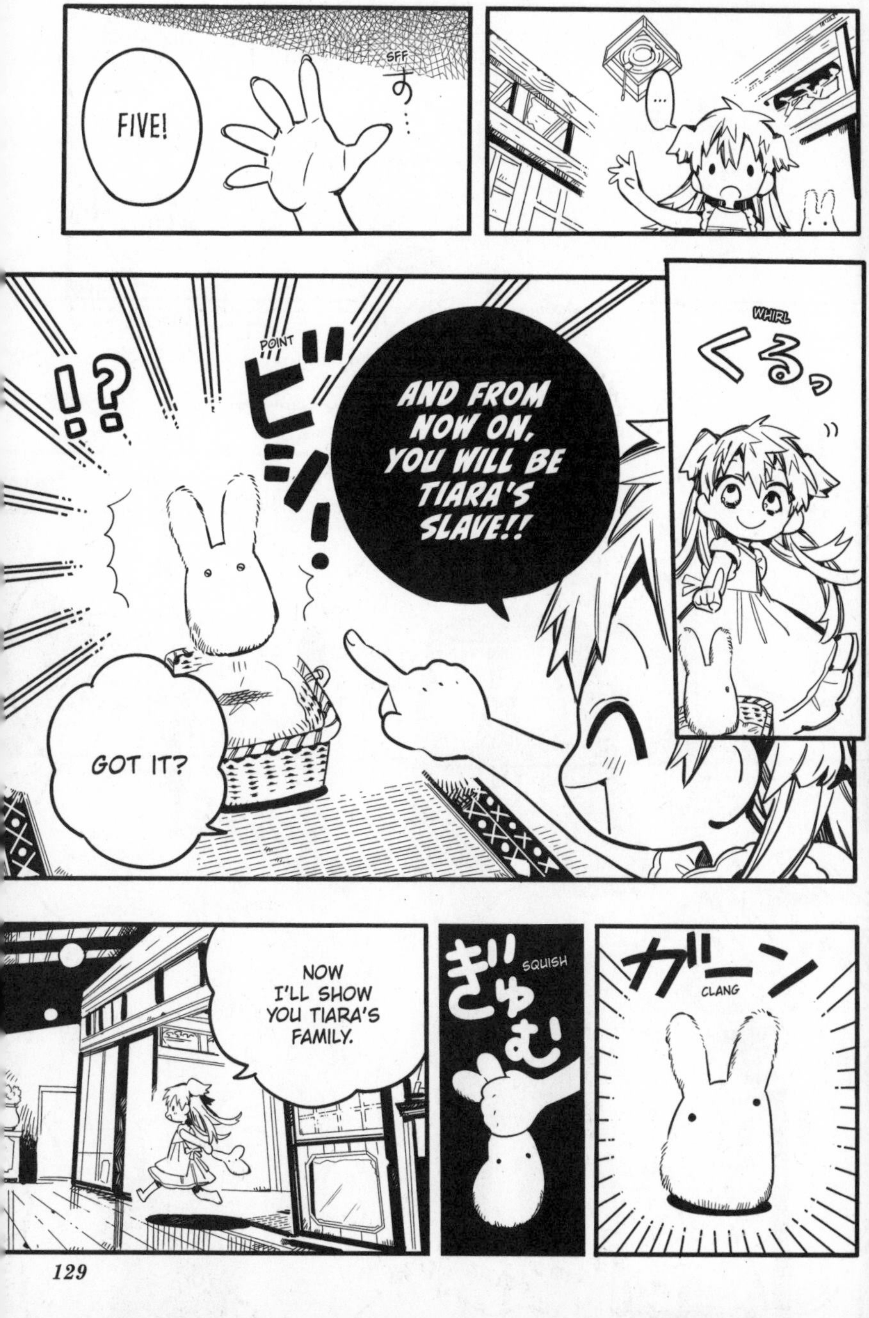
…
す…
SFF
FIVE!
くるっ
WHIRL
AND FROM NOW ON, YOU WILL BE TIARA'S SLAVE!!
ビシッ!
POINT
!?
GOT IT?
ガーン
CLANG
ぎゅむ
SQUISH
NOW I'LL SHOW YOU TIARA'S FAMILY.

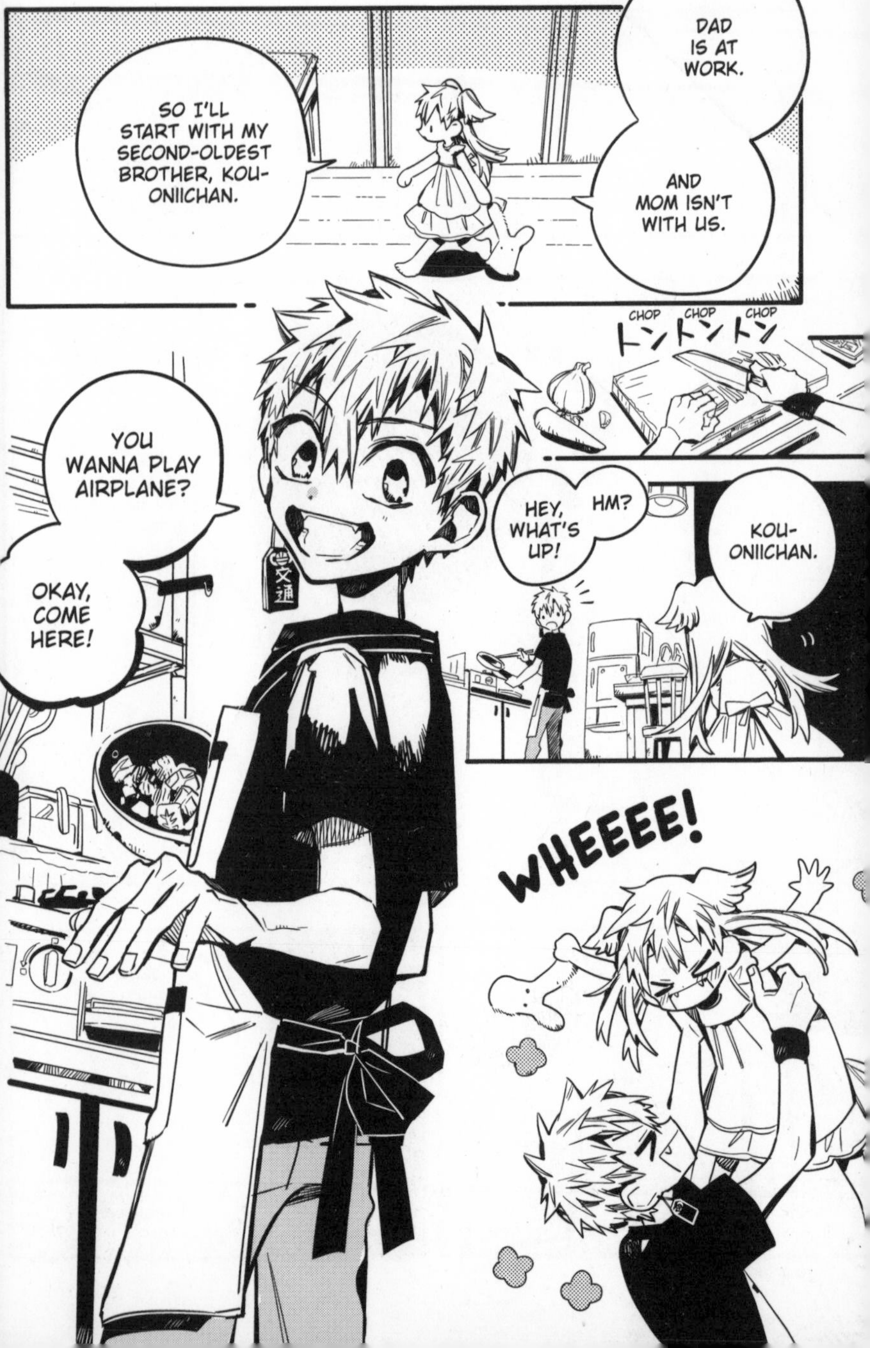
DAD IS AT WORK.
AND MOM ISN'T WITH US.
SO I'LL START WITH MY SECOND-OLDEST BROTHER, KOU-ONIICHAN.
CHOP CHOP CHOP
トントントン
KOU-ONIICHAN.
HM?
HEY, WHAT'S UP!
WHEEEEE!
YOU WANNA PLAY AIRPLANE?
OKAY, COME HERE!

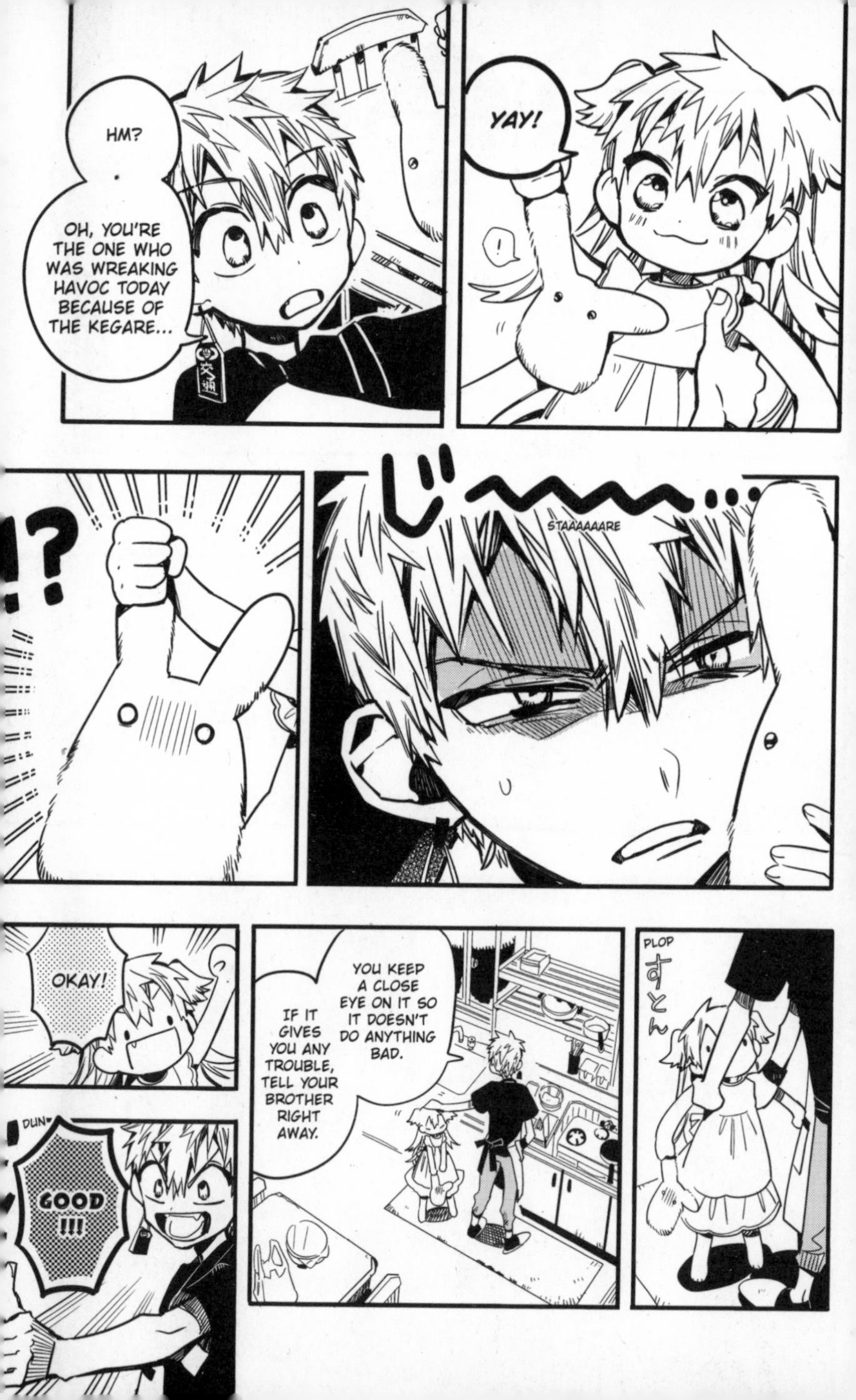
YAY!
!
HM?
OH, YOU'RE THE ONE WHO WAS WREAKING HAVOC TODAY BECAUSE OF THE KEGARE...
じ〜〜〜...
STAAAAAARE
!?
PLOP
すとん
YOU KEEP A CLOSE EYE ON IT SO IT DOESN'T DO ANYTHING BAD.
IF IT GIVES YOU ANY TROUBLE, TELL YOUR BROTHER RIGHT AWAY.
OKAY!
DUN
GOOD!!!

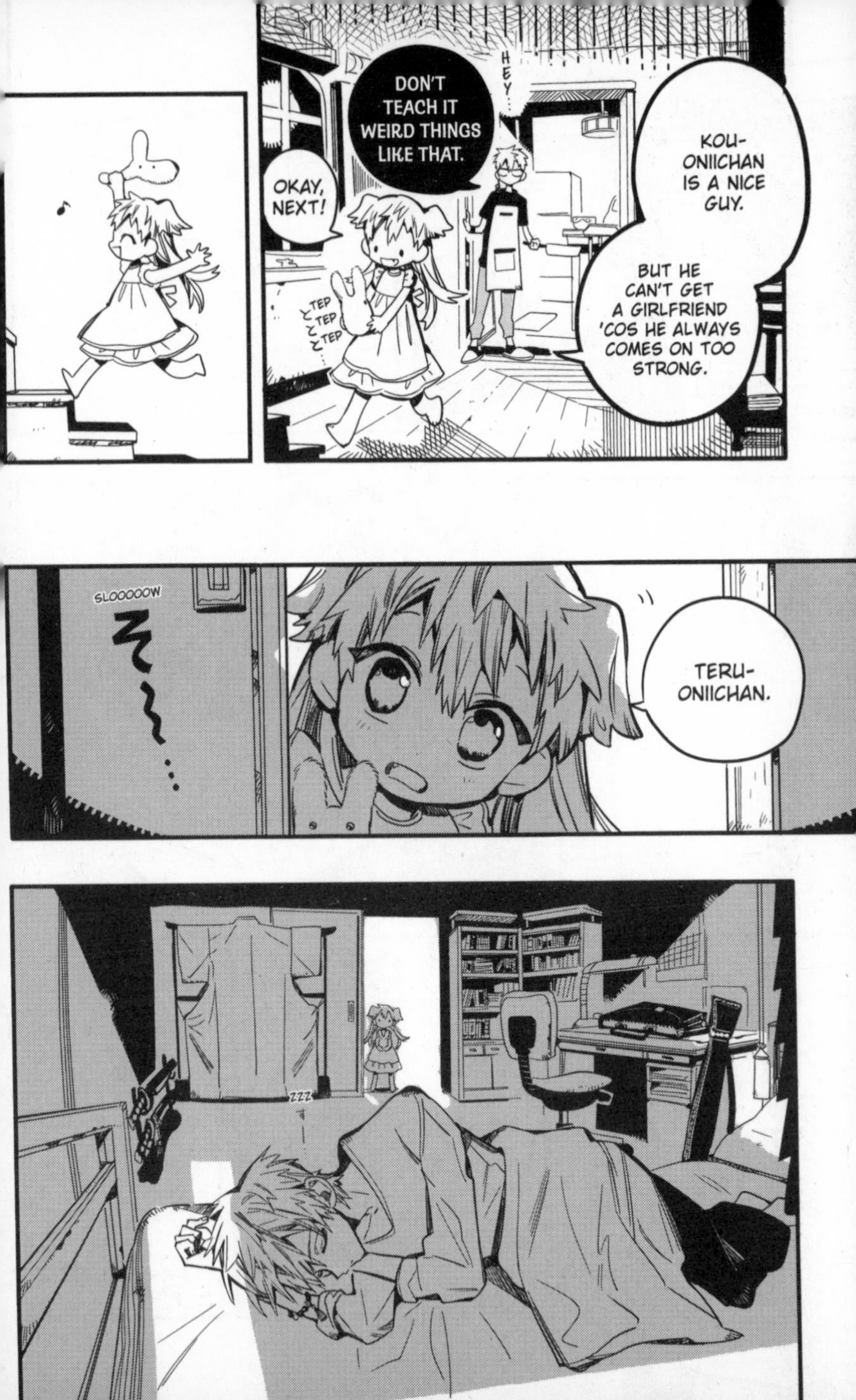
KOU-ONIICHAN IS A NICE GUY.
BUT HE CAN'T GET A GIRLFRIEND 'COS HE ALWAYS COMES ON TOO STRONG.
HEY...
DON'T TEACH IT WEIRD THINGS LIKE THAT.
OKAY, NEXT!
TEP TEP TEP
TERU-ONIICHAN.
SLOOOOOW
ZZZ

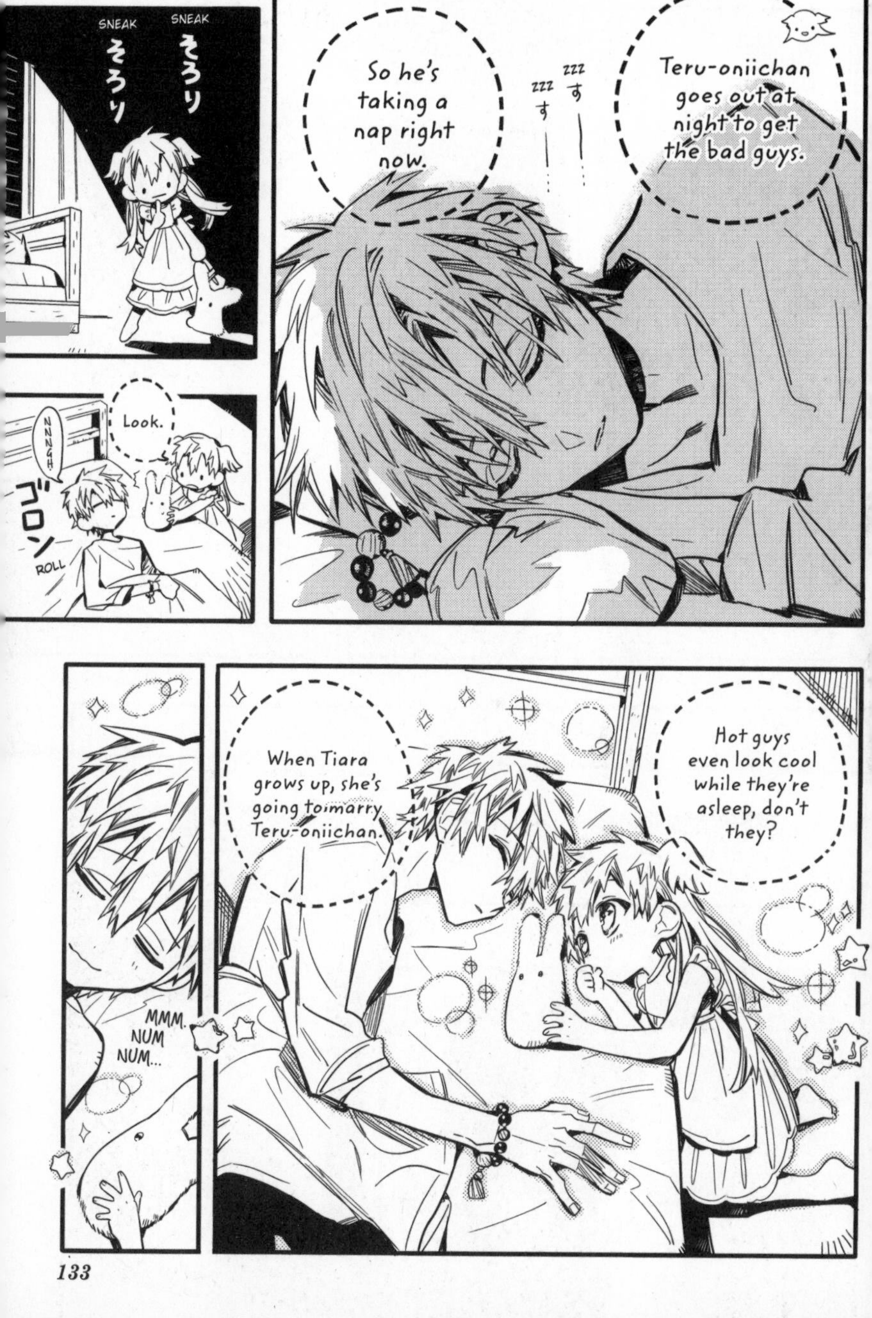
Teru-oniichan goes out at night to get the bad guys.
ZZZ
すー
ZZZ
すー
So he's taking a nap right now.
SNEAK
そろり
SNEAK
そろり
Look.
NNNGH
ゴロン
ROLL
Hot guys even look cool while they're asleep, don't they?
When Tiara grows up, she's going to marry Teru-oniichan.
MMM. NUM NUM...

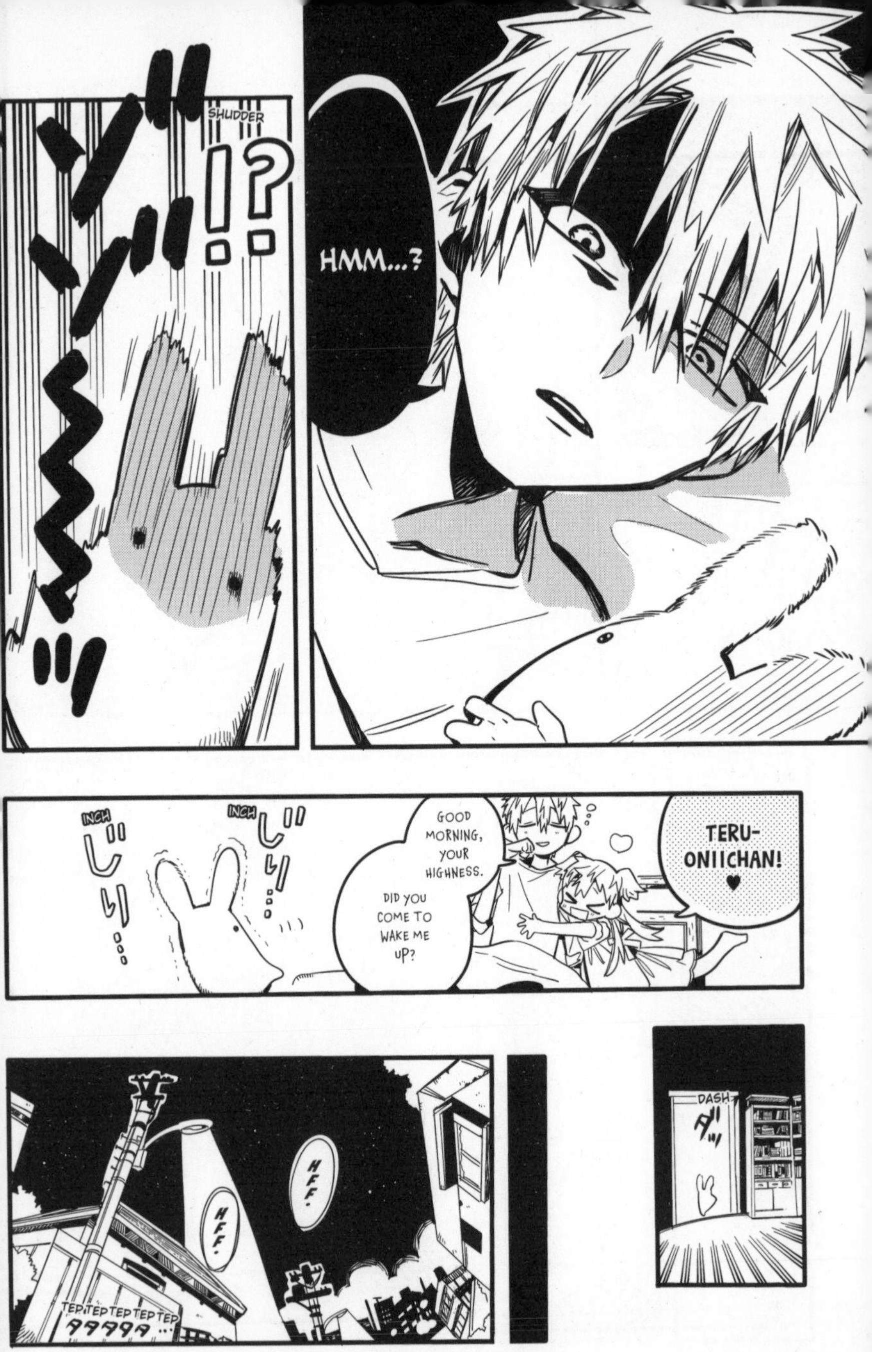
HMM...?
SHUDDER
!?
TERU-ONIICHAN! ♥
GOOD MORNING, YOUR HIGHNESS.
DID YOU COME TO WAKE ME UP?
INCH
INCH
DASH
HFF.
HFF.
TEPTEPTEPTEPTEP

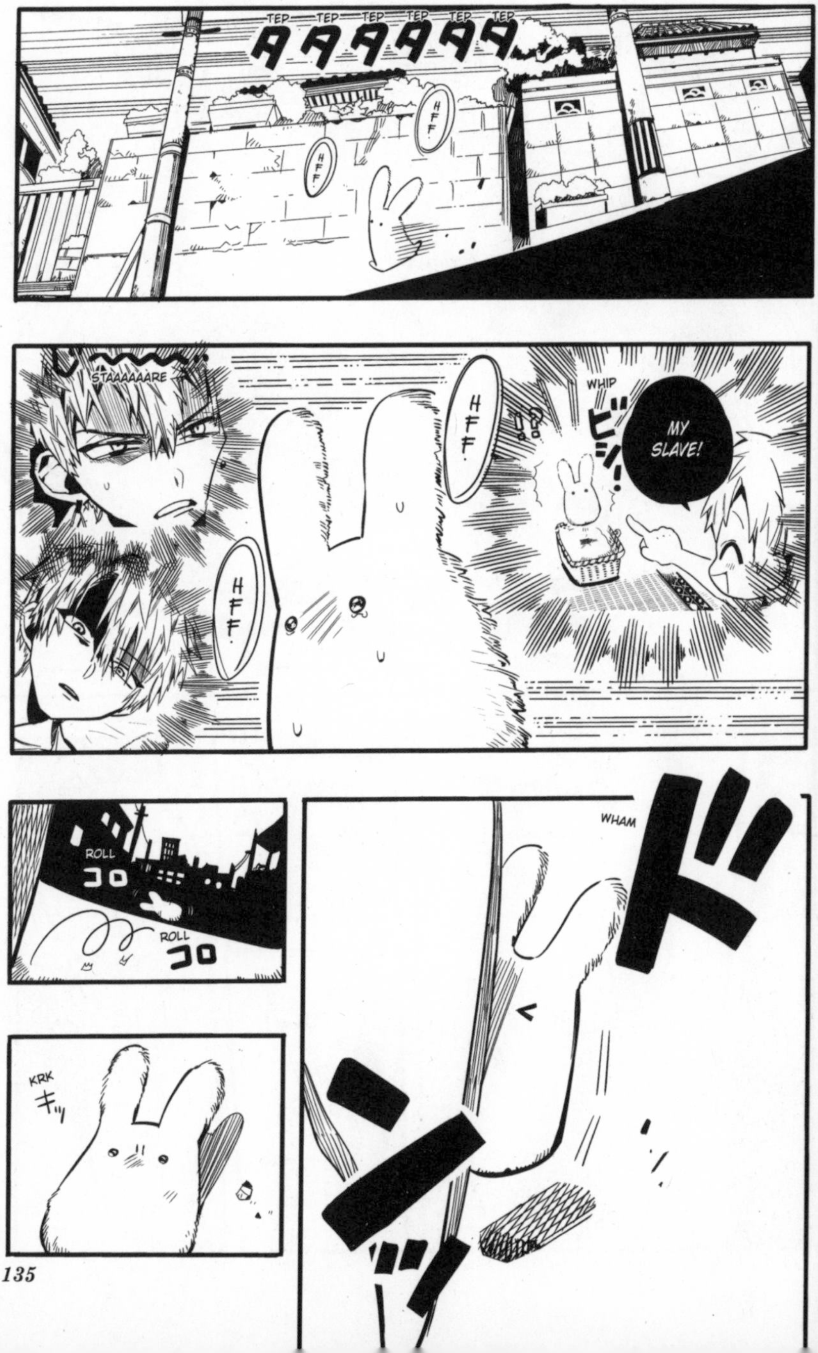
TEP TEP TEP TEP TEP TEP
HFF
HFF
WHIP
MY SLAVE!
HFF
HFF
STAAAAAARE
WHAM
ROLL
ROLL
KRK

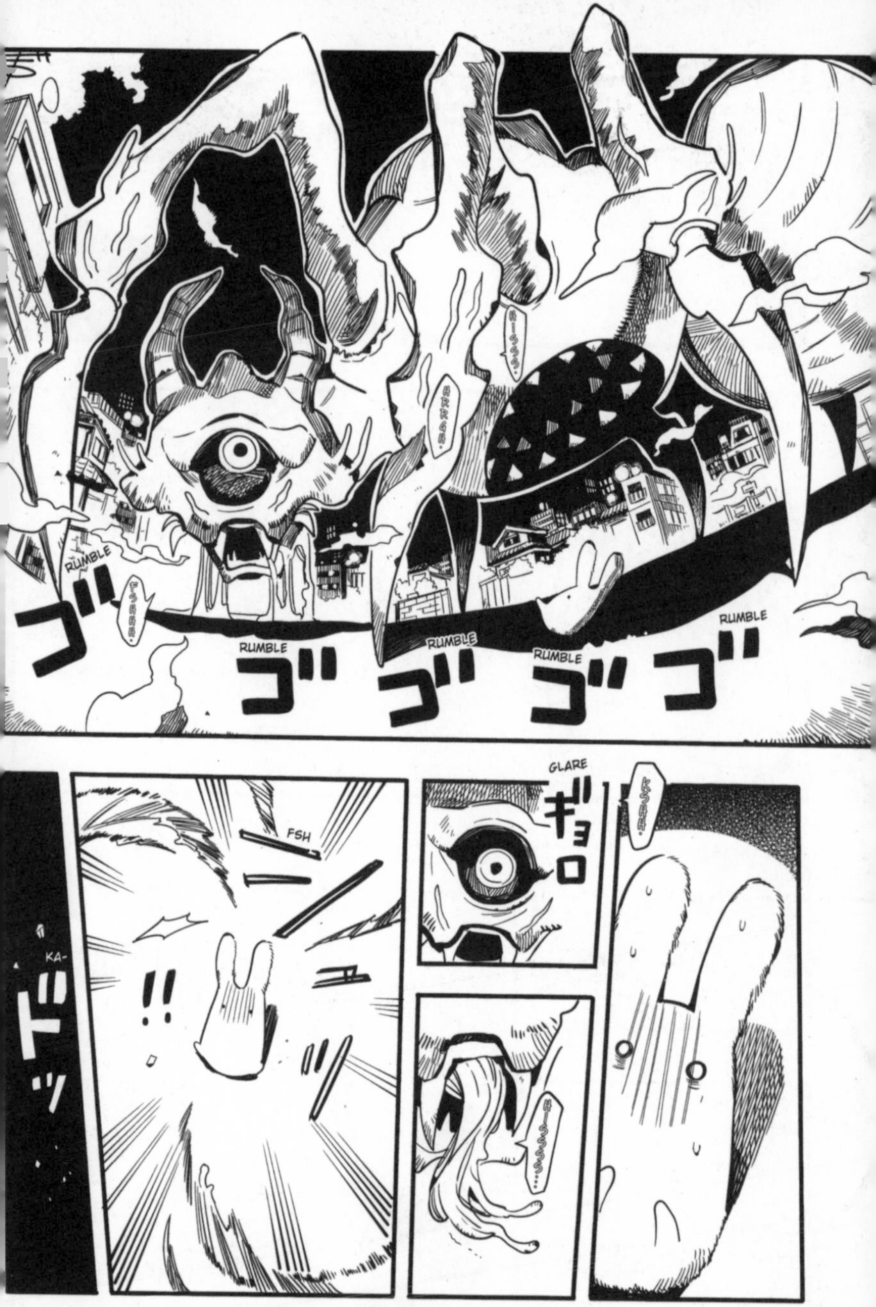
RUMBLE
ゴ
HISSS.
HRRGH.
RUMBLE
ゴ
RUMBLE
ゴ
RUMBLE
ゴ
FSHHH.
RUMBLE
ゴ
KSHH.
GLARE
ギョロ
HISSSS...
FSH
!!
KA-
ッ

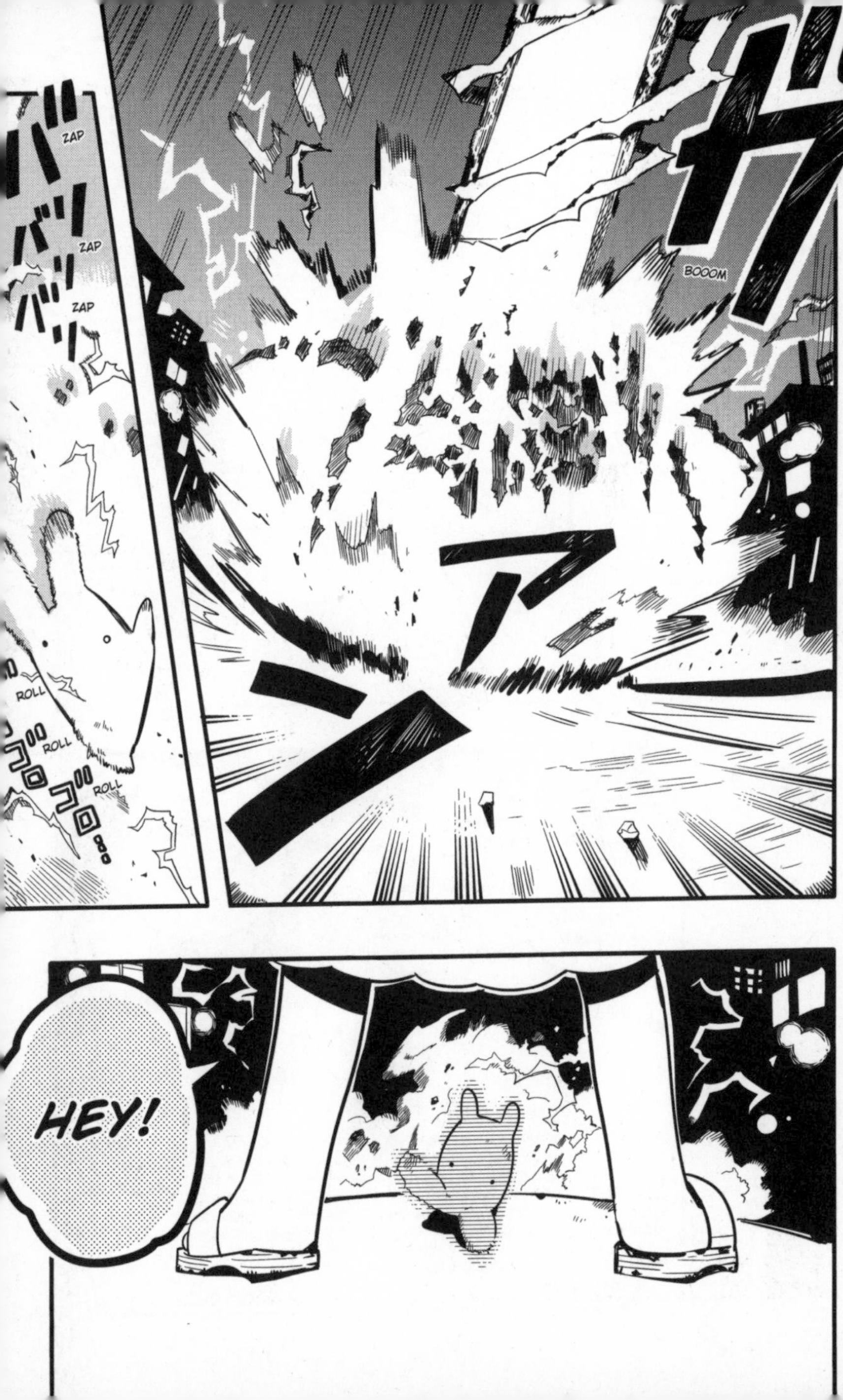
BOOOM
ZAP
ZAP
ZAP
ROLL
ROLL
ROLL
HEY!

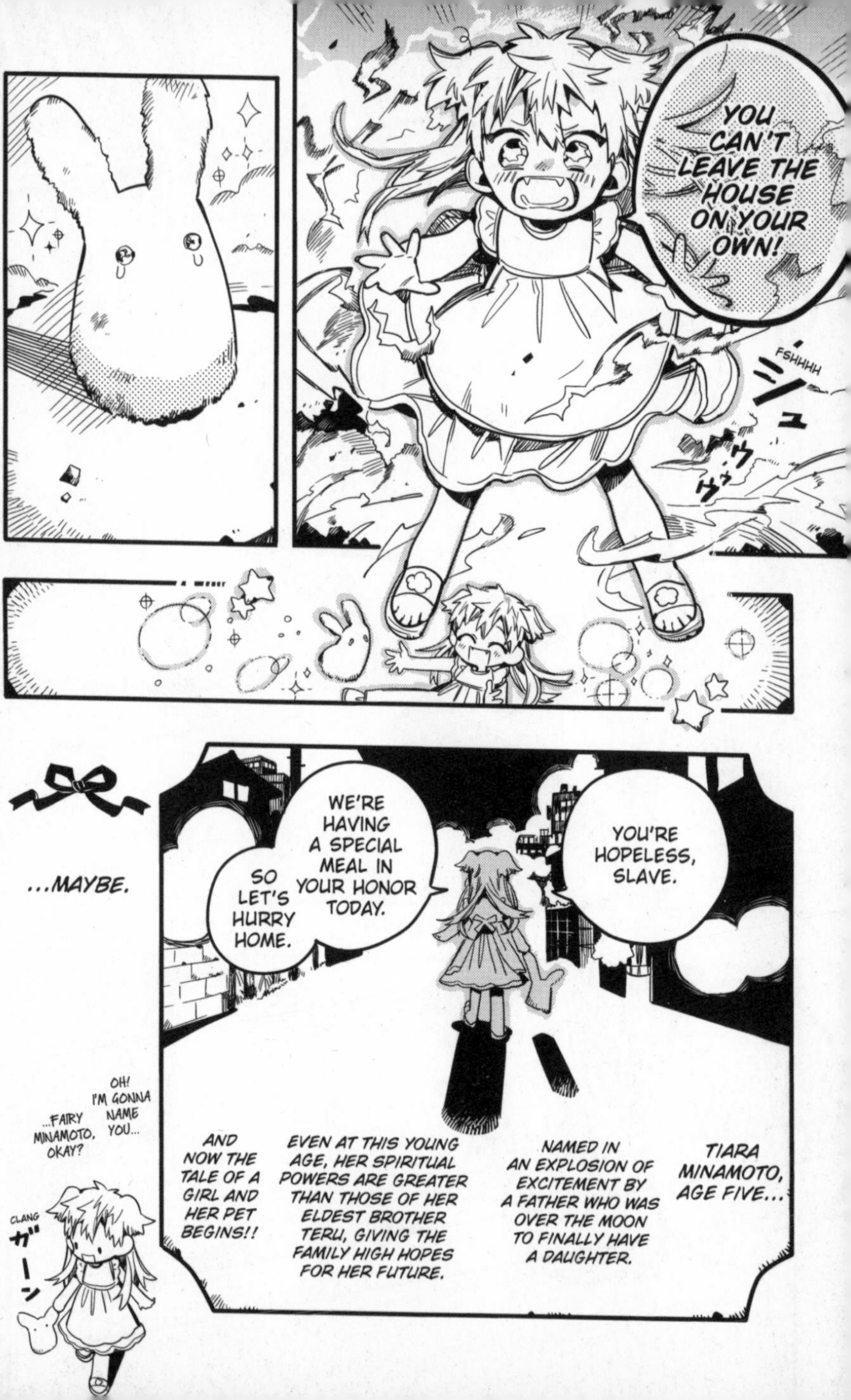
YOU CAN'T LEAVE THE HOUSE ON YOUR OWN!
FSHHHH
YOU'RE HOPELESS, SLAVE.
WE'RE HAVING A SPECIAL MEAL IN YOUR HONOR TODAY.
SO LET'S HURRY HOME.
TIARA MINAMOTO, AGE FIVE...
NAMED IN AN EXPLOSION OF EXCITEMENT BY A FATHER WHO WAS OVER THE MOON TO FINALLY HAVE A DAUGHTER.
EVEN AT THIS YOUNG AGE, HER SPIRITUAL POWERS ARE GREATER THAN THOSE OF HER ELDEST BROTHER TERU, GIVING THE FAMILY HIGH HOPES FOR HER FUTURE.
AND NOW THE TALE OF A GIRL AND HER PET BEGINS!!
...MAYBE.
OH! I'M GONNA NAME YOU...
...FAIRY MINAMOTO, OKAY?
CLANG

After•School
Hanako-Kun

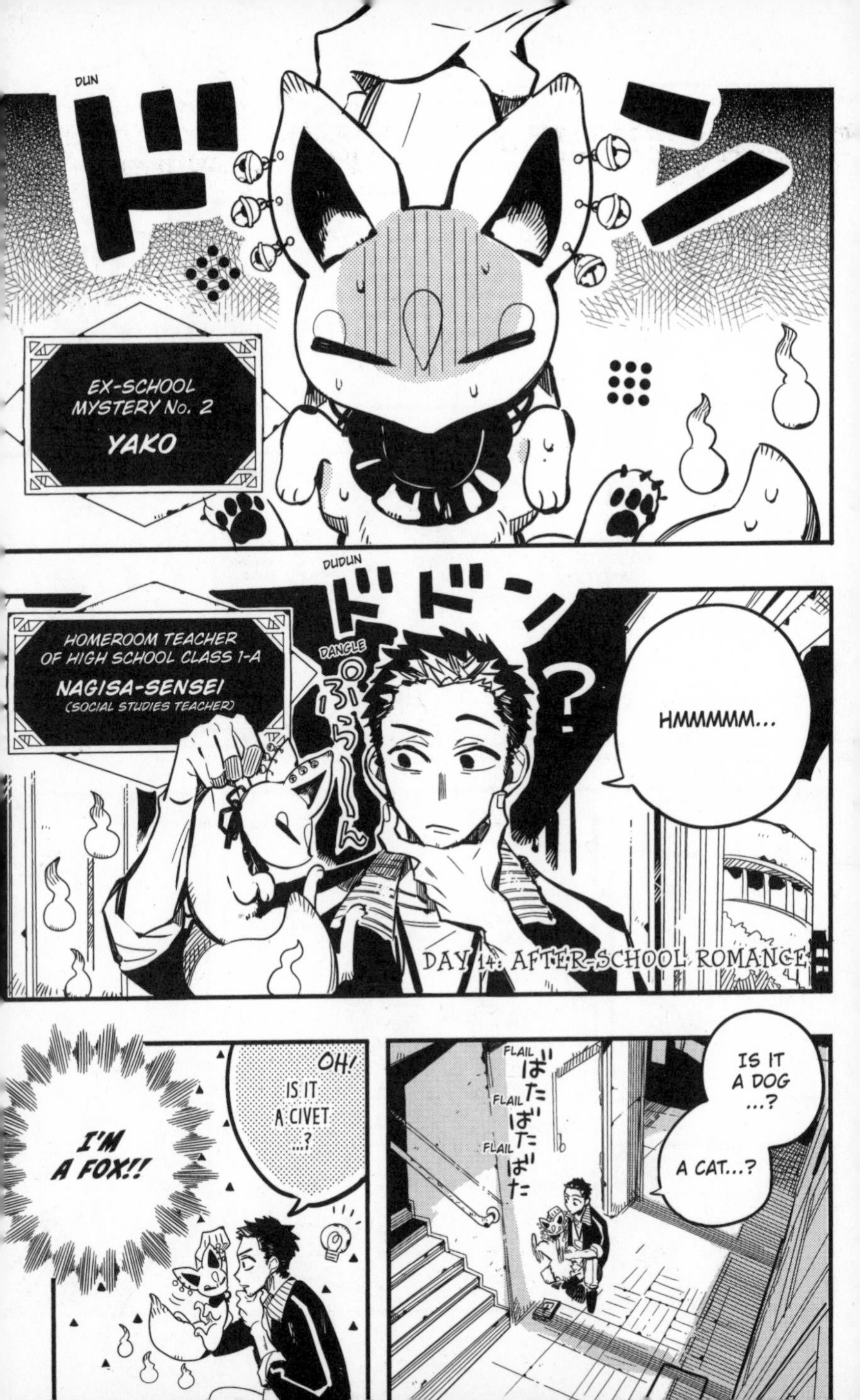
DUN
ドン
EX-SCHOOL MYSTERY No. 2
YAKO
HMMMMMM...
DUDUN
ドドン
DANGLE
ぷら～ん
HOMEROOM TEACHER OF HIGH SCHOOL CLASS 1-A
NAGISA-SENSEI
(SOCIAL STUDIES TEACHER)
DAY 14: AFTER-SCHOOL ROMANCE
IS IT A DOG ...?
A CAT...?
FLAIL
ばた
FLAIL
ばた
FLAIL
ばた
OH!
IS IT A CIVET ...?
I'M A FOX!!

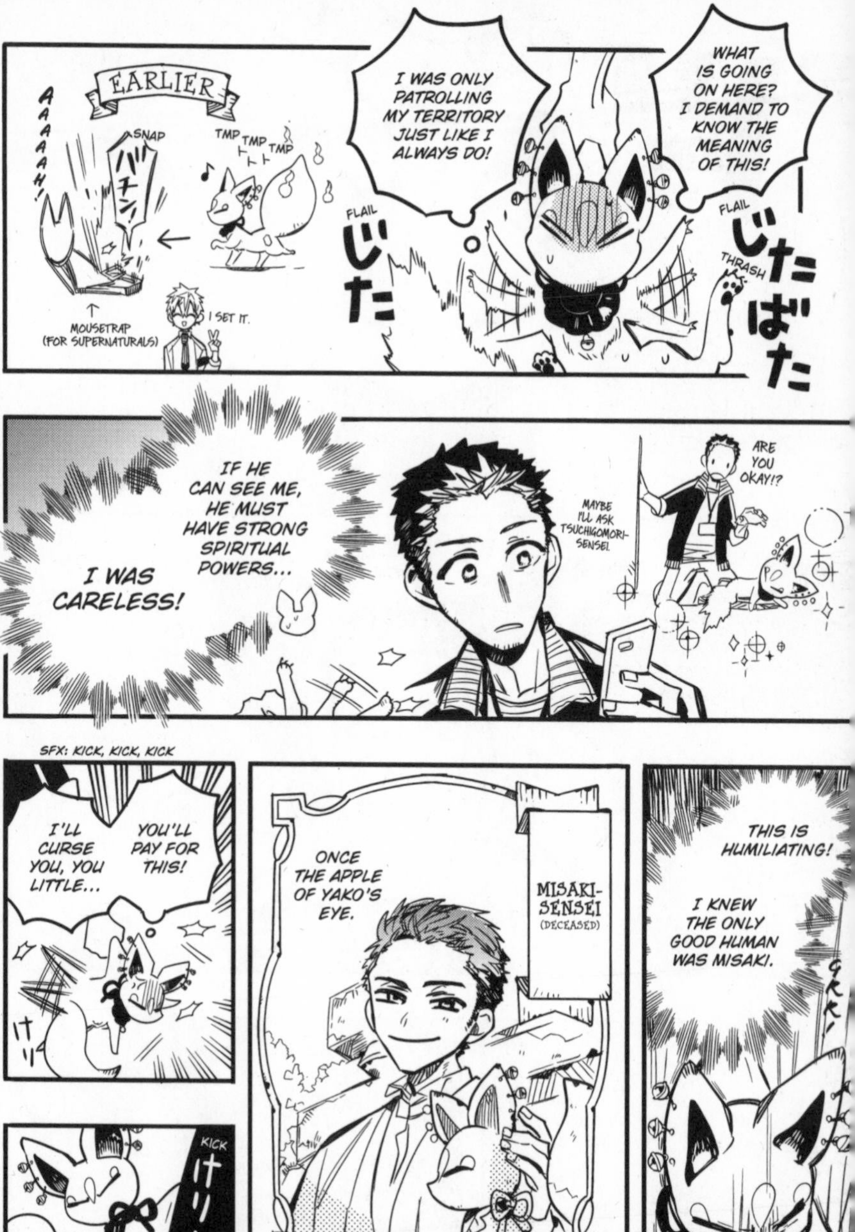
WHAT IS GOING ON HERE? I DEMAND TO KNOW THE MEANING OF THIS!
I WAS ONLY PATROLLING MY TERRITORY JUST LIKE I ALWAYS DO!
FLAIL
じた
FLAIL
THRASH
じたばた
EARLIER
TMP TMP TMP
トトト
SNAP
バチン!
AAAAAAH!
MOUSETRAP (FOR SUPERNATURALS)
I SET IT.
ARE YOU OKAY!?
MAYBE I'LL ASK TSUCHIGOMORI-SENSEI.
IF HE CAN SEE ME, HE MUST HAVE STRONG SPIRITUAL POWERS...
I WAS CARELESS!
THIS IS HUMILIATING!
I KNEW THE ONLY GOOD HUMAN WAS MISAKI.
GRR!
MISAKI-SENSEI (DECEASED)
ONCE THE APPLE OF YAKO'S EYE.
SFX: KICK, KICK, KICK
YOU'LL PAY FOR THIS!
I'LL CURSE YOU, YOU LITTLE...
けり
KICK
けり...
...YOU...

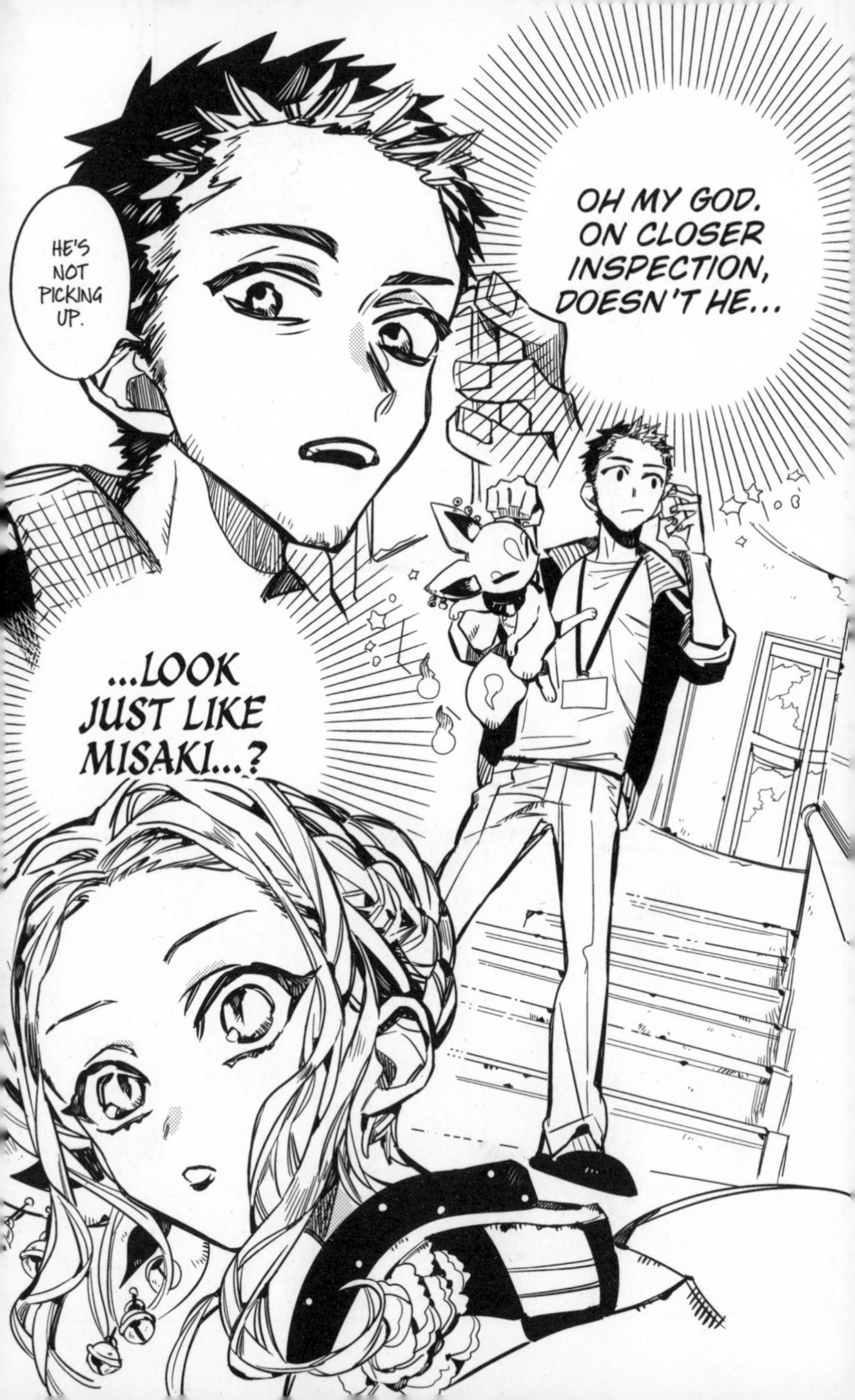
OH MY GOD. ON CLOSER INSPECTION, DOESN'T HE...
HE'S NOT PICKING UP.
...LOOK JUST LIKE MISAKI...?

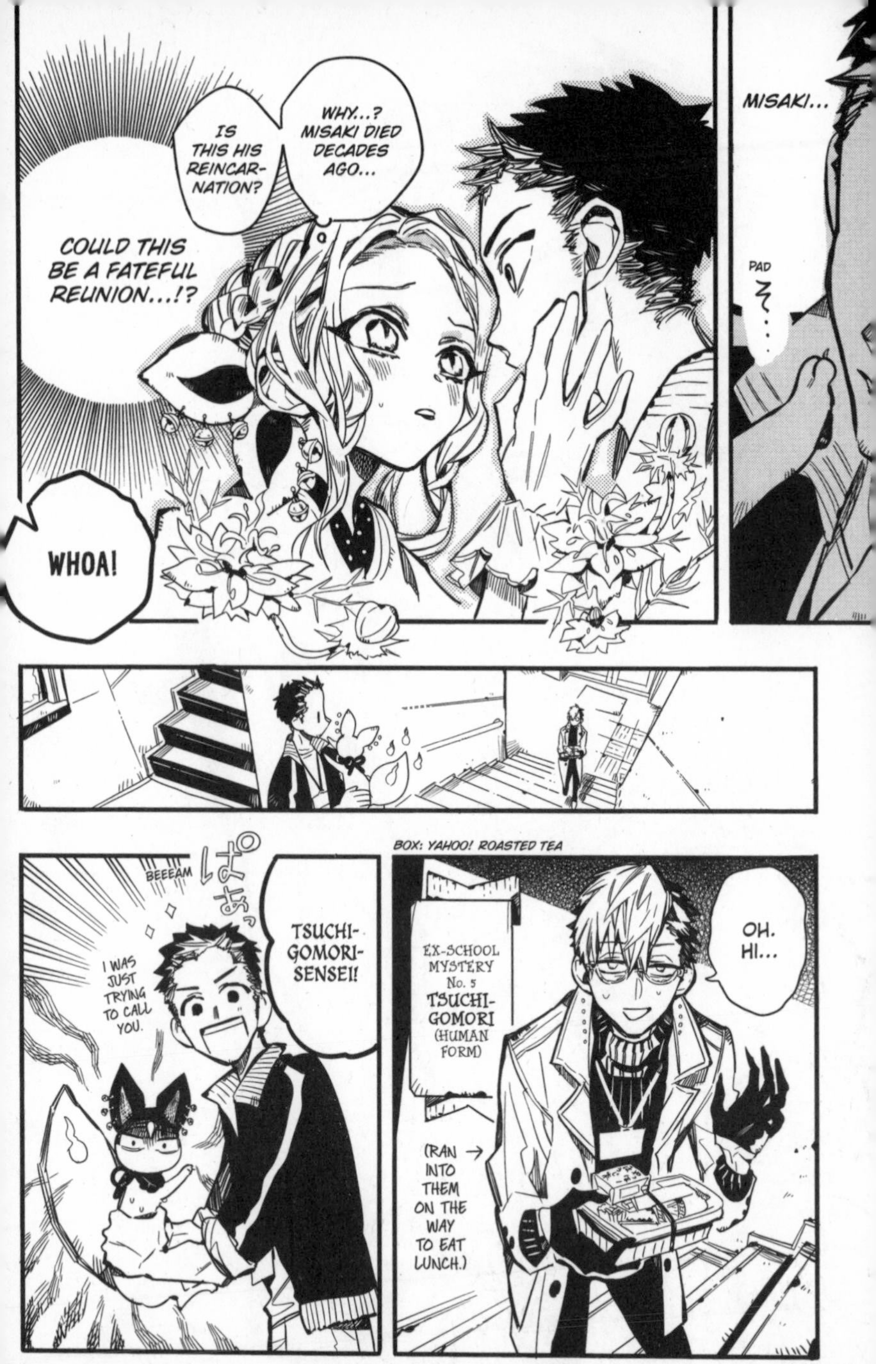
MISAKI...
PAD
WHY...? MISAKI DIED DECADES AGO...
IS THIS HIS REINCAR-NATION?
COULD THIS BE A FATEFUL REUNION...!?
WHOA!
BOX: YAHOO! ROASTED TEA
OH. HI...
EX-SCHOOL MYSTERY No. 5 TSUCHI-GOMORI (HUMAN FORM)
(RAN INTO THEM ON THE WAY TO EAT LUNCH.)
TSUCHI-GOMORI-SENSEI!
BEEEAM
ぱあっ
I WAS JUST TRYING TO CALL YOU.

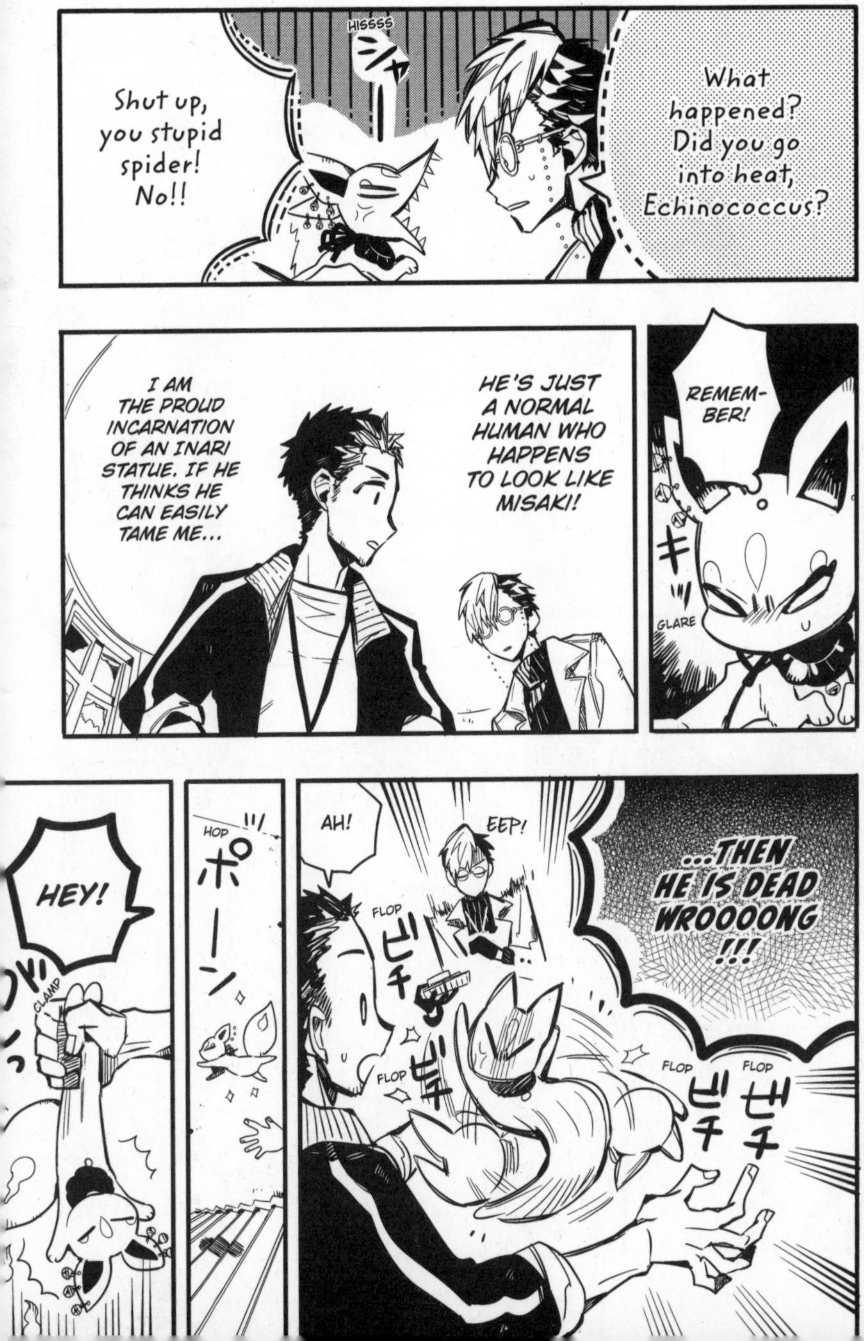
What happened? Did you go into heat, Echinococcus?
HISSSS
Shut up, you stupid spider! No!!
REMEMBER!
GLARE
HE'S JUST A NORMAL HUMAN WHO HAPPENS TO LOOK LIKE MISAKI!
I AM THE PROUD INCARNATION OF AN INARI STATUE. IF HE THINKS HE CAN EASILY TAME ME...
...THEN HE IS DEAD WROOOONG!!!
EEP!
AH!
FLOP
FLOP
FLOP
FLOP
HOP
HEY!
CLAMP

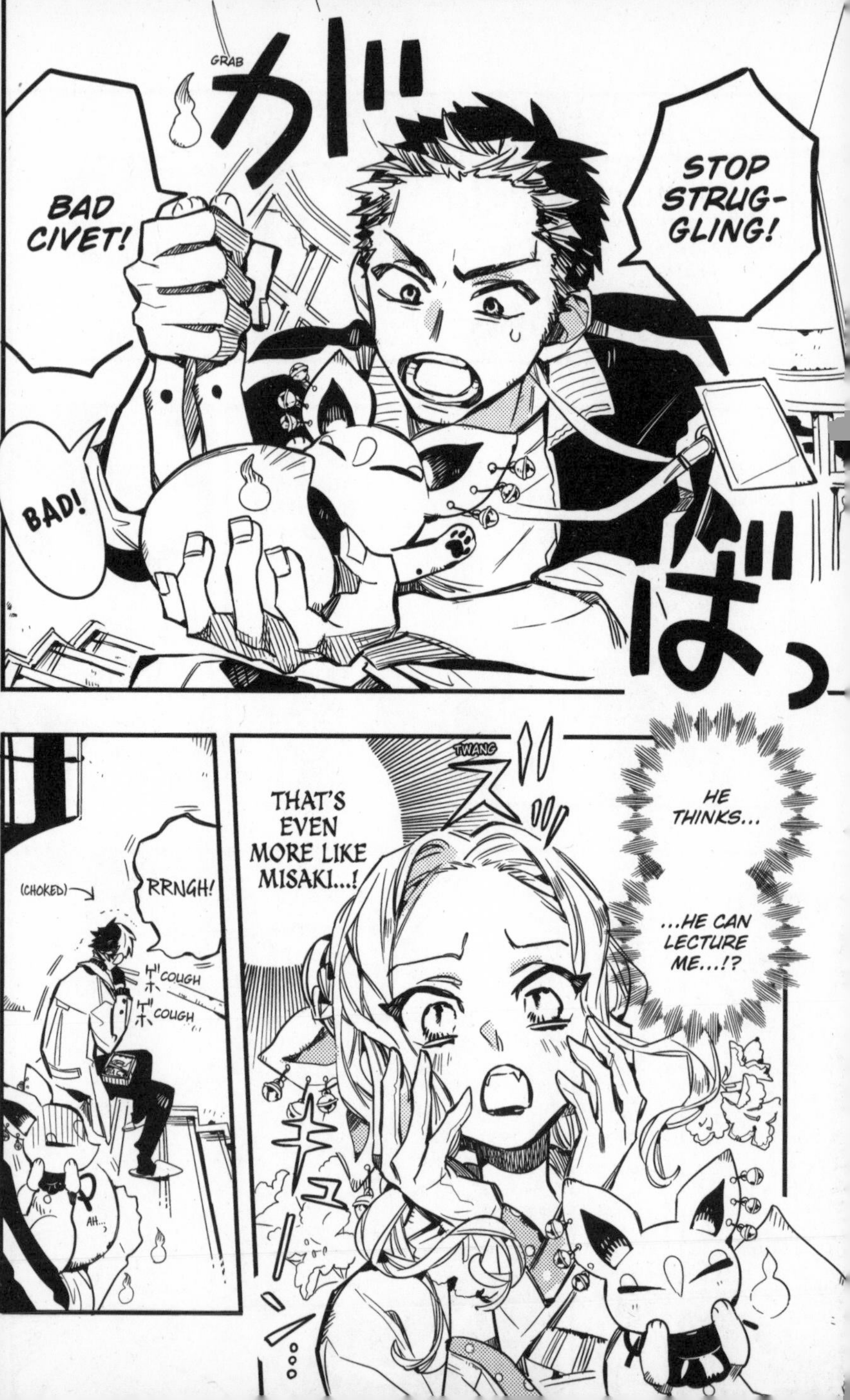

STOP STRUG-GLING!
ぱっ
GRAB
BAD CIVET!
BAD!
HE THINKS...
...HE CAN LECTURE ME...!?
TWANG
THAT'S EVEN MORE LIKE MISAKI...!
RRNGH!
(CHOKED)
COUGH
COUGH
AH...

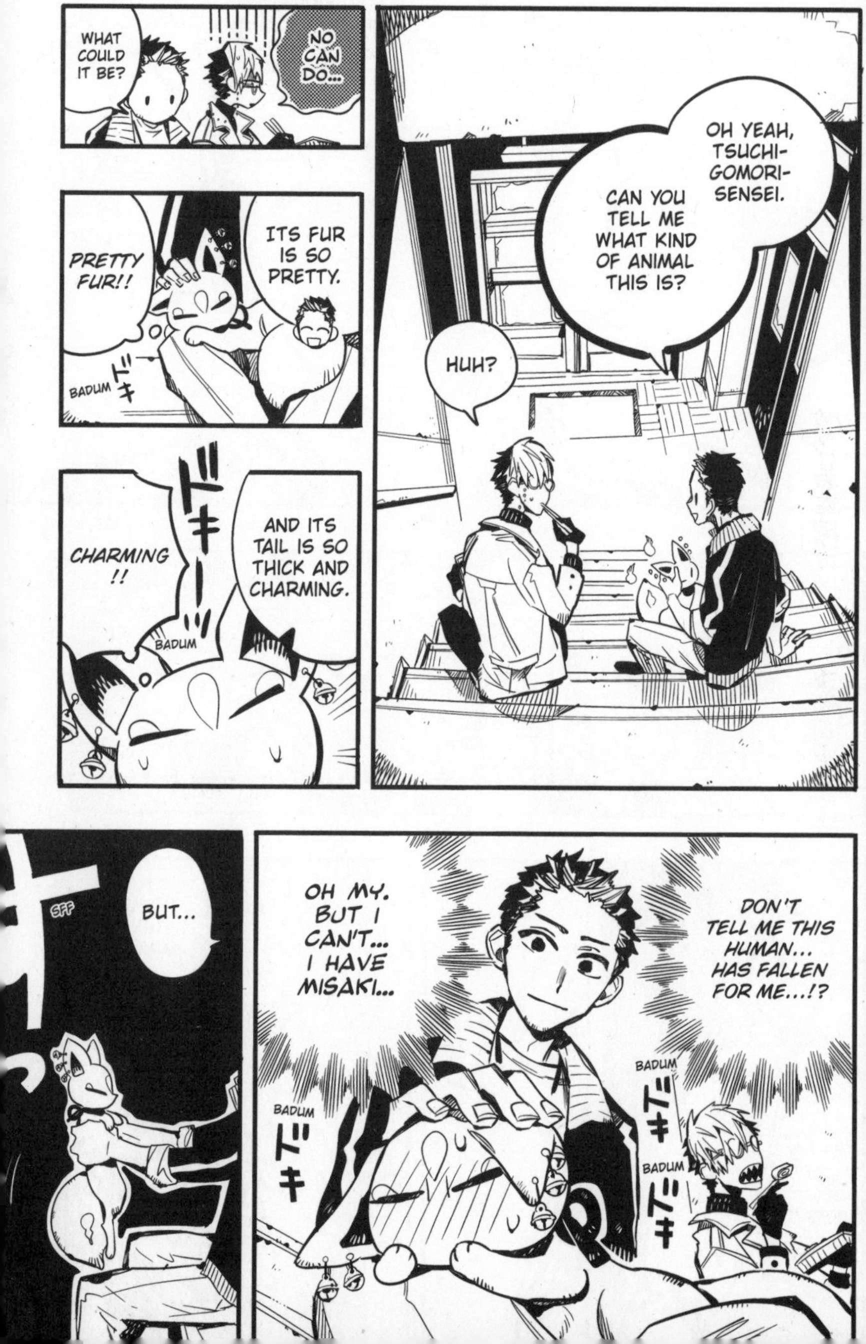
OH YEAH, TSUCHI-GOMORI-SENSEI.
CAN YOU TELL ME WHAT KIND OF ANIMAL THIS IS?
HUH?
NO CAN DO...
WHAT COULD IT BE?
ITS FUR IS SO PRETTY.
PRETTY FUR!!
BADUM
AND ITS TAIL IS SO THICK AND CHARMING.
CHARMING!!
BADUM
DON'T TELL ME THIS HUMAN... HAS FALLEN FOR ME...!?
BADUM
BADUM
OH MY. BUT I CAN'T... I HAVE MISAKI...
BADUM
BUT...
SFF

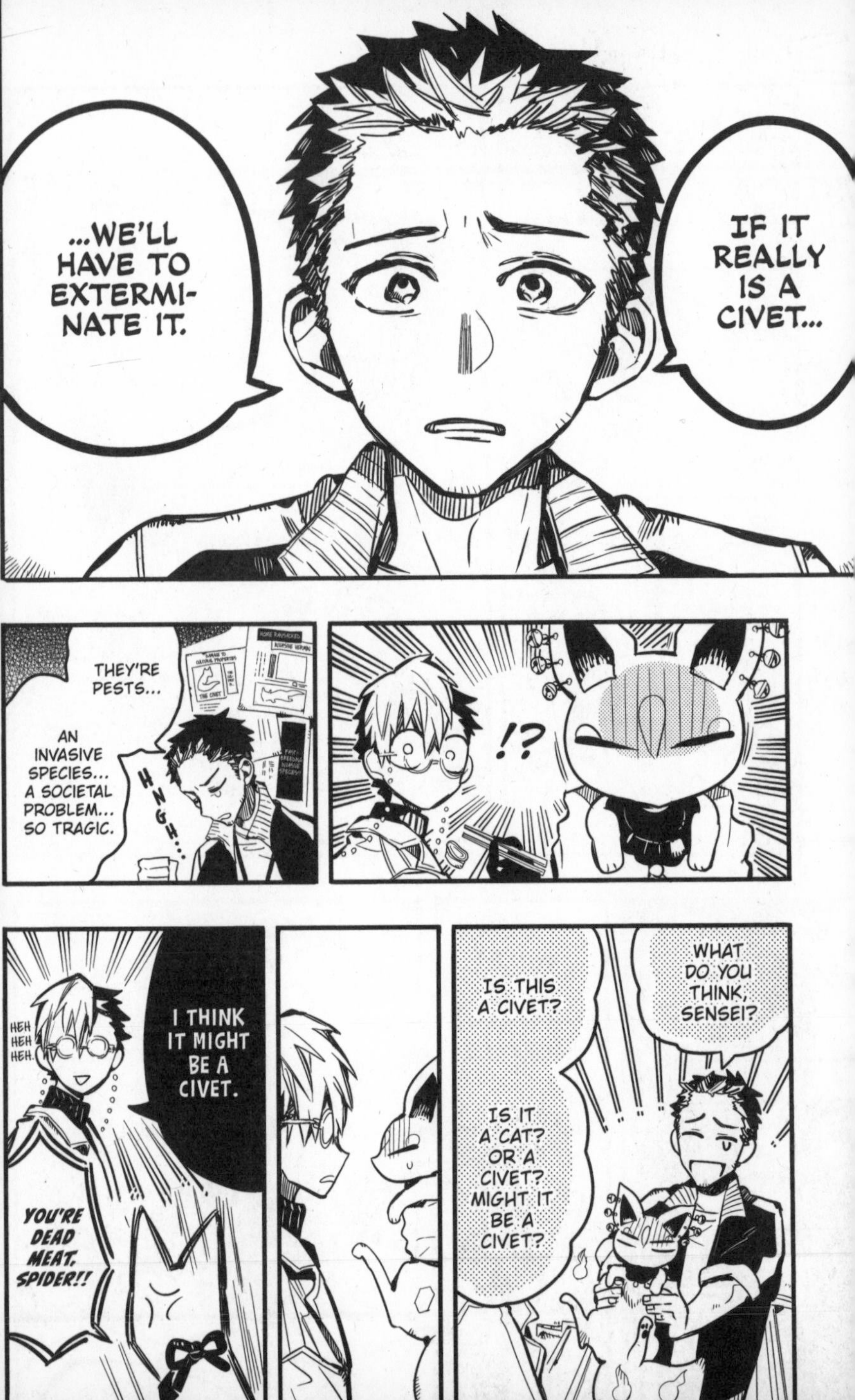
IF IT REALLY IS A CIVET...
...WE'LL HAVE TO EXTERMINATE IT.
!?
THEY'RE PESTS...
AN INVASIVE SPECIES... A SOCIETAL PROBLEM... SO TRAGIC.
HNGH...
WHAT DO YOU THINK, SENSEI?
IS THIS A CIVET?
IS IT A CAT? OR A CIVET? MIGHT IT BE A CIVET?
I THINK IT MIGHT BE A CIVET.
HEH HEH HEH.
YOU'RE DEAD MEAT, SPIDER!!

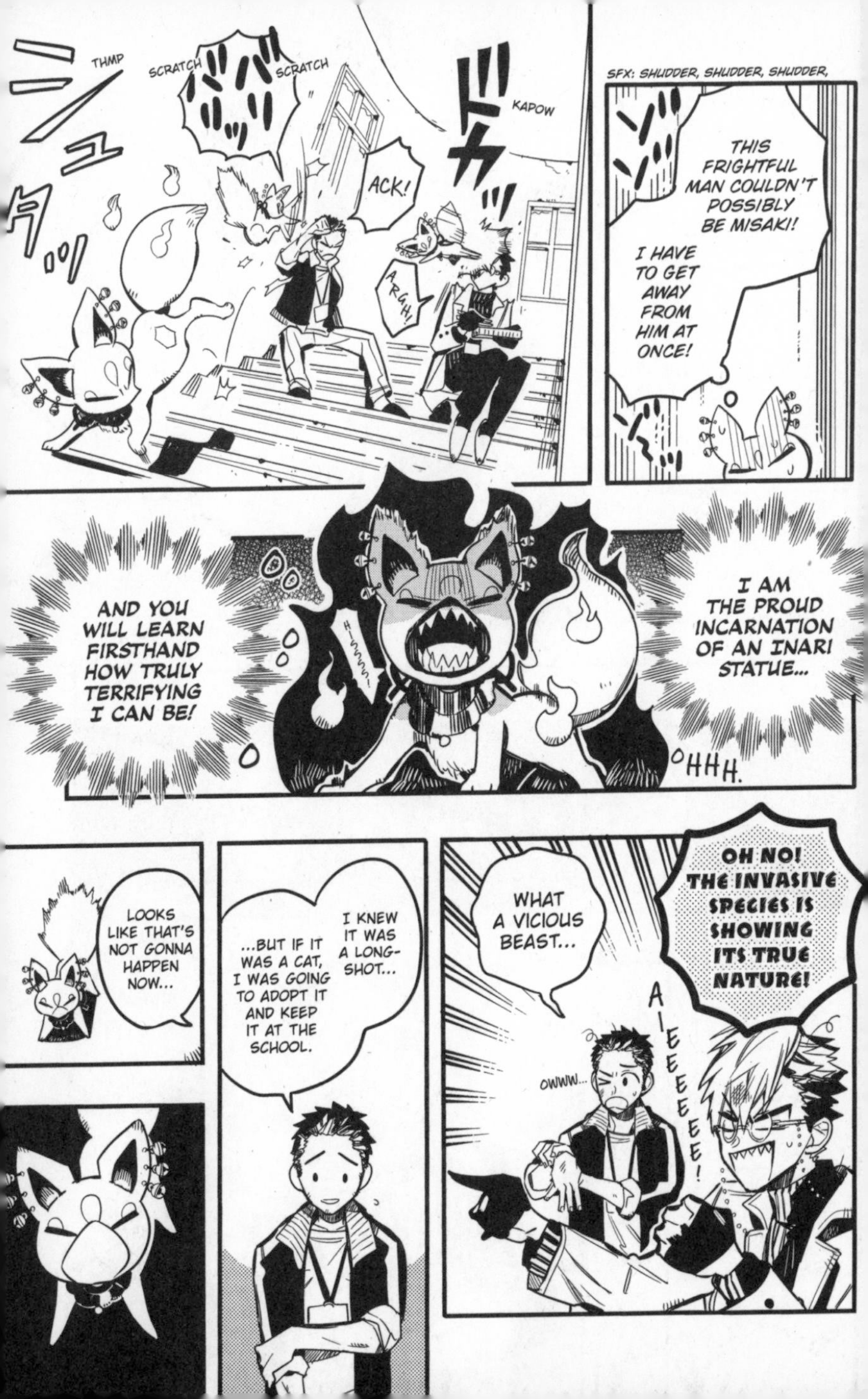
SFX: SHUDDER, SHUDDER, SHUDDER,
THIS FRIGHTFUL MAN COULDN'T POSSIBLY BE MISAKI!
I HAVE TO GET AWAY FROM HIM AT ONCE!
KAPOW
SCRATCH
SCRATCH
THMP
ACK!
ARGH!
I AM THE PROUD INCARNATION OF AN INARI STATUE...
HISSSSS!
OHHH.
AND YOU WILL LEARN FIRSTHAND HOW TRULY TERRIFYING I CAN BE!
OH NO! THE INVASIVE SPECIES IS SHOWING ITS TRUE NATURE!
WHAT A VICIOUS BEAST...
AIEEEEEE!
OWWW...
I KNEW IT WAS A LONG-SHOT...
...BUT IF IT WAS A CAT, I WAS GOING TO ADOPT IT AND KEEP IT AT THE SCHOOL.
LOOKS LIKE THAT'S NOT GONNA HAPPEN NOW...

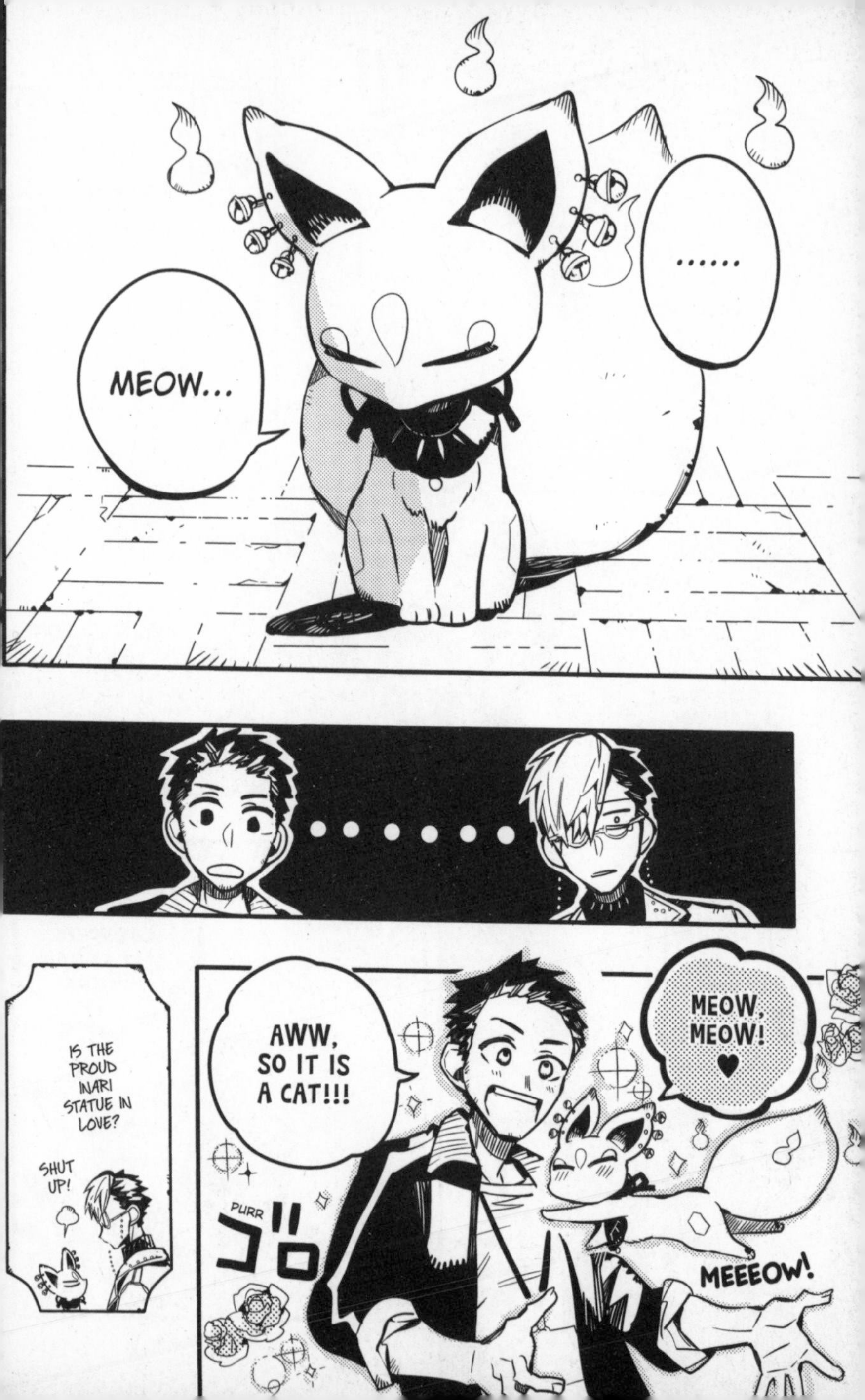
......
MEOW...
••••••
MEOW, MEOW! ♥
AWW, SO IT IS A CAT!!!
MEEEOW!
PURR ゴロ
IS THE PROUD INARI STATUE IN LOVE?
SHUT UP!

After•School
Hanako-Kun

TRANSLATION NOTES

Common Honorifics

no honorific: Indicates familiarity or closeness; if used without permission or reason, addressing someone in this manner would constitute an insult.

-san: The Japanese equivalent of Mr./Mrs./Miss. If a situation calls for politeness, this is the fail-safe honorific.

-sama: Conveys great respect; may also indicate that the social status of the speaker is lower than that of the addressee.

-kun: Used most often when referring to boys, this indicates affection or familiarity. Occasionally used by older men among their peers, but it may also be used by anyone referring to a person of lower standing.

-chan: An affectionate honorific indicating familiarity used mostly in reference to girls; also used in reference to cute persons or animals of either gender.

-senpai: A suffix used to address upperclassmen or more experienced coworkers.

-sensei: A respectful term for teachers, artists, or high-level professionals.

-oniichan: A familiar, somewhat childish way to refer to one's older brother.

Page 21

We see why Tsuchigomori's kanji drill order might be justified when Hanako forgets how to write the difficult second character in *shoumetsu* ("erasure" or "extinction") and has to phonetically spell it out. This has been translated as him forgetting how to spell "obliterated" and going for a simpler word instead.

Page 34

A *torii* is a shrine gate; it looks like the symbol for pi with an extra horizontal bar, as can be seen on the Kokkuri-san board.

Page 79

Natsuhiko's "poem" follows a three-seven-three syllable structure in Japanese, which is atypical but allowed in modern verse. Since the five-three-five structure is so heavily associated with Japanese poetry for English-speaking audiences, that more standard version was used for this translation. It is also a *senryuu*, which comically explore the foibles of human nature, rather than a *haiku*, which take the natural world as a subject and tend to be more serious.

Page 98

Manju are small cakes made of mochi and filled with red bean paste.

Page 100

Candy sculptures are *amezaiku*, intricately detailed figures molded from hot sugar and painted with edible dyes.

Page 131

In Japanese, *kegare* is a homophone for "impurity" but written with different kanji so as to read "spirit withering." This *kegare*-infected Mokke is what caused the candy zombie outbreak in Vol. 8.

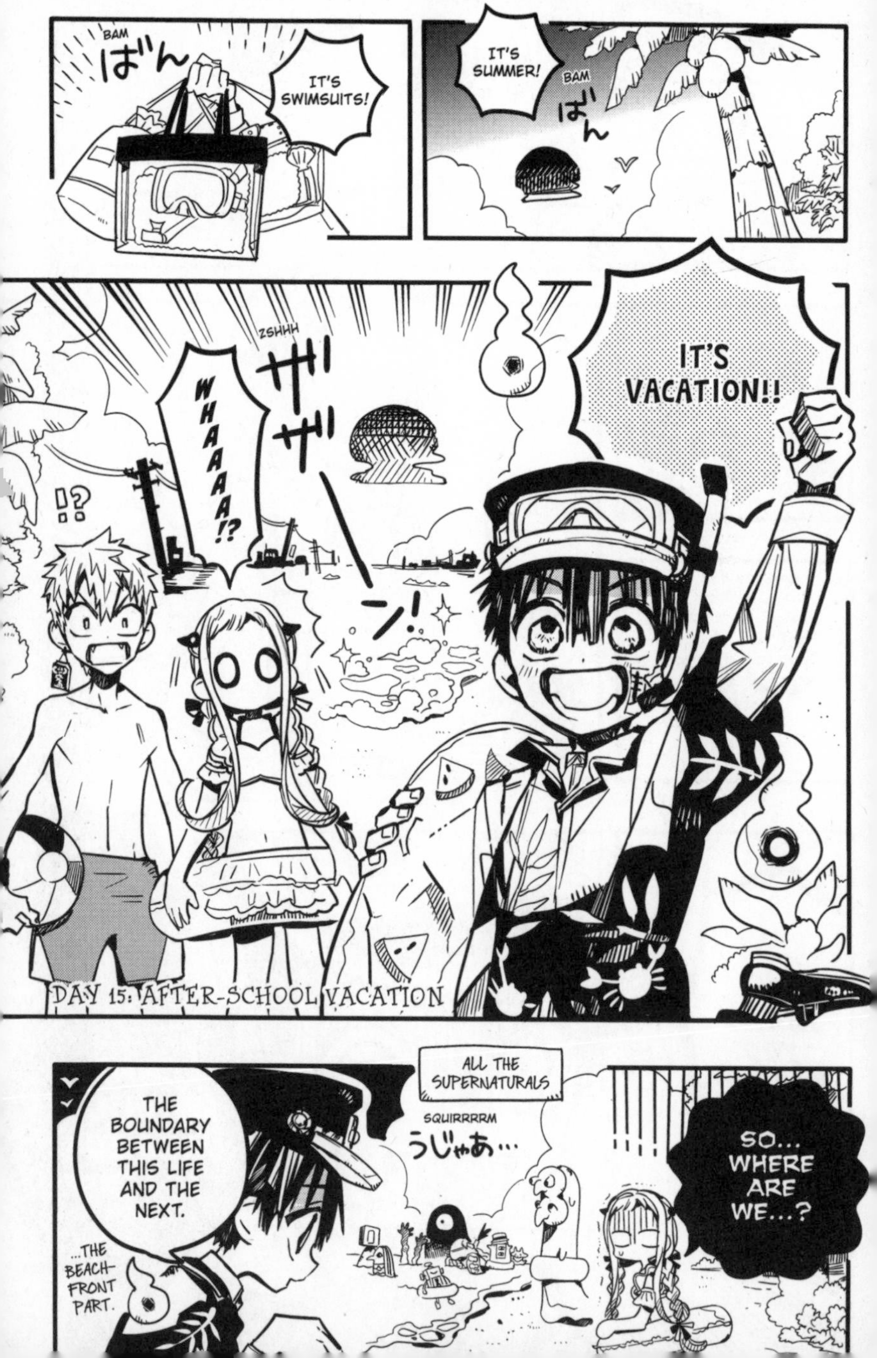
IT'S SUMMER!
BAM
ばん
BAM
ばん
IT'S SWIMSUITS!
IT'S VACATION!!
ZSHHH
ザザーン!
WHAAAAA!?
!?
DAY 15: AFTER-SCHOOL VACATION
SO... WHERE ARE WE...?
ALL THE SUPERNATURALS
SQUIRRRRM
うじゃあ…
THE BOUNDARY BETWEEN THIS LIFE AND THE NEXT.
...THE BEACH-FRONT PART.

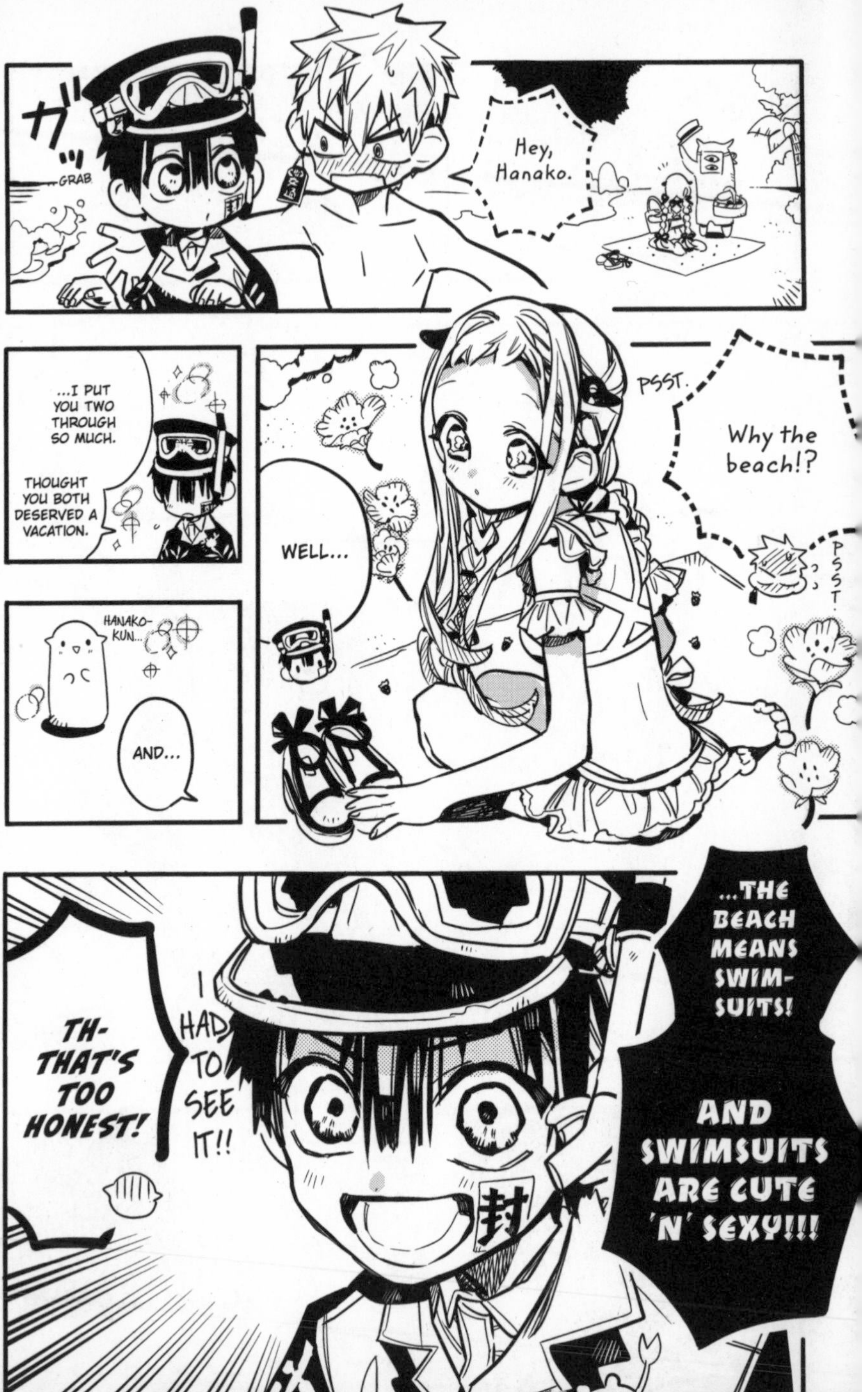
Hey, Hanako.
ガッ
GRAB
PSSST.
Why the beach!?
PSSST.
WELL...
...I PUT YOU TWO THROUGH SO MUCH.
THOUGHT YOU BOTH DESERVED A VACATION.
HANAKO-KUN...
AND...
...THE BEACH MEANS SWIM-SUITS!
AND SWIMSUITS ARE CUTE 'N' SEXY!!!
I HAD TO SEE IT!!
TH-THAT'S TOO HONEST!

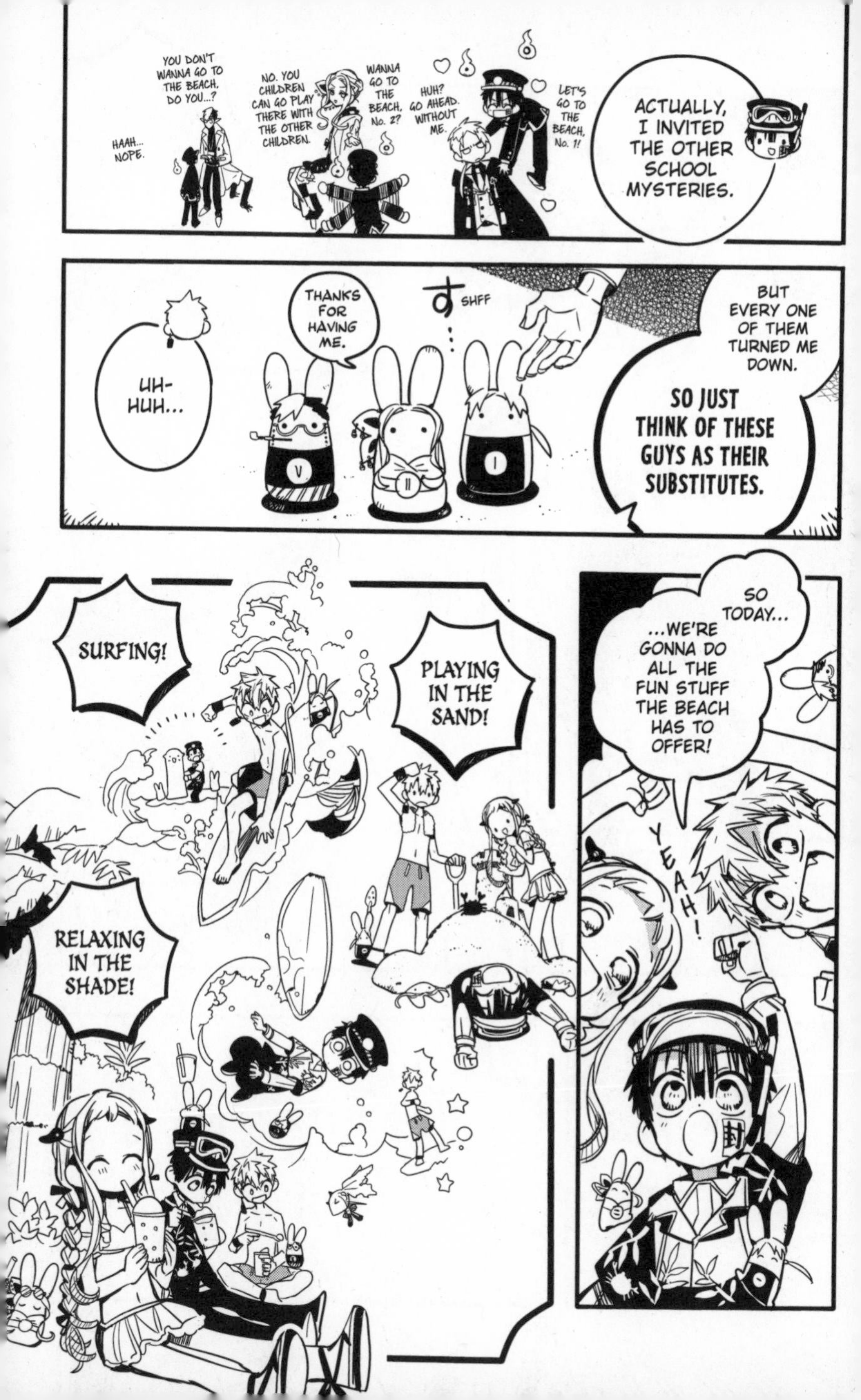
ACTUALLY, I INVITED THE OTHER SCHOOL MYSTERIES.
LET'S GO TO THE BEACH, No. 1!
HUH? GO AHEAD. WITHOUT ME.
WANNA GO TO THE BEACH, No. 2?
NO. YOU CHILDREN CAN GO PLAY THERE WITH THE OTHER CHILDREN.
YOU DON'T WANNA GO TO THE BEACH, DO YOU...?
HAAH... NOPE.
BUT EVERY ONE OF THEM TURNED ME DOWN.
SO JUST THINK OF THESE GUYS AS THEIR SUBSTITUTES.
す SHFF
THANKS FOR HAVING ME.
UH-HUH...
SO TODAY...
...WE'RE GONNA DO ALL THE FUN STUFF THE BEACH HAS TO OFFER!
YEAH!
PLAYING IN THE SAND!
SURFING!
RELAXING IN THE SHADE!

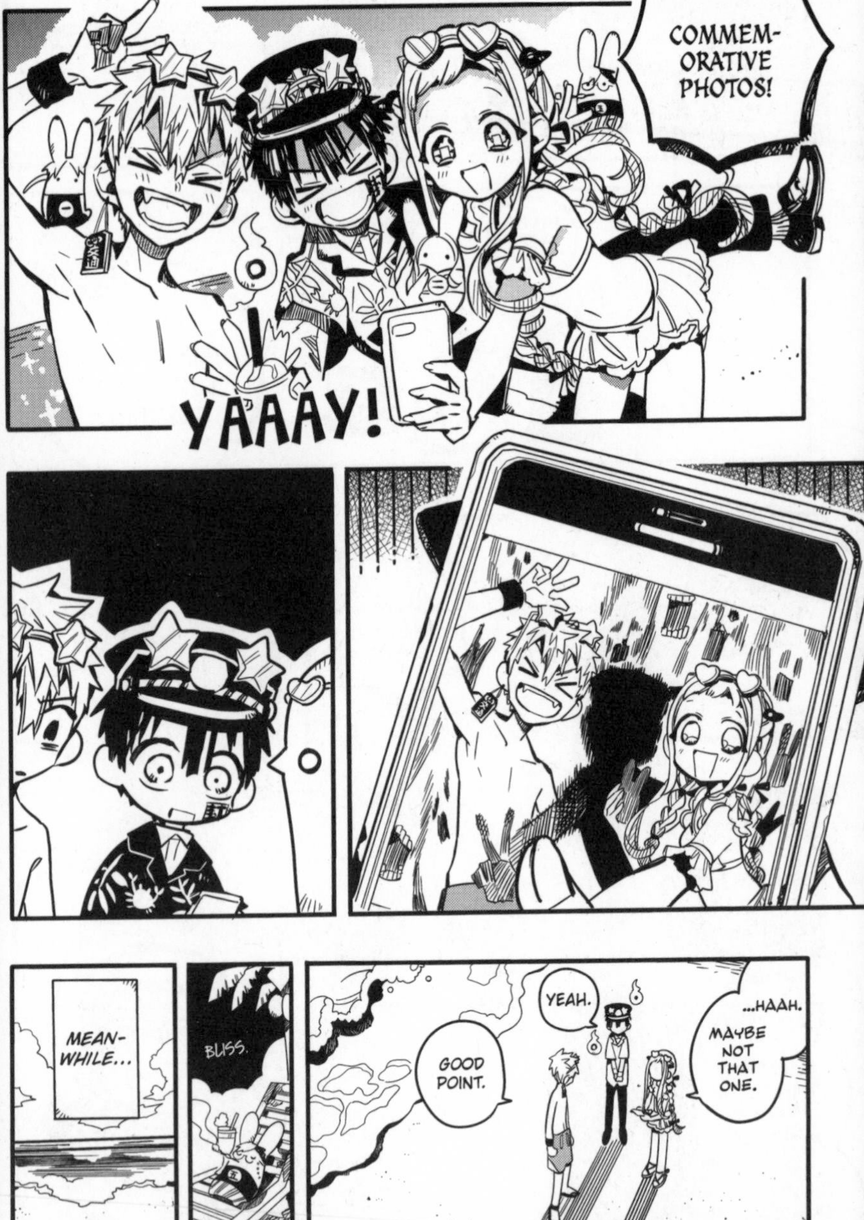
COMMEM-ORATIVE PHOTOS!
YAAAY!
...HAAH. MAYBE NOT THAT ONE.
YEAH.
GOOD POINT.
BLISS.
MEAN-WHILE...

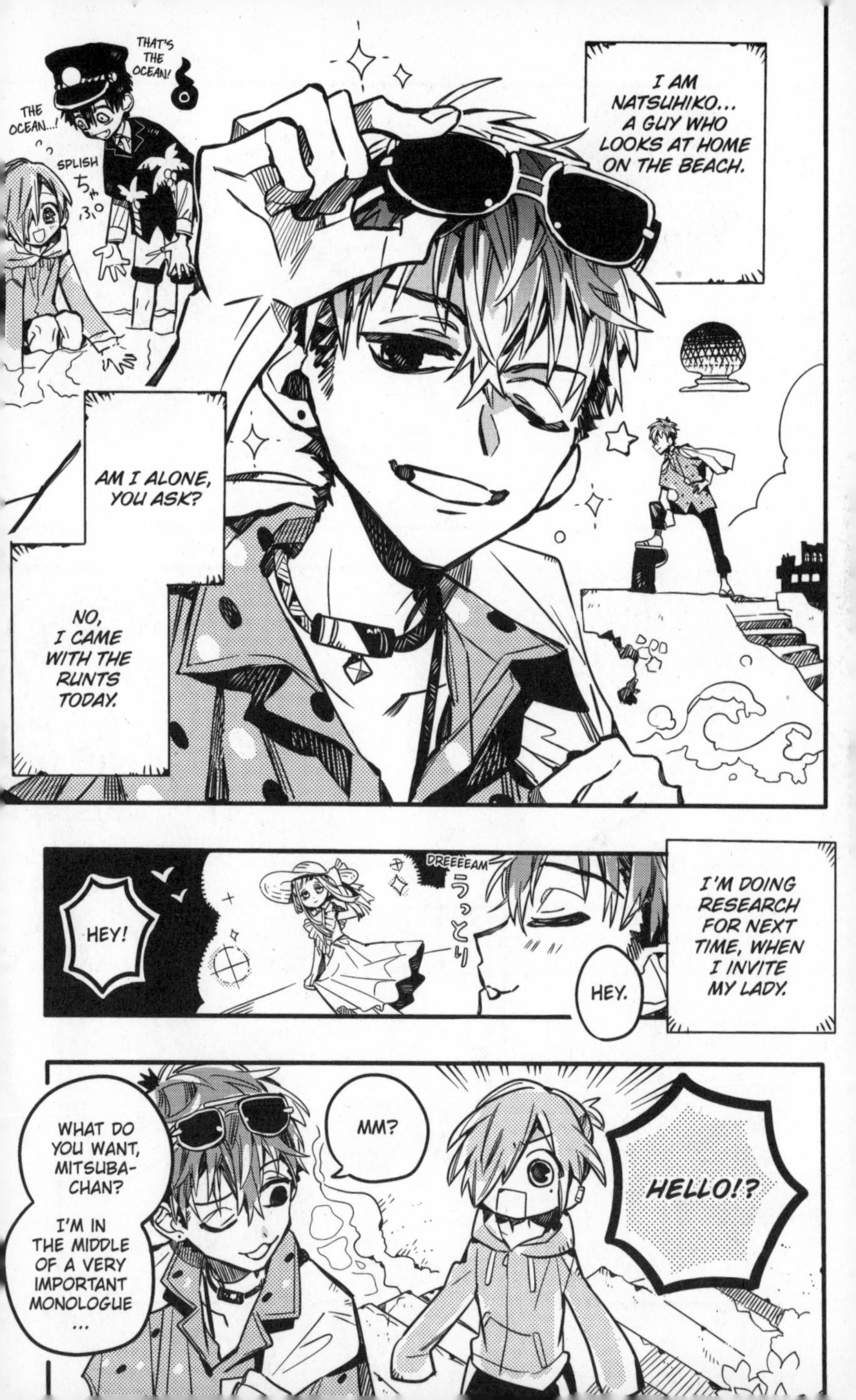
I AM NATSUHIKO... A GUY WHO LOOKS AT HOME ON THE BEACH.
THAT'S THE OCEAN!
THE OCEAN...!
SPLISH
AM I ALONE, YOU ASK?
NO, I CAME WITH THE RUNTS TODAY.
I'M DOING RESEARCH FOR NEXT TIME, WHEN I INVITE MY LADY.
HEY.
DREEEEAM
うっとり
HEY!
HELLO!?
MM?
WHAT DO YOU WANT, MITSUBA-CHAN?
I'M IN THE MIDDLE OF A VERY IMPORTANT MONOLOGUE...

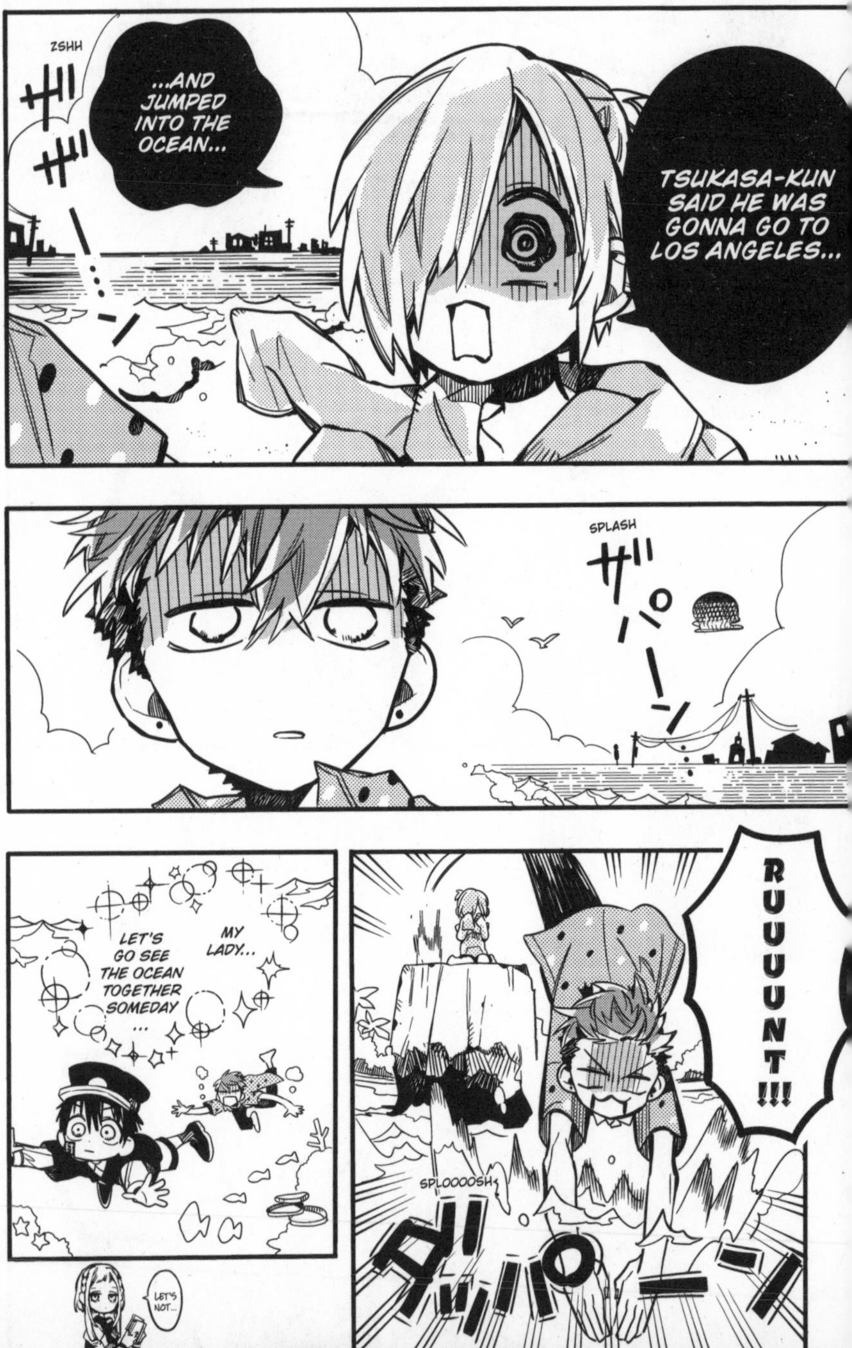
TSUKASA-KUN SAID HE WAS GONNA GO TO LOS ANGELES...
...AND JUMPED INTO THE OCEAN...
ZSHH
SPLASH
RUUUUNT!!!
SPLOOOOSH
MY LADY...
LET'S GO SEE THE OCEAN TOGETHER SOMEDAY...
LET'S NOT...

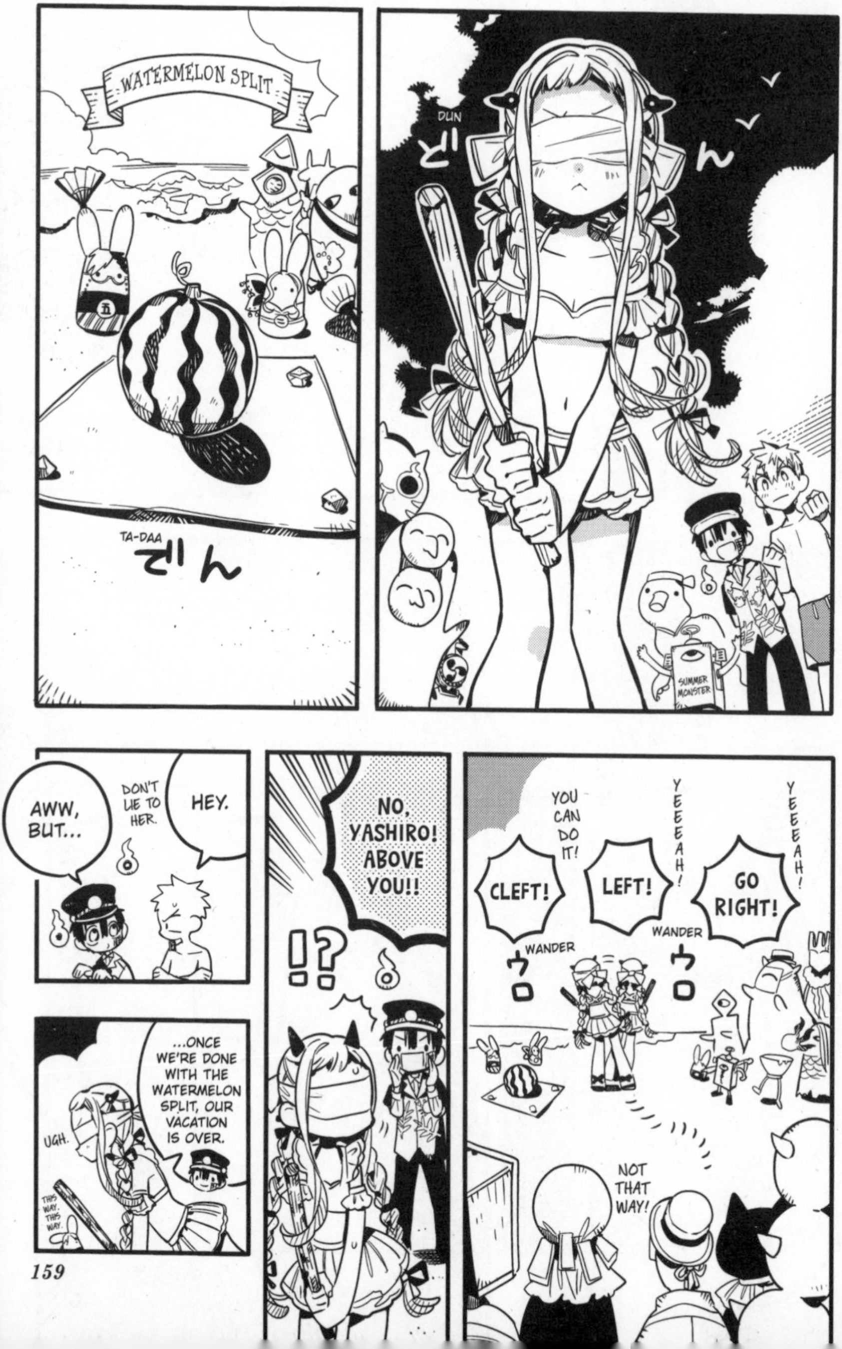

DUN
SUMMER MONSTER
WATERMELON SPLIT
TA-DAA
YEEEAH!
GO RIGHT!
YEEEAH!
LEFT!
YOU CAN DO IT!
CLEFT!
WANDER
WANDER
NOT THAT WAY!
NO, YASHIRO! ABOVE YOU!!
!?
HEY.
DON'T LIE TO HER.
AWW, BUT...
...ONCE WE'RE DONE WITH THE WATERMELON SPLIT, OUR VACATION IS OVER.
UGH.
THIS WAY. THIS WAY.

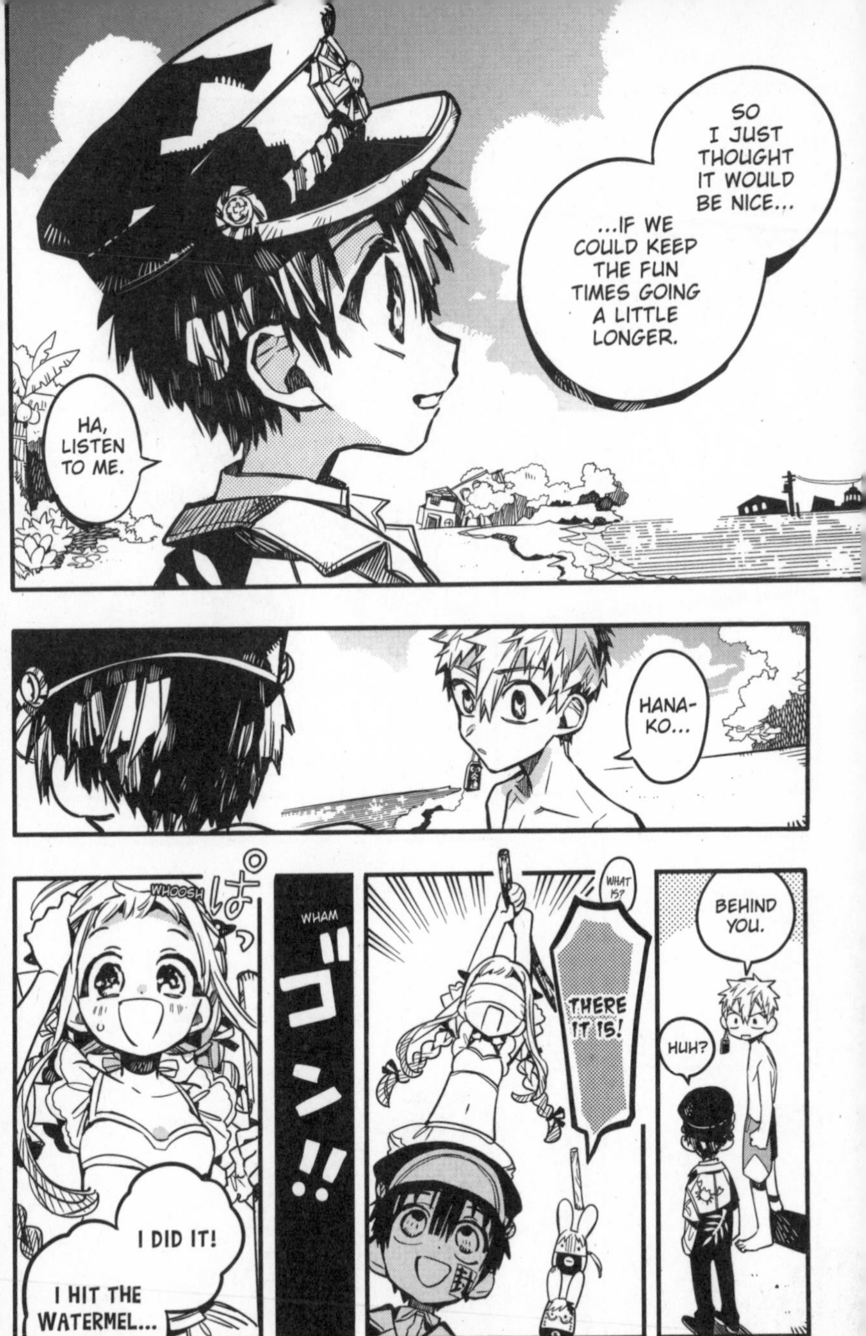
SO I JUST THOUGHT IT WOULD BE NICE...
...IF WE COULD KEEP THE FUN TIMES GOING A LITTLE LONGER.
HA, LISTEN TO ME.
HANA-KO...
BEHIND YOU.
HUH?
WHAT IS?
THERE IT IS!
WHAM
ゴン!!
WHOOSH
ぱっ
I DID IT!
I HIT THE WATERMEL...

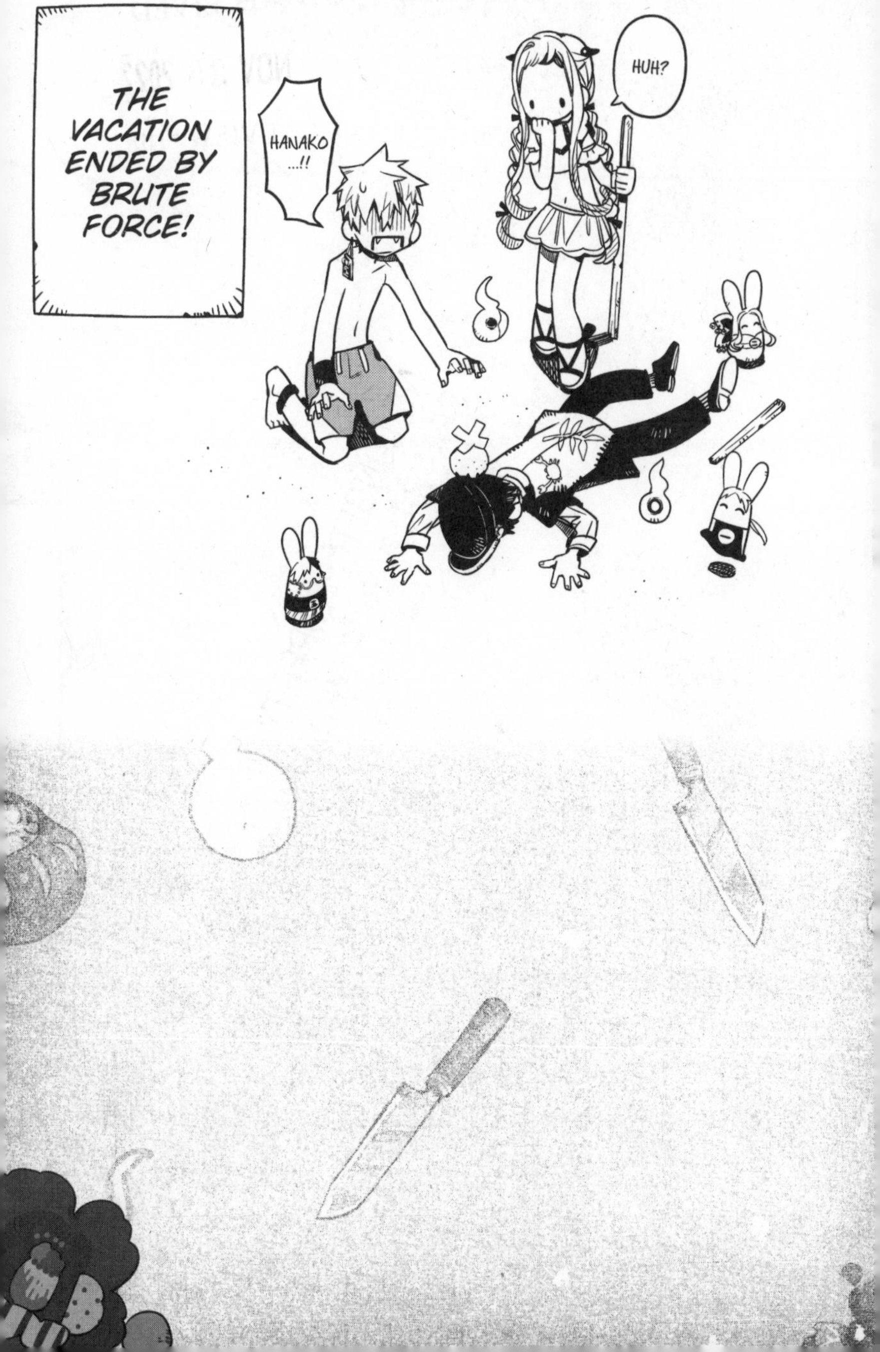
HUH?
HANAKO ...!!
THE VACATION ENDED BY BRUTE FORCE!

After-School Hanako-Kun

AidaIro

❖

Translation: Alethea Nibley
Lettering: Phil Christie

❖

HOKAGO SHONEN HANAKO-KUN
©2019 Aidalro / SQUARE ENIX CO., LTD.
First published in Japan in 2019 by SQUARE ENIX CO., LTD. English translation rights arranged with SQUARE ENIX CO., LTD. and Yen Press, LLC through Tuttle-Mori Agency, Inc.

English translation © 2021 by Yen Press, LLC.

Yen Press
150 West 30th Street, 19th Floor
New York, NY 10001

Visit us at yenpress.com • facebook.com/yenpress • twitter.com/yenpress • yenpress.tumblr.com • instagram.com/yenpress

First Yen Press Edition: April 2021

Yen Press is an imprint of Yen Press, LLC.
The Yen Press name and logo are trademarks of Yen Press, LLC.

The publisher is not responsible for websites (or their content) that are not owned by the publisher.

Library of Congress Control Number: 2020953027

ISBN: 978-1-9753-2435-3 (paperback)
978-1-9753-2436-0 (ebook)

10 9 8 7 6 5 4 3 2

TPA

Printed in South Korea